GREENSPAN

GREENSPAN

•

THE MAN
BEHIND MONEY

•

JUSTIN MARTIN

PERSEUS PUBLISHING
Cambridge, Massachusetts

Many of the designations used by manufacturers and sellers to distinguish their products are claimed as trademarks. Where those designations appear in this book and Perseus Publishing was aware of a trademark claim, the designations have been printed in initial capital letters.

A CIP record for this book is available from the Library of Congress.
ISBN 0-7382-0275-4

Perseus Publishing is a member of the Perseus Books Group.

Text design by Jeff Williams
Set in 11-point Galliard by the Perseus Books Group

First printing, September 2000

Perseus Publishing books are available at special discounts for bulk purchases in the U.S. by corporations, institutions, and other organizations. For more information, please contact the Special Markets Department at HarperCollins Publishers, 10 East 53rd Street, New York, NY 10022, or call 1-212-207-7528.

Find us on the World Wide Web at http://www.perseuspublishing.com

1 2 3 4 5 6 7 8 9 10—03 02 01 00

To the three strong women in my life:
my mother, Donna Martin;
my mother-in-law, Sylvia Charlesworth;
and my wife, Liza Charlesworth

Contents

Acknowledgments

I feel a great deal of gratitude toward my editor Jacqueline Murphy, for the care and consideration lavished on this book. From the kernel of an idea to a finished biography this was truly a collaboration, and a most satisfying one. I'm also grateful to Marco Pavia, Arlinda Shtuni, Lissa Warren, Michelle Wynn, and the rest of the talented team at Perseus Publishing for getting behind this project.

I wish to thank my agent, Lisa Swayne of the Swayne Agency. She helped me at the outset to shape a saleable proposal, and she was there throughout the process offering her wise counsel. I also want to thank my friend Richard Laermer for pushing me to write a book in the first place.

My research assistant for this project was Stephen Norton, a reporter with National Journal's Congress Daily. As Frank Lloyd Wright famously said, "God is in the details." Stephen helped dig them up in spades.

I had the opportunity, while working on this book, to spend a very pleasant week in Ann Arbor, Michigan, on a grant provided by the Gerald Ford Foundation. I want to thank the able staff at the Gerald R. Ford Library including Geir Gundersen, Donna Lehman, and Kenneth Hafeli. The Juilliard Archive was most helpful; my thanks to Jane Gottlieb and Jeni Dahmus. The New York Public Library is quite simply a national treasure.

I am also indebted to the Conference Board, former employer to both me and my subject, Alan Greenspan. Thanks to Ken Goldstein for vetting the book with an eye toward economic veracity. Thanks to Randy Poe—once my boss, long my friend, forever a music aficionado — for vetting the book with an eye toward jazz veracity. I also appreciate the valuable assistance I received from Lucie Blau, Delos Smith, and Frank Tortorici.

For helping me to make sense of Greenspan's time in Ayn Rand's inner circle, my thanks to Chris Wolski and archivist Jeff Britting at the Ayn Rand Institute and also to the Objectivist Center. Fred Cookinham's Ayn Rand-themed walking tours of New York City provided an invaluable window into the author's life and times.

For helping me to pin down various and sundry aspects of New York City, my thanks to Alan Wolk, my old friend and true New Yawker, as well as James Renner, local historian for Washington Heights. On this score, my book also benefited greatly from the input of Kathleen Hulser of the New-York Historical Society.

Historian and sympathetic fellow biographer Robert Hessen—one of the world's most widely ranging readers—kept me constantly apprised of articles about Alan Greenspan in way-off-the-beaten-path journals that otherwise would have escaped my notice.

Of course, a special measure of gratitude is due the book's countless sources. Literally hundreds of people gave generously of their time and shared their insights about this book's subject. They're too numerous to list, but among the many who helped me along the way were: Martin and Annelise Anderson, James Baker, Anirvan Banerji, George Bentson, Bill Callejo, Allan and Joan Mitchell Blumenthal, Barbara Branden, Nathaniel Branden, Kathryn Eickhoff, Bert Ely, Gerald Ford, Milton Friedman, Leonard Garment, Carolyn and Wesley Halpert, Lee Hilton, Henry Jerome, Martin Johnson, Robert Kavesh, Don Kennedy, Donald Kettl, Henry Kissinger, Ernest Kurnow, Allen Matusow, Paul McCracken, David Munro, Donald Rumsfeld, Paul Samuelson, Stanford Sanoff, Sylvester Schieber, L. William Seidman, Bernard Shull, Richard Sylla, Murray Weidenbaum, and Wyatt Wells.

I also wish to thank a trio of institutes: American Enterprise, Cato, and Hoover as well as some people associated with Harvard University—James Aisner, Samuel Hayes, Hendrik Houthakker, and Roger Porter.

For translation services, *grazie* to Aldo Moreno of V&T Pizzeria.

Thanks to my brother Andrew Martin for a keen grasp of language and to my aunt Diane Caldwell for calling my attention to a priceless Greenspan cartoon. And thanks to Rex Martin, my father, for inspiration, guidance, and for fostering my love of history.

Preface

The crisis began with a whimper in a far-off corner of the world. On July 2, 1997, Thailand threw in the towel and gave up defense of its currency, the baht. Federal Reserve Chairman Alan Greenspan was well aware of the event but didn't think it cause for alarm—yet. The perspective from Washington, D.C., suggested that the problem was very much a localized one.

Thailand had been on a borrowing binge for years—sopping up international investment money and using it to finance everything from skyscrapers to shopping malls to golf courses. As the country's economic policy grew increasingly cavalier, managers of U.S. mutual funds and other overseas investors began to suspect that they would not see adequate returns on their money. They started pulling out of Thailand en masse throughout the first half of 1997. That prompted currency speculators to rush in to bet against the baht. Thailand's central bank fell under immense pressure to stave off a devaluation.

In desperation, the country turned to the International Monetary Fund (IMF) for relief. That unexpected cry for help was a signal heard around the world. As the value of the baht fell by 10 percent against the dollar, it became apparent that Thailand was in deep trouble. The first seeds of a global crisis were planted.

Malaysia, Thailand's neighbor to the south, was next to topple. Culturally, the two nations are fairly dissimilar—Thailand is a Buddhist country, while Malaysia's population is predominantly Muslim. Come summer of 1997, however, they shared some conspicuous economic similarities. Each had achieved supercharged gross domestic product

(GDP) growth during the 1990s, sometimes in excess of 10 percent a year. Both countries had been engines in an apparent East Asian economic miracle, which had drawn $500 billion worth of foreign investment capital between 1987 and 1997. More notably, both had built their booms on what amounted to quicksand—lax business-sector regulation and easy credit terms on bank loans.

As Thailand caved under increasing scrutiny from the international investment community, so too did Malaysia. On July 24, 1997, Malaysia's currency—the ringgit—imploded. Prime Minister Mahathir Mohamad blamed his country's woes on "rogue speculators." He even went so far as to single out one in particular, calling billionaire hedge-fund manager George Soros a "moron." But Mohamad's comments only served to further increase the scrutiny on the entire region. The Philippine peso was next to plummet.

As the list of stricken currencies lengthened, the crisis gained momentum. Headlines in the United States began to hint at a frightening prospect: The problem might soon wash up on American shores. Before long the press gave the strange and menacing new phenomenon a name: the "Asian Contagion." Christen it, and it begins to take on a life all its own.

Greenspan monitored the situation from 9,000 miles away. As Fed chief for a decade by this point, he knew the value of a wait-and-see attitude. React too soon, or worse yet overreact, and fear of a crisis might quickly turn into a self-fulfilling prophecy. The United States was in the midst of a long economic expansion and he wanted to do everything possible to keep it going.

Indonesia was the next domino. In 1996, at the height of that country's boom, supermodels Claudia Schiffer and Naomi Campbell had jetted into Jakarta, the capital city, for the grand opening of a Fashion Café. Beginning in August 1997, the currency began a precipitous fall: It would shed 80 percent of its value in the space of six months. The economic turmoil led to rioting; 1,200 people were killed in Jakarta alone. Faced with a spiraling crisis, Indonesian president Suharto would first fire the nation's central banker and then step down himself after a thirty-two-year reign. The Asian Contagion was growing virulent.

Then bang, bang: Just like that, the crisis slipped into China and hopped continents to the United States. A paroxysm in Hong Kong's Hang Seng index one day shook the U.S. market on the very next. On

October 27, 1997, the Dow plunged 554 points to 7,161, down 7 percent. It was the stock market's worst day in a decade.

At the close of trading that day, Treasury Secretary Robert Rubin read a prepared statement. Standing on the steps of the Treasury Building in Washington, directly beneath a statue of Alexander Hamilton, Rubin declared: "Remember that the fundamentals of the U.S. economy are strong."

The next morning, Greenspan testified before Congress. He, too, delivered a carefully worded statement. As he read it, an aide handed him notes on the state of the Dow. Greenspan wanted to make sure that nothing he said roiled the skittish markets. The Fed chief—famous for tortured verbiage—was unusually clear during his testimony. At one point, he stated: "The foundation for good business performance remains sound."

Greenspan and Rubin's assurances had their desired effect. The two had built up a great deal of clout, thanks to their stewardship of the U.S. economy during the 1990s. Merely uttering soothing words was enough to temporarily stabilize the markets. The Dow recovered much of the lost ground during the ensuing weeks, and the U.S. boom continued unabated. But a deep undercurrent of anxiety remained.

In November 1997, South Korea fell. By dint of so-called crony capitalism, the country had spurred its economy into hyperdrive via widespread corruption and acts of political favoritism. The government routinely encouraged the nation's banks to give preferential treatment to a handful of large conglomerates, known as *chaebols*. Throughout 1997, one by one, various multibillion-dollar *chaebols* had declared themselves insolvent. When the number of belly-up *chaebols* hit seven, critical mass was achieved.

The vulnerability of South Korea came as a shock to global investors. It was the world's eleventh largest economy, and a major trading partner for the United States and Japan.

The Fed quietly stepped in. Among its varied duties, the Federal Reserve has regulatory authority over a portion of U.S. banks. It urged lenders to refinance some of the short-term debt held by South Korea, thereby buying time for the country and relieving some pressure. This was pivotal in keeping a bad situation from getting worse.

Meanwhile, there was growing concern that the contagion would spread to Japan, already mired in a long recession. Japanese banks had an estimated $44 billion worth of bum loans on their books—many of them for various abortive projects in Thailand, Indonesia, and South Korea. On top of that, the region's financial woes had seriously contracted demand for Japanese exports.

Throughout the winter of 1997–1998, Greenspan remained watchful. The news from overseas was nerve-racking. Fully 40 percent of the world's economies were now in recession. Some were victims of the Asian Contagion; others simply had the misfortune to be in a down cycle. But the U.S. economy kept humming along.

As Fed chief, Greenspan was called upon to strike a very careful balance. The Fed's most powerful tool is control over two short-term interest rates that influence long-term rates—on bonds, business loans, and mortgages—often causing them to move in tandem.

Greenspan knew the Fed could give the economy an immediate shot in the arm by lowering interest rates, which would have the effect of inoculating the United States against the Asian Contagion. But if the contagion didn't make another appearance in the United States, it would be more like administering an overdose. The economy might grow too fast, spurring inflation that could bring the expansion crashing to a halt.

The Fed chairman was torn between two potential dangers: the threat of Asian Contagion on one side, and the threat of the economy overheating on the other. During testimony before the House Banking Committee in February 1998, he described the U.S. economy as poised between "finely balanced, though powerful forces."

Greenspan decided to err on the side of caution. He prevailed on his colleagues at the Fed to hold off on lowering interest rates, for the time being.

In May 1998, Greenspan and Rubin jointly testified before Congress, urging approval of a Clinton administration request to add $18 billion to the IMF's reserves. The organization had lately taken on an extraordinary number of new commitments and had only about $15 billion left in its coffers. It had already agreed to a $17.2 billion rescue package for Thailand and $42 billion in aid for Indonesia. It had also finalized a $57 billion package for South Korea on December 3, 1997—a day the country's citizens deemed "National Humiliation Day." The world literally couldn't afford any additional economic turmoil.

Then, on August 17, 1998, Russia announced that it was defaulting on a portion of its sovereign debt. This was stunning news. The country was refusing to honor certain bonds it had issued. It was the equivalent of the U.S. government putting a moratorium on paying obligations on Treasury bills. Russia signaled a turning point. The contagion had leapt out of Asia in a very big way.

Russia, as it turned out, had been tarred with the same brush as various Asian countries that had experienced meltdowns. Investors were becoming increasingly skittish about emerging markets, period. They were dumping questionable investments from their portfolios, whether in Thailand, Indonesia, Russia, or elsewhere. There to fill the vacuum were currency speculators. Hot on the heels of Russia's crisis, in fact, Brazil and Argentina came under pressure.

In late August, Greenspan attended an annual conference the Federal Reserve holds in Jackson Hole, Wyoming. He remained outwardly nonchalant. The press was on hand and he didn't want to say anything that might spook the markets. But privately, he admitted to being very concerned.

The most conspicuous warning signal was an increase in spreads between U.S. Treasuries and bonds issued by emerging-market countries. Such spreads had stood at around 6 percent as recently as the beginning of the year. In the wake of Russia's default, they had widened to as much as 17 percent. This meant investors were demanding a giant premium to put money into emerging markets.

More troubling still, investors were even fleeing high grade U.S. corporate debt in favor of U.S. Treasuries. In Wall Street parlance, this is known as a "flight to quality." U.S. investors were battening down, preparing for another wave of financial chaos.

Greenspan confided to colleagues that he had never seen anything quite so extreme during his half century of observing the economy.

As investors grew increasingly nervous, spreads grew larger. There was a growing gulf between ultrasecure U.S. Treasuries and almost everything else. It was this process that ushered in a devastating encore appearance of the Asian Contagion. And it struck in a way that no one could have imagined or anticipated.

In September 1998, the crisis that had begun the previous year in Thailand showed up in Greenwich, Connecticut, striking a hedge fund called Long-Term Capital Management (LTCM). Hedge funds are basically mutual funds with a limited number of very wealthy investors. As such, they are free to pursue a myriad of complicated investment schemes without regulatory supervision.

LTCM was the brainchild of John Meriwether, former head of Salomon Brothers bond-trading department. His antics—suggesting a $10-million-a-hand card game, for example—had already earned him a prominent role in the best-selling book *Liar's Poker*. The staff of LTCM included former Fed vice chairman David Mullins, two Nobel laureates in economics—Robert Merton and Myron Scholes—and a brigade of Ph.Ds.

LTCM's modus operandi was to use computer models to identify anomalies in spreads between various investment vehicles. A computer model might, for example, identify U.S. Treasuries and junk bonds as out of whack, spreadwise. Step two was to place bets—by means of mind-bendingly complicated derivative investments—that those spreads would return to normal range.

But following Russia's default, spreads widened drastically. In the blink of an eye, the hedge fund lost $4 billion on a series of wrong-way bets. All of LTCM's brainpower and computer wizardry was for naught.

Meriwether and Mullins called William McDonough, president of the New York City branch of the Federal Reserve. They tipped him off to their firm's problems.

McDonough, in turn, consulted with Greenspan. The two feared that LTCM's $4-billion loss was just the tip of the iceberg. The firm had woven a complicated web of failed derivatives bets, and there was no telling how many other companies might be similarly exposed. Greenspan and McDonough worried that a chain reaction might occur, dragging down the entire U.S. financial system. It was a frightening prospect—and one that was entirely possible.

On September 23, 1998, McDonough arranged a meeting on the 10th floor of the New York Fed's building at 33 Liberty Street. In attendance were representatives from seventeen major financial-services companies, including Merrill Lynch, J. P. Morgan, and Travelers Group. Ultimately, fourteen of the companies present agreed to fork over $3.6 billion to buy stakes in the hedge fund to keep it afloat.

But by now, the Asian Contagion was having a discernible effect on the U.S. economy. The markets were pretty much in a holding pattern.

Investor confidence was plummeting, and the economy was in danger of sliding into a recession or worse.

Time to pull the trigger.

The Fed initiated a quarter-point interest-rate cut on September 29, 1998, dropping what's known as the "Federal funds rate" to 5.25 percent.

The decision to make an incremental move was deliberate. In Greenspan's estimation, a deeper cut ran the risk of using up the Fed's leverage too quickly.

But the quarter-point easing failed to calm the economy's jitters. So Greenspan took an unusual step. Acting on his own authority, he enacted another rate cut without waiting for the next regularly scheduled Fed meeting. This sent a strong signal to the market: Greenspan was on top of the problem and willing to take decisive action.

The Fed announced the cut at 3:15 P.M. on October 15, 1998. During the last hour of trading, the Dow launched into a vigorous rally, climbing 331 points to 8,299. This time the medicine was starting to work.

The Fed did one last quarter-point cut on November 17. Just to be certain, Greenspan backed up action with words. The Fed issued a statement that included the following assurance: "Financial conditions can reasonably be expected to be consistent with fostering sustained economic expansion while keeping inflationary pressures subdued."

Everything was under control. The threat of a financial disaster—pressing just weeks before—had been contained through a combination of soothing words and savvy interest-rate policy.

The Asian Contagion was repelled, exiting the United States as quickly as it had appeared. America's boom kept right on rolling, and the Dow soon shot through the 10,000 mark. Meanwhile, Congress pushed through an increase in IMF reserves. Bailout money continued to flow, helping Thailand, Indonesia, Russia, and the other afflicted countries start the long, slow process of rebuilding their economies.

During the nervous days of 1998, Greenspan showed infallible instincts in steering the U.S. economy. It was a masterful performance, and a crucial one. Had the United States succumbed, the Asian Contagion would have rampaged through the economies of the rest of the world. "Greenspan saved the day. He prevented a thorough meltdown," says William Griggs, a veteran Fed watcher and managing director of the Wall Street firm Griggs and Santow.

Afterward, Greenspan was hailed as a hero, and even attained an odd measure of celebrity—a first for a Fed chairman.

But Greenspan did not simply burst onto the public stage—an unflappable economist with a gift for calming markets. First he traveled a path that was winding and weird, colorful and fraught with controversy. Quelling the Asian Contagion was simply one high note in an extraordinarily varied life and career.

Greenspan was named to his first term as Fed chairman in 1987. But during the 1940s, he did a stint as a professional jazz musician. He also spent fifteen years in the inner circle of author Ayn Rand. And he was an economic adviser to Richard Nixon and Gerald Ford.

Alan Greenspan has had numerous personal and professional victories. He has also made multiple missteps and has been embroiled in contretemps aplenty.

In the course of a lifetime, Greenspan has halted stock market crashes, played the clarinet and saxophone professionally, and gotten married twice; he's scrapped with George Bush, earned millions, been caricatured on the TV show *The Simpsons*, and presided over the longest stretch of economic prosperity in U.S. history.

His is quite a tale. Given the vagaries of the economy, it's also a story very much in progress, with the last chapters yet to be written. His legacy is still in question. But one thing is certain: Greenspan has attained a remarkable level of power and mystique. The world hangs on his every word. To get an idea of where Greenspan is headed, it's well worthwhile to travel back and follow his story from the very beginning.

GREENSPAN

1

WASHINGTON HEIGHTS

A few years prior to the great stock market crash of 1929, Alan Greenspan's parents moved into an apartment in the Washington Heights section of Manhattan. The area is so named because it offers the highest natural elevation on the island, and as a consequence, General George Washington chose it as the site of his headquarters during some key Revolutionary War battles. For decades thereafter, Washington Heights remained a surprisingly rural part of New York City, containing only a handful of large country estates, including one that belonged to the naturalist John James Audubon.

The colonization of Washington Heights began in earnest in 1906 with the completion of a subway line. Soon after, people intent on escaping the teeming slums of Manhattan's Lower East Side began moving uptown in search of larger apartments and better living conditions. Then in the 1920s, when flush times sparked a boom in housing and construction in northern Manhattan, new residents flooded in.

The section came to be known as "Frankfurt on the Hudson," a term of mild derision that served to point to the considerable number of Jewish immigrants from Germany who called the neighborhood home. The area also became home to large pockets of Irish and Greek immigrants.

Into this thriving community at the northern end of Manhattan, Alan Greenspan was born on March 6, 1926. He weighed nine pounds. His father, Herbert Greenspan, was a businessman who later

1

became a stockbroker and economic consultant. He was medium in height, slender in build, and bore a decided resemblance to the movie star Gene Kelly. Alan's mother, Rose, was a petite, dark-haired woman, possessed of an innate sweetness and natural optimism. In keeping with the times, Rose was a full-time homemaker.

Herbert Greenspan's forebears hailed from Germany. Rose, née Rose Goldsmith, was of Polish descent. Nathan and Anna Toluchko—Rose's parents—had come to the United States at the beginning of the twentieth century and had Americanized their name at immigration services, changing it to Goldsmith. Rose came from a large family of seven siblings, all born in the United States, except for the oldest sister, Mary, who had been born in Poland.

Young Alan's parents had a tumultuous marriage. It was generally agreed that the couple had wed too young, when Rose was just seventeen. They were mismatched in temperament as well. Herbert was something of a dreamer, given to aloofness and abstraction, while Rose was vivacious, brimming with energy and zeal.

The young couple were already at odds, but it was the crash of 1929 that sealed their fate. During the ensuing depression, money was tight in the Greenspan household, causing financial anxieties that served to drive the two further apart.

When Alan was five years old, Rose and Herbert divorced. Rose took Alan and moved back in with her own parents, strict disciplinarians with old-country values and manners. The four lived together in a one-bedroom apartment in a six-story red brick building at the corner of Broadway and West 163rd Street—600 West 163rd, to be exact. Conditions there were extremely cramped. Nathan and Anna Goldsmith slept in the bedroom, while Alan and Rose shared a dining room that was converted into a second bedroom.

To help make ends meet, Rose took a job in the domestics department at Ludwig-Bauman, a furniture store at 149th and Third Avenue in the Bronx. Following the divorce, Herbert became very distant. Visits to his son were infrequent at best. "He disappeared from their lives very fast," recalls cousin Wesley Halpert. "Alan hardly got to see him. But I do remember the ecstasy that Alan exhibited on those rare occasions when his father visited."

Wesley and Marianne Halpert, the children of Rose's sister, Mary, lived half a block away from Alan. Alan spent a great deal of time with his cousins, and they grew as close as siblings. Wesley was older, Marianne younger. Their father, Jacob Halpert, became almost like a second father to Alan. An insurance broker by trade, Jacob managed to enjoy a fair amount of success during the Great Depression. Wesley recalls an aching and almost boundless neediness on the part of his cousin.

"Here was my father," says Wesley. "He was one father with two hands. But there were three kids: Alan, Marianne, and myself. We'd be walking down the street and Alan would kind of worm his way between me and my father and grab my father's hand."

Wesley also remembers that Alan would periodically pipe up and sing "Brother Can You Spare a Dime?" Little Alan's mournful rendition of the popular tune and unofficial anthem of depression-era America was guaranteed to tug at Jacob Halpert's heartstrings. Invariably, he'd dig into his pocket and toss Alan a dime.

As a young child, Alan showed a precocious intelligence. By the age of five, he was able to add up three-digit numbers in his head. His mother often trotted him out to do this trick to impress guests and neighbors.

His intellect served him in grammar school as well when he attended P.S. 169 at 169th Street and Audubon Avenue. He excelled as a student, reading at a level ahead of his classmates and memorizing multiplication tables in a snap. "Alan was good at everything he did," recalls Stanford Sanoff, a boyhood friend.

He adds that Alan was well behaved and polite even at an early age: "I never knew Alan to get into any trouble at all. He was a straight arrow right down the line."

At P.S. 169, one of Greenspan's teachers was a Mr. Small. Small brought pragmatism to teaching mathematics, taking the students on some unusual field trips. "He made it very interesting," Bill Callejo, another of Greenspan's childhood friends, recalls of Small. "He had us go down to banks and get copies of deposit slips as an introduction to math."

During summers, Greenspan and other neighborhood boys played sandlot baseball on a team they called the Titans. As a left-hander, Greenspan was naturally called upon to play first base. He modeled himself after Dolph Camilli, a slugger for the Dodgers who played the same position. Although Washington Heights was Yankees territory, Greenspan's heart lay with their crosstown rivals in Brooklyn. Growing up, his other favorite players were Dodgers shortstop Pee Wee Reese and third baseman Cookie Lavagetto. He even developed an extraordinarily complicated system for scoring ball games that he listened to on the radio, with intricate notations identifying the type of pitch thrown, the exact location to which the ball was hit, and so on.

In the summertime, Greenspan spent many happy weekends at the Halpert family's beach house in the Rockaway section of Queens. "We'd go beachcombing to find coins that had been dropped in the sand," says Wesley. "We were good. We did it without using machinery or anything. We'd just walk along the beach looking. Then we'd go buy candy."

The two boys also indulged an appetite for horror films. Just up the street from the Goldsmiths' apartment was the Audubon Theater, where Wesley often took Alan to the movies. This was the heyday of classic monster films starring Boris Karloff and Bela Lugosi. "I took Alan to see *Frankenstein*," recalls Wesley. "He was terrified."

When Alan was nine, his father—in the course of one of his increasingly infrequent visits—gave him a copy of a book that he had recently published called *Recovery Ahead!* It was a defense of Franklin D. Roosevelt's New Deal, in which he argued that government programs could help spur the economy out of depression. The book bore the following inscription from Herbert Greenspan to Alan Greenspan: "May this my initial effort with a constant thought of you branch into an endless chain of similar efforts so that at your maturity you may look back and endeavor to interpret the reasoning behind these logical forecasts and begin a like work of your own. Your Dad."

Young Alan put the book away and it was soon forgotten—he would not get around to reading it until years later. Already, he was moving in a direction that would take him about as far from economics as one can get.

Both the Goldsmiths and Halperts were very musical families. Nathan Goldsmith—the grandfather with whom Greenspan lived—was a cantor at a Bronx synagogue; Alan's mother, Rose, loved to play the piano and sing, belting out Cole Porter and Jerome Kern songs as well as novelties such as "The Big Brown Bear Went Woof." Her style was loose and energetic, reminiscent of the chanteuse Helen Morgan. She also worked some Yiddish songs into her repertoire, such as "Rozhinkes mit Mandlen" (Raisins and Almonds).

"Rose was such a vibrant, lively, lovely lady," recalls Alan's cousin, Claire Rosen. Claire grew up to be a professional singer, specializing in musical comedies. She worked various Radio City revues and during the mid-1940s appeared in the original Broadway production of *Annie Get Your Gun*, starring Ethel Merman.

And then there was Uncle Mario, born Murray Toluchko. First, his name was Americanized to Murray Goldsmith, then Murray Smith, and finally he changed it to Mario Silva. A small, round man with a swarthy complexion, he wanted to pass for Italian and hoped to build a career in the opera. Silva wrote a play that actually appeared on Broadway, called *Song of Love*, about the composer Robert Schumann.

Surrounded by all this passion for music, young Alan had no alternative. He chose the clarinet as his instrument.

From the time he was very young, Greenspan showed an idiosyncratic but highly developed sense of morality. During the mid-1930s, when he was just ten or eleven years old, he and his friend Bill Callejo founded a secret society called the Detective Scouts of Washington Heights. The two boys had a vague sense that something was amiss in the world, and they planned to do something about it.

Prohibition was then in full force, spurring all kinds of gangland activity. In Manhattan, District Attorney Thomas Dewey—hard-boiled predecessor to Rudolph Giuliani—was busy prosecuting racketeers and crime syndicates such as Murder Incorporated. Meanwhile, unsettling news from Germany continually filtered into the boys' Washington Heights neighborhood. Alan and Bill didn't understand the specifics, but they knew they wanted to help clean up a world that seemed to be going increasingly mad.

The two devoted an entire afternoon to designing their Detective Scouts of Washington Heights ID cards. Greenspan derived great pleasure from printing in tiny letters; into adulthood, his handwriting would remain unusually small and rococo. He filigreed the ID cards with all kinds of slogans and secret codes and symbols. By the end of the afternoon, Alan and Bill had drawn up impressive secret-agent credentials.

"We wanted to ferret out evil," recalls Bill Callejo with a laugh. "It was just one of those things kids dream up with their wild imaginations. I think we wound up being the only two members of the damn thing."

Greenspan attended Edward W. Stitt Junior High School at 164th Street and Edgecombe Avenue in Manhattan. He was placed in rapid advanced classes and managed to skip a grade, completing the seventh-through ninth-grade curriculums in two years.

Classroom seating was done by height. At the back of the class sat the very tallest students. Greenspan and Callejo filled in the second-to-last row. Greenspan was sprouting up. Surprisingly, he was not a gangly, spastic beanpole. He was actually rather well built and athletic, quite out of keeping with his image of later years.

It was during junior high that Greenspan developed a crush on a girl named Corinne Eskris. "All the kids knew it," recalls old classmate Leila Kollmar—Leila Ross at the time. But she's not certain that Greenspan ever even approached the object of his affections. "He didn't talk much," says Kollmar. "He was a very quiet person."

In these years, Greenspan also began to show real signs of aloofness—a bequest of his father and unquestionably one of his own defining traits in adulthood.

"He had a classwide reputation for being a little snobbish," recalls Callejo. "I think it was coming from the fact that he was an introspective person." Sanoff agrees that "he was a thinker even at that age."

One way Greenspan asserted his intellectual independence was by refusing to be bar-mitzvahed. Although he was never to renounce his heritage, he was moving away from religious practice, and for the rest of his life, he would be what is sometimes called a "secular Jew."

"It may have been our grandparents who turned him off," says Wesley Halpert. "Our grandfather had certain authoritarian ideas. Children should be seen, not heard. Our grandmother was a very nervous person. She would get hysterical." Halpert also remembers that "Alan estranged himself from them in the same apartment. I remember many times being over there and he'd be in the bedroom, door closed, listening to the radio. He totally separated himself."

Rose, by contrast, was very lax. "She put no pressure on him and left him to his own devices," says Wesley Halpert.

In the autumn of 1940, Greenspan entered George Washington High School. The school's most prominent feature is a high tower that offers a stunning panoramic view, sweeping up and down Manhattan, into the Bronx and Queens, and across the Hudson to New Jersey. Throughout his junior-high years, Greenspan had been privy to adolescent rumors about the tower. Supposedly, it was a venue for unimaginable acts by lust-crazed high-school girls. Thus was the school nicknamed "The Whorehouse on the Hill."

Upon arriving at George Washington High, however, Greenspan found the tower being put to very different use. It was occupied by armed members of the U.S. Navy. At the top of it, they had positioned a powerful telescope. The site offered a great vantage point from which to survey the Hudson and Harlem Rivers. There was concern that a German U-boat might sneak up one of those waterways. The evils that the Detective Scouts had vowed to fight were becoming all too pressing and ominous at a time when America was on the brink of war.

Between 1933 and 1941, 20,000 German and Austrian Jews poured into Washington Heights, fleeing the Nazis. In 1938, among them was a young boy named Heinz Alfred Kissinger, who arrived from the Bavarian village of Fürth. He changed his name to Henry and lived with his family in a cramped little apartment on West 187th Street, not far from Greenspan.

Kissinger attended George Washington High two classes ahead of Greenspan. Their time at the school overlapped, but they did not meet one another until many years later. Kissinger actually attended school at night, an option in that era. By day he worked as a delivery boy for a shaving-brush manufacturer, earning $10.89 a week, $8.00 of which he gave to his parents. Despite a backbreaking schedule, Kissinger made straight A's and hoped to become an accountant.

Greenspan was also a good student, though he didn't manage straight A's. Among his favorite courses were history and current events. He was also a real joiner during high school. He was president of his home room, class 8–1, and served in a group known as lunch squad. George Washington High was extremely crowded during the early 1940s, mainly due to the massive influx of new immigrants. Lunch squad's main duty was to break up numerous fights that occurred in the cafeteria.

Greenspan played clarinet in the school orchestra, sporting a blue sweater emblazoned with a white "GW." He was also a member of a school dance band organized by classmate Hilton Levy. The band went by the name Lee Hilton and His Orchestra–"Lee Hilton" being young Hilton Levy's stage name.

Levy was extremely entrepreneurial. He managed to finagle a letter of introduction from bandleader Glenn Miller and, armed with this letter, Levy would case the Brill Building—the famous song-writing factory in Times Square—wandering from floor to floor, hitting people up for free sheet music for the band. Thus, Lee Hilton and His Orchestra's repertoire included standards such as "Bye Bye Blackbird," "Wait Till the Sun Shines, Nellie," and "Sweet Georgia Brown." In deference to their benefactor—and also because it was a huge crowd-pleaser—the orchestra ended each show with Glenn Miller's "In the Mood."

Levy, Greenspan, and an ever-changing roster of anywhere from seven to ten musicians played school dances and proms at George Washington High. They also tooled around their neighborhood performing at socials held by temples and churches. Standard pay was $2 a show per band member.

Levy, who remained in the music business for many years, and legally changed his name to Lee Hilton, remembers bandmate Greenspan as rather abstruse. "He never said anything definitively. It was always double-talk—very much like today." But he also remembers that they had a good time together. "We thoroughly enjoyed what we were doing, and we were getting paid for it," says Hilton.

As one might expect, Greenspan didn't get into much trouble during high school and didn't exactly run with a rowdy crowd. Besides, this was the 1940s, a time long before the advent of malls and cineplexes. Nevertheless, Greenspan enjoyed frequenting a candy store near George Washington High, renowned for its chocolate egg creams, and he put in occasional appearances at a spot in Riverside Park where neighborhood kids congregated—known simply as "the wall."

"We used to say, 'I'll meet you at the wall,'" recalls Sanoff. "It was just a place to meet. There was nothing much to do. You have to remember, this wasn't the same world as today, with fast food restaurants and such."

In general, Greenspan's classmates found him quiet and reserved. "I think Alan and I were a little more concerned about towing the line," adds Sanoff. "If we were expected to be home Saturday night by midnight, we were home by midnight. Somebody else might come in at 3 A.M. and not care."

During his teens, Greenspan continued to spend long stretches of the summer with his cousin Wesley Halpert. By this time, the Halperts had a beach house on Lake Hiawatha in New Jersey. At night, all the kids would congregate at the Blue Front Diner, where Greenspan could be counted on to cue up Glenn Miller and various other swing bands on the jukebox. He loved to dance the lindy-hop and, as his cousins recalled, was surprisingly graceful.

Lake Hiawatha was the place that Greenspan had the most luck with meeting girls, more so than at George Washington High. "As I recall, during the summers he had more dates than me," says Halpert. "He always selected girls that looked like his mother."

Outside of school, Greenspan was growing increasingly serious about music. He was beginning to entertain dreams of playing professionally. To supplement the instruction he received at George Washington High, he began taking lessons from Bill Sheiner, one of the leading music teachers in New York City.

Sheiner was a multi-instrumentalist, fluent in the clarinet, saxophone, flute, and oboe. Lessons were held in a studio behind the Bronx Musical Mart at 174th Street and Southern Boulevard. Besides providing music instruction, Sheiner also did session work with a variety of popular orchestras.

Most students who worked with Sheiner were "doublers," meaning that they were trying to learn two similar instruments. Greenspan's were clarinet and saxophone. In teaching him, Sheiner employed a couple of books that are still standard texts: *The Universal Complete Saxophone Method* and *Klosé Complete Clarinet Method*.

"Bill did not have the ability to teach creativity. Very few do," says Ron Naroff, a music teacher who took lessons from Sheiner during the 1940s. "But guys who worked with him—provided they had solid study habits—were guaranteed to become good players. They'd be able to play with anyone."

In fact, a variety of notable musicians used Sheiner's vigorous instruction to lay the foundations of their careers, including Lenny Hambro, Red Press, and Stan Getz. Through Sheiner's lessons, Greenspan and Getz actually got to know one another and grew friendly. Both had similar backgrounds—Getz's family was also lower middle class and Jewish. His family lived on Hoe Avenue in the Bronx, where Getz attended James Monroe High School; his father was a printer who often had trouble finding work during the Great Depression.

Greenspan and Getz took to hanging around together, trading licks on the saxophone. They also engaged in fevered discussions about their idol, Benny Goodman. Greenspan was one year older than Getz, but in terms of musical talent, Getz was light years ahead. He was first to take the plunge into the music business, dropping out of school at age fifteen to join Jack Teagarden's orchestra. Getz eventually became one of the most important figures in jazz history, revered for a trademark breathy saxophone style at once lushly romantic and restlessly experimental. His 1963 single "Girl from Ipanema" was a crossover sensation and one of the biggest pop hits of all time.

Despite a love of music and dreams of going pro himself, Greenspan stayed in school. He graduated from George Washington High in 1943, a member of the Arista honor society and recipient of a special citation from the school's music department. His photo in the yearbook shows him looking suitably serious, hair combed back in a mild pompadour, a popular look of the time.

Beneath his picture is a quote that reads: "Smart as a whip and talented, too. He'll play the sax and clarinet for you."

2

JAZZ DAYS

Greenspan's universe centered around music. He had become so taken with it that he made playing professionally his life's ambition. While friends such as Stanford Sanoff were bound for NYU and Cousin Wesley went to City College, Greenspan opted to apply to the Juilliard School.

There, he hoped to expand and refine the work he had begun under the tutelage of Bill Sheiner. But Juilliard was a rather elitist institution, particularly in those days—and though Greenspan enjoyed the school, he was never quite suited to its pomp. Founded in 1905 by Frank Damrosch, godson of composer Franz Liszt, Juilliard's goal was to serve as an American rival to the great classical conservatories of Europe. This was a serious institution for serious musicians. Throughout its history, the school has churned out famous graduates including cellist Yo-Yo Ma, violinist Itzhak Perlman, and pianist Van Cliburn. Greenspan would need to check any frivolous Benny Goodman ambitions at the door.

Admissions standards were extremely stringent—one had first to pass muster with an examining jury composed of members of the faculty. Greenspan, now seventeen years old, went before them, clarinet in hand. He was asked a series of questions, designed to probe his knowledge of the classical repertoire and was required to play passages from Bach and Mozart to demonstrate technical proficiency on his instrument.

Greenspan managed to satisfy the jury and was accepted into the school as a clarinet major in the winter term of 1943. He was now part of a very small and select group, made smaller still by the fact that World War II was raging. His class—slated to graduate in 1945—was fewer than fifty, and mostly women.

Greenspan attended Juilliard's then uptown campus, the Institute of Musical Art at 122nd Street and Claremont Avenue in the Morningside Heights section of Manhattan, an easy trip by subway or bus from his apartment in Washington Heights. Piano, chorus, music theory, elementary dictation, and sight singing were all part of his course load. As a clarinet major, his adviser and primary teacher was a man named Arthur Christmann.

Christmann, a finicky and exacting man, was himself a Juilliard graduate who had received additional schooling at Columbia University and Union Theological Seminary's School of Sacred Music. He was a musical polymath. Along with the clarinet, he was proficient in the piano, organ, violin, and viola. His most significant contribution to the field of music was highly specialized and thoroughly esoteric—the invention of a "double-tongued" method for playing the clarinet.

By all appearances, Greenspan didn't exactly catch fire at Juilliard. The school paper of that era—the *IMA News*—rigorously chronicled the doings of the members of Greenspan's tiny class. It covered performances of student concerts, social events, and blood drives organized to benefit injured soldiers, as well as providing announcements on who made the honor roll and who won scholarships. There is not one mention of Greenspan.

Years later, Christmann compiled a list of students he was particularly pleased to have taught during his long and distinguished career. Greenspan was not on that list. He never really connected with Christmann—certainly not in the way he would in years to come, at other academic institutions, with other distinguished teachers.

One of Greenspan's classes was "Survey of Music as a Profession." According to the course catalog, it would help prepare students for a challenging and competitive career in the field of music. But Greenspan was already beginning to grow restless. One day late in 1943, Greenspan received a call from Bill Sheiner. A traveling swing band was looking for someone to play saxophone and clarinet, and his onetime teacher suggested that he audition.

Greenspan was taken by the idea. Why stay at Juilliard? Why spend several years getting a credential—taking courses like "Survey of Music as a Profession"—when there were opportunities to be had? Even at this young age, Greenspan showed a penchant for pragmatism.

When Greenspan auditioned for the swing band at Nola's Studios on West 57th Street, he was called upon to show his chops to bandleader Henry Jerome and Jerome's right-hand man, Leonard Garment. During his audition, Greenspan managed to make a favorable impression on both of them. That his resume didn't boast any significant professional experience—swing, jazz, or otherwise—was not viewed as a drawback. The pair liked the fact that he was a "legit" player with a degree of training. Jerome offered him a job at $62 a week. Greenspan accepted, and on January 6, 1944—less than a year after he'd been admitted—he dropped out of Juilliard.

Just like that, he'd become a member of Henry Jerome and His Orchestra.

"Alan was good, although he wasn't primarily a jazz player," recalls Jerome, age eighty-one. "I hired him because he was an excellent musician, but I didn't use him as an improviser."

"He was a very good section musician," concurs a seventy-five-year-old Garment. "He played the notes correctly and was part of a section. You don't even hear individual section players. The *idea* is not to hear them. They're supposed to be part of an ensemble."

Jerome and Garment were two of the most fascinating characters Greenspan was to meet during a lifetime filled with fascinating characters.

Jerome had begun his professional life as a trumpeter at twelve years old, touring around New England. During high school, he'd taken four months off to play on a transatlantic ocean liner. He, too, had gone to Juilliard; he, too, had dropped out, whereupon he'd formed his own band and toured ceaselessly from the late 1930s onward, playing the swing-music equivalent of the chitlin' circuit. He'd done gigs aboard steamships, in casinos, at the Paradise Ballroom in the Bronx, and at Nevele, a Borscht Belt institution up in the Catskills. He no doubt seemed immensely sophisticated to the teenage Greenspan.

Nineteen-year-old Lenny Garment was a member of the swing band's sax section and was also Jerome's good friend and talent scout. A New York City native who had grown up under circumstances very similar to Greenspan's, Garment had spent his childhood playing stick-ball and stoopball in the Brownsville section of Brooklyn. Like Greenspan, Garment was Jewish. His father and mother had emigrated from Eastern Europe.

Both Greenspan and Garment shared the experience of having a doting mother and absentee father. But Greenspan's dad had truly abandoned the family, whereas Garment's merely worked incessantly and had become estranged from his children.

Garment's mother, like Rose Greenspan, had a passionate love of music. Upon coming to America, one of her first jobs was as a waitress at the Wallenstein and Gershwin Restaurant on the Lower East Side. Sometimes, she would baby-sit for the Gershwin family's young son, George. Gershwin's success with masterpieces such as *Porgy and Bess* and *Rhapsody in Blue* gave her a palpable sense of just what was possible in her adopted country of America.

Henry Jerome's peripatetic outfit included five brass, four saxes, piano, drums, assorted other instruments, and a vocalist. Greenspan was called upon to play clarinet, tenor saxophone, and occasionally the flute. While Greenspan was now part of a big band, it was a far cry from the bands of Benny Goodman, Glenn Miller, or Artie Shaw. For one thing, Henry Jerome couldn't approach these acts in talent or popularity. His orchestra, though competent, wasn't exactly known for inspired arrangements or dazzling musicianship.

For Greenspan, this was actually a blessing of sorts. He enjoyed the ensemble's music, and given that it wasn't brimming with talent, he was actually able to hold his own.

Within the swing-band constellation, Jerome's outfit was what's known as a "sweet" band. It played the so-called businessman's bounce at hotels and casinos and similarly unhip, unhopping venues. Middle-aged couples took to the floor and danced languidly to the strains of "All the Things You Are" and "Stardust." If anything, Henry Jerome's band was closer in style and spirit to Guy Lombardo's band, celebrated for its saccharine New Year's Eve staple, "Auld Lang Syne."

In fact, Henry Jerome and His Orchestra had its own staple, a song called "Nice People." And it was plenty saccharine. The band used the song to kick off each and every show:

> *Nice people, hello and good cheer*
> *Nice people, we're glad that you're here*
> *It's always fun to get together again*
> *Just like the sun you bring fair weather again.*
>
> *Nice people, be happy awhile*
> *Nice people, let's start with a smile*
> *It will seem like forever 'til we run into*
> *Such nice, nice people like you.*

Greenspan toured all over the Eastern half of the United States during his time with Jerome. Sometimes the band traveled by bus, sometimes by train, sometimes in a caravan of borrowed cars, a truck loaded down with instruments bringing up the rear. The orchestra's base was New York City, but they were often on the road for months at a time. They didn't tend to do one-night stands; more often, they'd land engagements of a few nights or even weeks at places like the Claridge Hotel in Memphis; Jimmy Brink's Lookout House in Covington, Kentucky; or the Blue Room of the Hotel Roosevelt in New Orleans.

Greenspan and Garment, city boys both, had never had the opportunity to do much traveling. They thoroughly enjoyed the experience of touring. A highlight for Greenspan was spending lazy afternoons swimming and getting suntanned before gigs at Virginia Beach's Surf Club.

But for Jerome—the band's leader and a hardened veteran at age twenty-six—life on the road was getting to be a grind. "It's the old tired cliché," says Jerome. "After a while every city seems the same. You wake up in the morning and you're in a hotel. It becomes a routine."

Jerome was growing weary of the endless touring, the lack of money, the elusiveness of stardom. By this time, too—in the mid-1940s—the swing era was coming to an end. It had been the reigning style for a decade, ever since Benny Goodman's legendary stand at the Palomar Ballroom in Los Angeles had launched the music into prominence. But people were growing tired of the lindy hop and jitterbug. They were ready for something different. The next big thing was bebop. And for Greenspan, it would mark a truly bizarre chapter in his brief musical career.

Along the evolutionary arc of popular jazz music, it was natural for bop to follow swing. It was swing in a new and improved formulation: more rigorous, more demanding, more complex.

Bop, like swing, got its start among black musicians. Swing's true progenitors were Count Basie, Duke Ellington, and Fletcher Henderson. But it was Goodman and other white artists who popularized swing with a mainstream audience. While swing was peaking, bop's pioneers Earl Hines, Charlie Parker, Dizzy Gillespie, and Dexter Gordon began pushing into new musical territory.

Bop basically upped the ante. This was music made by young musicians who had grown up listening to Louis Armstrong and Duke Ellington. Now they wanted their own voice. They fashioned a sound that was distinctly in-your-face and urban, in keeping with the continued migration of blacks into large Northern cities. Bop also tended to demand a more active and introspective listening experience. Where swing was essentially good-time dance music, bop was for connoisseurs.

Heading in a bebop direction would be challenge enough for the Glenn Millers of the world—not to mention Henry Jerome. For Greenspan, it would be especially difficult, given that he was less than enamored of the new style and wasn't exactly a virtuoso performer, besides. But bop was the next big thing and Greenspan—a pro and a good sport—stuck around for the ride.

Garment was actually the one responsible for the band's change in direction. Every chance he got, the intrepid Garment had been out crawling the clubs in New York City. He went to Minton's and Monroe's Uptown House in Harlem, visited Kelly's Stable and the Three Deuces downtown on West 52nd Street, known as Swing Alley. He loved what he heard. Garment was getting exposed to the first rumblings of a musical revolution.

Excited and inspired, Garment approached Jerome late in 1944 with a brainstorm. "Look what's happening, Henry," he told Jerome. "The trend is going to be bop. This is what's going to replace swing. The pure musicians—this is all they want to play. This is what's in their hearts."

It was a crazy notion. But Jerome was just fed up enough to be willing to take a chance. There was not much to lose. Other bandleaders—Tommy Dorsey, say, or Claude Thornhill—had achieved enough success to have to satisfy their audience's expectations. They couldn't afford to head off in a wild new direction that might backfire. But Henry Jerome and His Orchestra were going nowhere fast.

Greenspan had joined a sweet band and was now about to be part of a peculiar bebop big band. In short order, he was issued his new uniform—startlingly yellow jacket, brown trousers, brown tie. Jerome deep-sixed "Nice People" as an opening number.

True to Garment's word, anyone with chops wanted to play bop. The new band quickly attracted some very talented young musicians, including Al Cohn and Norman "Tiny" Kahn, a couple of buddies from Garment's old neighborhood. Kahn was a drummer who had earned the nickname "Tiny" because he weighed more than 300 pounds. Cohn was a tenor saxophone player.

Another ringer was Johnny Mandel. Mandel was just nineteen when he signed on with Henry Jerome's band as an arranger and trombone player. He would later go on to win an Academy Award, four Grammies, and three Emmy nominations and would work with everyone from Frank Sinatra to Michael Jackson to Natalie Cole.

Circa 1944, bookings were a problem, though. Over the years, Loew's State Theater in Hartford, Connecticut, had been a dependable venue for Jerome. They just shook their heads, puzzled. Nobody knew what to make of his new bebop act. About the only gig Jerome could drum up was at Child's Restaurant in Times Square, where he'd played when he was first getting started as a bandleader.

Child's was a giant cafeteria, capacity 1,500, directly beneath the Paramount Theater. It was like a bomb shelter, all concrete and plaster. The acoustics were terrible. When the band took the stage, the crowd was primed to do some businessman's bouncing to the familiar strains of "Stardust." Instead, they were greeted with a barrage of honking saxes, clarinet squeals, and wild drum bursts. They remained seated as they ate their meals, trying to tune out the din.

The Child's Restaurant performances didn't do much for the band's reputation as a radio act, either. In that era, prime-time radio was devoted to mysteries and sitcoms. Then came the news. At 11:00 P.M., the networks would often carry live feeds from performances of various big bands. Although Henry Jerome and His Orchestra had never been stars, they had always gotten their share of radio coverage. As the Child's stand wore on, their appearances on radio grew less frequent and were picked up later and later at night.

Garment had promised that bop was a type of music that held appeal for musicians. As it was turning out, musicians were about the only people who cared about Henry Jerome's new outfit. The band itself was packed with talented musicians now. On any given night, the audience was certain to be filled with the band members' musician friends. And word spread. "Everybody came to see us," recalls Mandel. "It was like a Who's Who as far as the young jazz fraternity went."

Mandel remembers that one night, Dizzy Gillespie showed up at Child's to check out the band. It's entertaining to think that a true jazz eminence looked on as future Fed Chairman Greenspan blazed away on his saxophone. But Greenspan was merely a section player. He was never called upon to step up and execute a solo. Most likely, Gillespie's eyes and ears were trained instead on Mandel or Al Cohn.

With the influx of raw youth and bold talent, Henry Jerome's orchestra was growing wilder by the moment. Typically, the band played for thirty minutes, then took a thirty-minute break. To Garment and Greenspan fell the task of gathering up the band members before the break ended. "We had to locate the musicians and get them back on stage," says Garment. "They were frequently stowed away somewhere in a cloud of smoke."

A favorite spot was a tunnel that connected the Paramount Theater to a Walgreen's drugstore, where the phone booths were located. Garment remembers going into the tunnel and spotting a bunch of canary yellow jackets, all lined up in a row. The musicians were pretending to make phone calls but were actually passing a joint around.

Greenspan was never party to the partying. In fact, as the band grew wilder, he grew straighter. He began to exhibit latent and long-repressed accounting tendencies and even took to doing the band's books and helping fellow musicians with their taxes. During set breaks, he started reading treatises on economics borrowed from the public library. The topic gripped him.

"Alan was in the books all the time," says Mandel. "I remember an element of great sincerity. When he spoke you knew he meant whatever he said."

Greenspan pretty much kept to himself. Aside from Garment—with whom he had a cordial relationship—about the only person he really spent time with was Evan Aiken, a baritone sax player.

Aiken was quiet and intense. He was a big believer in a movement called Technocracy, which had created a sensation during the 1930s. The answer, according to Technocracy, was to relinquish all power to an elite group of scientists who would create a utopia based on economic units called energy determinants. Pretty muddled stuff. But in 1932, at the height of the Great Depression, it was all the rage. Technocracy's founder, Howard Scott, was a charismatic charlatan, equal parts fundamentalist preacher and snake-oil salesman.

Greenspan and Aiken would engage in quiet, deeply serious conversations. Jackie Eagle, a trumpeter with the band, recalls that Aiken seemed more science nerd than jazzman. "He and Greenspan were probably the only guys into anything besides music." Eagle adds: "We had a lot of hip musicians in those days who were pretty wild in their own way. Greenspan was a nice guy, but he wasn't one of the guys. He didn't hang out. We'd be telling jokes and laughing, but all the while he'd be reading, doing his thing."

One day in 1945, Greenspan's boyhood friend Bill Callejo dropped by Child's Restaurant. Callejo had enlisted underage in the National Guard and had later gained admission to an aviation cadet school. He had no idea Greenspan was part of Henry Jerome and His Orchestra; the two had lost touch during the chaos of the war years. Callejo was just a typical military grunt on leave, cooling his heels in a Times Square nightspot.

"I look up and there's Alan playing licorice stick," he says. "Everybody's gone, everybody's in the service somewhere. I don't know where anyone is anymore. The last thing in the world I expected to see was Alan up there playing clarinet. I waved to him and he waved back."

During the band's next half-hour break, the two of them caught up.

"You're in uniform," was the first thing out of Greenspan's mouth.

"And you're not," said Callejo.

Greenspan explained that he'd been designated 4-F by the military when an X-ray discovered a spot on his lung. It ultimately turned out to be nothing.

The two friends were full of questions and hurriedly reconstructed the turns their lives had taken since high school. Then the break was over. Greenspan returned to the bandstand. Callejo resumed life in uniform, waiting to be assigned to an aircraft carrier in the Pacific or perhaps a base in the Philippines.

Greenspan's band never cut a record. Both earlier and later incarnations of Jerome's bands did, but not the bop lineup. They faced a triple whammy. First, an experimental teenage orchestra didn't scream "next big thing," at least not in 1945. Even if it had, a musicians' recording strike was in effect. The strike had begun in the summer of 1942 at the urging of American Federation of Musicians head James Caesar Petrillo, who worried that if people bought records, they would stay home and refuse to go to live dances.

When the strike finally ended near the close of the war, there was a new problem. Shellac—that stiff and eminently shatterable material used in old-fashioned 78 rpm records—was in short supply and was needed for the war effort. To stretch out the supply, companies such as Columbia Records began making records that consisted of a cardboard disk covered with a thin veneer of shellac. Certainly, no one considered Henry Jerome's orchestra worthy of its precious shellac ration.

Even though the band didn't formally cut a record, there were recordings made near the end of World War II, when the military enacted its so-called V-disk program. The "V" in this case was for vinyl, a new material for making records. To keep morale high, kits featuring a phonograph, a packet of styluses, and a stack of V-disks were shipped off to the fighting men overseas. Some of the day's great acts cut V-disks, including Frank Sinatra, Bing Crosby, and Harry James. Henry Jerome and His Orchestra added their music to the list in support of the war effort.

Greenspan appears, too, on private recordings made by Jerome. This was the 1940s, a period before the advent of cassettes, so it wasn't possible to simply turn on a tape recorder and capture a performance. Instead, Jerome cut instant records, employing a machine that used a stylus to etch directly onto a material called glass acetate.

He'd do this on nights when the band was really hot. It was like a game tape in football—a private recording so his band could relive moments when they were at the top of their form. Jerome recorded two hours' worth of his bop band on glass acetate disks.

Years later, when many of the members of the band had gone on to renown, Jerome transferred four songs from glass acetate to a compact disk. He shopped it around as a demo to various record companies but couldn't find any takers. But the Institute of Jazz Studies at Rutgers University—one of the world's premier musical archives—has a copy of *A Taste of Crazy Rhythm,* featuring Greenspan, Jerome, Garment, Cohn, Mandel, Tiny Kahn, and the rest. The four songs are "Vitalize," "Tea for Two," "Etonize," and "It's a Wonderful World."

In 1945, Jerome pulled the plug on his bop experiment. "Commercially speaking, it was a big mistake," he says. "Timing is everything and the timing was premature. People didn't know what we were doing."

Nevertheless, the band earned a small place in music history. "Henry Jerome did not have one of the greatest bands" says Loren Schoenberg, a conductor and jazz historian. "The reason to talk about Jerome, the reason he's important, is that some marvelous musicians passed through his outfit."

There's Johnny Mandel, of course. Also Al Cohn, who joined Woody Herman's so-called Second Herd and was part of a famous saxophone quartet—also including Stan Getz, Zoot Sims, and Serge Chaloff. Later, as a solo act, he carved out a place as one of jazz's great sax players.

Tiny Kahn—literally a huge talent, and one who shone all too briefly—went on to play with such notable artists as Buddy Rich and Boyd Raeburn. At twenty-nine, he died of a heart attack brought on by too much Benzedrine and too many candy bars.

Then there was Gerry Mulligan. He never collected a paycheck from Jerome, but he sat in on a few sessions. Mulligan went on to collaborate with Miles Davis on the landmark *Birth of the Cool* recording, and during the 1950s, he teamed up with Chet Baker and cut some extremely influential sides.

Several Henry Jerome alums besides Greenspan earned acclaim outside of music. Sax player Larry Rivers achieved great success as a painter and East Village fixture; Jackie Eagle became a trumpet-playing comedian who managed to parlay that into a career as an actor in TV commercials for Xerox.

As for Jerome himself, he quickly moved on to the next thing. He formed a new band called Brazen Brass. Later, Jerome became a record executive and worked for Decca, MCA, and United Artists. He also found success as a composer—his songs have been recorded by musicians as diverse as Burt Bacharach, the Beatles, and Shania Twain.

Greenspan didn't actually stick around until the bitter end; he quit a few months before Henry Jerome's band dissolved. Playing in a bop band had never quite captured his fancy, and being thrown into the company of stellar talents such as Al Cohn revealed exactly what it took to be a great musician—and he realized that he didn't have it. As Greenspan would recall many years later: "I was a pretty good amateur musician, but I was average as a professional, and I was aware of that because you learn pretty quickly how good some professional musicians are. I realized it's innate. You either have it or you don't. . . . So I decided that, if that was as far as I could go, I was in the wrong profession."

Garment had a similar experience. He, too, was forced to stack himself up against Cohn night after night. It made both men painfully aware of their limitations.

Neither Greenspan nor Garment would ever attempt to play professionally again. They went off to pursue separate interests, but their divergent lives took strange twists and, at a very critical juncture, were destined to intersect once again.

3

NEW HORIZONS

After exiting Henry Jerome's band, Greenspan enrolled in New York University. Even after a term at Juilliard and a tour of the jazz world, he remained unsure of his real calling. Ultimately, he decided to abandon the musician's life to pursue his other passion—numbers.

During the 1940s, NYU was in certain respects the complete opposite of Juilliard. As mentioned earlier, the latter was founded to compete with the great conservatories of Europe in the rarefied realm of classical music. By contrast, NYU was chartered in 1831 with a far more modest and pragmatic aim. Nineteenth-century New York was on the brink of becoming a world city, one that rivaled Paris or London. What was needed was a university that could prepare people for the trades a great city required: accounting, retailing, and engineering.

Greenspan enrolled in NYU's School of Commerce, since rechristened the Stern School of Business. As times have changed, as a more advanced economy has raised the bar in business education, the Stern School has grown into an elite institution. But when Greenspan attended the School of Commerce, it was nicknamed "the factory" and churned out graduates who specialized in real estate, sales, insurance, and public-utilities management. The school was huge, too: In Greenspan's division of NYU alone, there were 9,000 students, largely a consequence of World War II veterans taking advantage of the GI Bill.

Classes for the School of Commerce were held at the Greenwich Village campus of NYU, in various buildings surrounding Washington Square Park. Greenspan was among the select few pursuing a degree in the more specialized field of economics. Along the way, he'd be exposed to a mixed bag of professors. There was Walter Spahr, for example, chairman of the economics department. Spahr was a nice enough man, but his teaching methods were less than inspiring.

He'd kick off each class by asking the students to open their textbooks.

"Are there any questions on page one?"

No answer.

"Are there any questions on page two?"

No answer.

"Any questions on page three?"

And so it went, usually culminating in: "Well, since all of you apparently know everything, close your textbooks, we're going to have a pop quiz."

Greenspan was eager to learn—he truly wanted to immerse himself in economics. As a consequence, he started reading books that weren't even on the assigned list. One was *The Economics of J. M. Keynes* by Dudley Dillard, among the first popular expositions of the noted British economist's work.

Keynes was cutting-edge stuff back then. He'd offered a challenging new prescription for managing economic downturns in his treatise *General Theory*, published in 1936. According to Keynes, there was no need to simply wait out a recession or depression, as had been the practice up to that time. Instead, governments could jump-start their economies by pouring money into public-works projects. Spending during tough times would create deficits, of course. When the economy was stable again, outlays could be cut back and the accrued government debt paid off.

Keynes's revolutionary ideas had been taken up by Roosevelt during the depths of the Great Depression. The U.S. government became the employer of last resort, paying people to build roads and paint walls. Within a few years, at the onset of World War II, the U.S. government's role was elevated to that of primary employer. Industrial production kicked into high gear to support the war effort, and the United States was jolted out of depression.

In the aftermath of World War II, there was concern that the economy—sans government stimulus—might slide right back into distress. To intervene or not to intervene—that became the great debate, and

Keynes's theory provided the terms and the context. "I remember Greenspan clutching that Dillard book," says Robert Kavesh, a friend and classmate from NYU.

Often Kavesh and Greenspan would arrange to meet between classes. Thanks to NYU's morning-to-midnight schedule, "between classes" could wind up being a long time. You could take a class at 10:00 A.M. and not have another until 2:00 P.M. Greenspan and Kavesh began taking long walks in Washington Square Park.

They'd while away the time whistling and humming classical tunes and trying to stump one another—playing "name that composer." The two engaged in endless debates about baseball. Kavesh was a Yankees fan; Greenspan remained loyal to the Dodgers. They'd argue about who was a better second baseman, Brooklyn's Eddie Stanky or Joe Gordon of the Bronx Bombers.

Sometimes they'd entertain themselves for hours by simply sitting in the park and watching the girls walk by. "We used to just sort of ogle, saying, 'she's pretty, she's pretty, she's pretty'—the stuff that guys do," recalls Kavesh.

Actually meeting any of these girls was a different matter. The war veterans—bona fide heroes with riveting tales of exotic lands—had Greenspan and Kavesh totally trumped. "Greenspan really wasn't very gregarious," recalls one classmate, Betty Schwimmer, née Betty Shapiro. "He hung out in the economics office more or less. He was big on shirts and ties, always dressed up, not like the rest of us . . . I thought he was kind of nerdy."

For his part, Kavesh took to pursuing girls in Rockaway, Queens, where he'd grown up. There, at least he had a home-field advantage. Greenspan followed the same strategy, trying to meet girls back in Washington Heights, where he was still living at home with his mother and grandparents. He didn't have a great deal of luck there either in those days, as Kavesh recalls. "I think this is one of those times in his life when the pickings were lean, as they say."

But these were golden days, nonetheless. During those walks and talks in Washington Square Park, Greenspan and Kavesh forged a life-long friendship. Kavesh would go on to earn a Ph.D. in economics, ultimately teaching at NYU. He'd also wind up being Greenspan's teacher when he did advanced course work at NYU during the 1960s and 1970s.

Another of Greenspan's teachers during his undergrad days at NYU was Geoffrey Moore. Moore was on a year's leave from the National Bureau of Economic Research (NBER) and proved to be a notoriously poor lecturer. Often he'd do little more than stare at his shoes and mumble. Unlike some of Greenspan's other NYU professors, however, he was incredibly knowledgeable about the subject matter. Moore went on in 1995 to win the American Economic Association's Distinguished Fellow Award—an honor second only to the Nobel Prize—for his work on leading economic indicators. Moore's future inflation gauge (FIG) would prove to be one of Greenspan's favorite indicators as Fed chairman.

Moore taught statistics during his NYU stint. One of the textbooks he employed was *Measuring Business Cycles,* published by Arthur Burns and Wesley Mitchell in 1946. Like Keynes's *General Theory*, this was a landmark work. Mitchell was one of the founders of the NBER, and Burns, an eminent professor at Columbia. In reading *Measuring Business Cycles*, Greenspan and the other students got a taste of the NBER's rigorous approach to collecting economic data and generating statistics.

When the celebrated Moore was traveling or delivering a lecture, a young associate professor named Ernest Kurnow took over the statistics class. He has vivid memories of Greenspan: "He had an intellectual curiosity that was unquenchable. He was always restless, fidgety, couldn't learn enough. I had a feeling deep down that this man was going to go somewhere."

Kurnow became a full professor at NYU in 1960. He taught there for the entire second half of the twentieth century. During that time, he encountered only one other student who, in his estimation, exhibited the same thirst for learning as Greenspan. That student was Harvey Golub (NYU class of 1961), who went on to become CEO of American Express.

Greenspan was a real joiner at NYU, much as during his days at George Washington High, but quite unlike his brief stint at Juilliard. He played clarinet in the orchestra and sang in the glee club. He was also president of something called the Symphonic Society. It held as its mandate "To elevate and cultivate musical tastes and standards among business students." The society met every third Thursday, whereupon Greenspan would play phonograph records and students would try to guess the composition—a more formal take on the game he and Kavesh played in Washington Square Park. There were occasional guest speakers, too, drawn from NYU's music school.

Greenspan was also president of the Economics Society, an organization that arranged monthly lectures by professional economists. Notable guests included Solomon Fabricant from the NBER and Martin Gainsbrugh, senior economist at the National Industrial Conference Board, a business research organization.

NYU was a good experience for Greenspan. He even got a mention in a *New York Times* article that cited a paper he had written, entitled "Profits of Small Corporations." It was the first of literally millions of times that his name was to appear in print.

Greenspan graduated summa cum laude in 1948, with a B.S. in economics. He would have managed straight A's had it not been for two B's during his first term.

The next step for Greenspan was graduate school at Columbia University. In the late 1940s, Columbia offered one of the best economics programs in the country, neck-in-neck with Harvard and Princeton. Exposure during Geoffrey Moore's course to the NBER's statistical methods helped push Greenspan toward the school, an acknowledged seat of the empirical approach to economics. Wesley Mitchell and Arthur Burns—coauthors of the textbook used by Moore—were in large part responsible for the high profile enjoyed by the university's economics department.

Mitchell favored a rigorously scientific approach. Rather than viewing economics through the lens of abstract theory, he urged that theories be built up through data and observation. His book *Business Cycles*, published in 1913, was one of the first ever to attempt a systemic study of changes in the economy over time. Up to that point, people generally had no narrative explanation for the ebb and flow of the economy. That it might actually move in a cyclical fashion was the province of just a handful of leading-edge thinkers.

Mitchell was driven to make sense of the economy. His only problem was that there wasn't much data available in those days. In 1920, Mitchell helped found the NBER. The intent was to gather fresh information and statistics so the economy could be better understood. The simple fact was that no one at the time knew how much people in

America earned on average, how many hours they worked in a standard week, or very much else of use, for that matter.

Arthur Burns was Mitchell's student at Columbia. After earning his Ph.D., he landed a teaching post at Rutgers University in New Jersey, where he in turn taught such future eminences as Geoffrey Moore and Milton Friedman. Later, Burns returned to Columbia as a professor and was granted tenure in 1944. Burns and his mentor Mitchell cowrote *Measuring Business Cycles*, an update of the seminal 1913 work. After Mitchell retired in 1945, Burns took over the NBER.

Burns—student of the great Wesley Mitchell, teacher of Friedman and Moore—would become Greenspan's teacher as well. He was a formidable and immensely intimidating presence. He parted his hair down the middle, like an old-fashioned banker, wore large round wire-rimmed glasses and was forever puffing on his pipe. Burns's famous pipe was a character unto itself, almost like an adjunct to his personality. As some poor student fidgeted before him, he would proceed to smoke it, clean it, tamp it, refill it—all these various motions acting as a fearsome prelude to whatever he was about to say. When he spoke, it was in a basso profundo directly out of the Old Testament.

Burns was one of the few critics of Keynes. The way in which the U.S. economy bounced back after World War II had pretty well sealed Keynes's stature, especially in academic circles. His theories would continue to hold sway into the 1970s, when the United States was gripped by a deep recession and inflation spiral that seemed to defy all the conventional remedies. But back in the 1940s and 1950s, Burns was practically a lone voice in the anti-Keynes camp, though a commanding one to be sure.

That Burns and Keynes would be in opposition made eminent sense. Burns was an empiricist, Keynes a theorist. In Burns's eyes, one data point—America's rocket-rise up out of the Great Depression—did not a theory confirm. Burns proceeded to challenge Keynes on a number of grounds.

For example, Keynes held that the economy had a deflationary bias. If the government didn't periodically intervene, the economy might slowly grind to a halt. That was the lesson of the Great Depression, in the view of Keynes's many supporters. Burns drew a different lesson. His dissertation, *Production Trends in the U.S. Since 1870*, catalogued the constant creation of new industries and technologies, both in good times and bad. This was evidence, in Burns's eyes, that the economy had the capacity to self-correct.

Even during the worst depressions, a new industry or innovation— something—could be counted on to set the stage for the next boom. Burns believed in a natural business cycle. By contrast, Keynes viewed the economy as something akin to a lazy horse that had to be constantly prodded and pushed by its rider.

At Columbia, Greenspan took a seminar from Burns on business cycles. On the very first day of class, Burns asked the students, "What causes inflation?"

He scanned the room in silence until the tension was palpable, then removed his pipe from his mouth and pronounced, "Excess government spending causes inflation."

Judith Mackey was a doctoral student at Columbia at the same time as Greenspan. The two took Burns's seminar together and became friends. She remembers what a powerful impression Burns's statement made on the students.

"It impressed everybody in the class including Alan," Mackey recalls. "Burns was brilliant. He was very interested in ideas tied to the real world, not the theoretical realm. His aim was to concretize the business cycle by means of rigorous statistical analysis. He really made you think."

Burns's contention—that government policy might actually be counterproductive to the economy—set young Greenspan's head spinning. Much of what he'd been exposed to up to that point in his life stressed the efficacy of government largesse. When he and Kavesh first met, Greenspan had been carrying around a popularization of Keynes's theory. His father had written *Recovery Ahead!* which championed the big-government initiatives of Roosevelt's New Deal. Now he was becoming versed in the other side of the argument.

Under Burns's tutelage, Greenspan would do an about-face. He'd start moving away from the benevolent-government perspective advocated by Roosevelt, Keynes, and his own father. He would grow to be a staunch supporter of laissez-faire and limited government. Later still, Greenspan would do another flip-flop. As Fed chairman, he'd be charged with actively managing the economy—although he'd continue to hew to a free-market philosophy on issues such as deregulation.

Accuracy and precision were of paramount importance to Burns. He blanketed students' papers with comments and criticisms. The rap on

Burns was that he checked everything, and then checked it all over again. Students had to be prepared to defend their work down to the smallest footnote.

But there was another side to Burns. He could be surprisingly warm and generous toward the handful of students who earned his respect. To them, he would open up and show a side that was rather at odds with his professorial persona. He was always willing to help a favorite student with problems, even those of a personal nature.

Milton Friedman got to see this other side of Burns, and over the years, the two grew very close. During an interview, the great economist, aged eighty-seven, described his onetime mentor as "almost a surrogate father."

Greenspan also managed to earn Burns's respect. Although not yet the polished data-sifter he'd later become, Greenspan impressed Burns with his dogged approach to statistical analysis. Burns encouraged Alan to be ever more vigorous, never committing to an idea unless it could be backed up by numbers.

"I know Burns regarded Greenspan's ability very highly," says Friedman.

"Burns clearly had great respect for Alan," concurs Mackey. "Both of them were concerned with very serious matters and both of them were interested in the economy and what made it tick. Burns became Alan's mentor, and they eventually grew very close."

Greenspan wasn't completely entranced with economics during this time. He made room for a social life. In 1952, he was set up on a blind date with a woman named Joan Mitchell. Hailing from Winnipeg, Canada, she was a petite blonde in her early twenties, elegant and highly cultured. She had only just arrived in New York and was planning to study art history at NYU's Institute of Fine Arts. A family friend, figuring she was in need of company, told her to expect a call from a man named Alan Greenspan. "This is a very intelligent, interesting young man," the family friend told Mitchell. "I think perhaps you would like to meet him."

But Mitchell wasn't big on blind dates; she figured she'd meet people on her own soon enough. When Greenspan called, she was fully prepared to turn him down. But he won her over. Whether through hesitance or savvy, he talked to her on the phone for quite a while before getting around to asking her on a date. By that point, she felt they'd established a rapport.

He proceeded to rattle off three possible plans. They could take in a movie, catch a ball game, or go to Carnegie Hall. Mitchell agreed to meet him, and for their first date they attended a concert featuring music by Bach and Gian Carlo Menotti. She continued to be impressed, finding him a pleasant companion, courtly and well spoken. "He was an interesting man to talk to," she recalls. "And he was very attentive to me."

The two began dating, although Mitchell didn't find Greenspan to be much of a romantic. He wasn't the flower-giving sort. But they found plenty to talk about. He was solicitous of her and learned all about art history. She learned a bit about economics. They enjoyed listening to classical music on the hi-fi in her tiny apartment and sometimes went out dancing. This was the 1950s; that was enough. Shortly, they were engaged.

Ten months after their first meeting, Greenspan and Mitchell were married in a small ceremony at the Pierre Hotel. Only their immediate families were in attendance. There had been considerable discussion about whether Greenspan's father was welcome at the event since the Goldsmith family still felt animosity toward him.

He finally wound up on the guest list. On an earlier occasion, he had managed to exchange a few words with his son's bride-to-be. He had told her not to worry and assured her that his son was nothing like him—Alan wasn't going to just up and run off the way he had. As for the wedding, he actually left early. Mitchell couldn't help but find him to be a cold and distant man. Herbert Greenspan, the man who touted beneficent and paternalistic government, had never been able to muster any real devotion to his own son.

The young couple moved into the top half of a duplex on Juno Street in the Forest Hills section of Queens where Greenspan and his mother had been living. Rose found another apartment in Manhattan.

By this time, Greenspan had dropped out of Columbia. He was having trouble coming up with money to pay for tuition. What's more, Arthur Burns had gone off to Washington, where he was serving as chairman of the Council of Economic Advisers (CEA) in the Eisenhower administration. So Greenspan went to work at what was then known as the National Industrial Conference Board, later called simply the Conference Board, a not-for-profit organization devoted to research on business practices. Greenspan earned a respectable salary, $4,000 a year.

The Conference Board had been founded in 1916 during a time of rampant societal change. The agrarian age was giving way to the industrial age and there was a sense that all the rules were changing, provoking immense anxiety. Strife between labor and management was on the upswing and was getting increasingly violent. Many at the time were of the opinion that class warfare was right around the corner.

To address such concerns, a meeting of business leaders was arranged by Magnus Washington Alexander, an engineer for General Electric. The purpose of the meeting was to discuss ways of cooling the tensions and fostering a greater understanding of the role that industry and technology played in society. This meeting led to other meetings and the Conference Board was founded.

At first, the new organization was viewed with great suspicion. There were worries that it might act as a tool of management and take on the labor unions directly. Such concerns might have proved founded, too, had it not been for a stroke of enlightened self-interest. If labor was unhappy, went the reasoning, it was best to find out why. Otherwise, absenteeism and strikes would cause businesses to suffer right alongside their employees. They'd feel the pain in their bottom line.

With this in mind, the Conference Board set about trying to study business issues with scientific rigor and objectivity. Over the years, it would be involved in everything from efficiency and productivity to health-care benefits and workplace safety.

Greenspan thoroughly enjoyed working at the Conference Board. His job involved analyzing the issues faced by heavy industries such as steel and railroads. He appreciated having access to the Conference Board's extensive library. He borrowed countless books—a number of which he never returned. Years later, in 1996, Greenspan was honored during a ceremony celebrating the Conference Board's eightieth anniversary. He was jokingly informed that he would need to fork over the fines for his overdue books, now totaling a decent percentage of the national debt.

Greenspan liked his Conference Board coworkers and became especially close to Al Sommers, an economist who had studied at NYU. Sommers was liberal-leaning and favored what he termed "affirmative government." But the two shared a passion for tennis, and Greenspan appreciated Sommers's far-ranging approach to economics, which integrated ideas from various disciplines in the social sciences.

While at the Conference Board, Greenspan also worked with the legendary Sandy Parker. The two shared a small office. Parker was trained as an economist, but he eventually moved on to *Fortune* magazine, where he became an editor. He introduced a section to the magazine devoted to economic forecasting, a journalistic innovation that proved to be very popular. Parker took to consulting with Greenspan on these forecasts. For Greenspan's part, he got to know a man who understood the economy up, down, and sideways. "Parker had a full-blown model of the U.S. economy in his head," recalls an acquaintance. "Anything you were working on, he knew what data was available and what wasn't, and how you should be looking at the various details."

While Greenspan was immersed in his job at the Conference Board, his new bride was already growing restless. During the 1950s—the era of the three-martini lunch—he was working modern-day investment banker's hours, and at a not-for-profit organization besides. He generally put in six-day weeks, and on Sundays, he usually played golf.

"I think he enjoyed the work tremendously," recalls Mitchell. "But I didn't quite like it, because I didn't see where he was going with it. I thought he might get lost and get stuck there for the rest of his life."

Quick to marry, Greenspan and Mitchell were just as rapidly growing apart. One of the biggest issues was that they were moving in separate social orbits, ones that in no way overlapped. Mitchell was spending time with a group of New York City intellectuals who were interested in a philosophy called objectivism. She could not interest Greenspan in fraternizing with her group. His world consisted of the Conference Board and golf. They didn't really fight, as such—Greenspan was much too calm and polite for that—they simply saw precious little of one another.

During this time, Arthur Burns offered Greenspan a job working as a staff economist at the CEA. The job would have necessitated a move to Washington, D.C., but Mitchell quickly put the kibosh on that. The couple couldn't seem to find any common ground.

When the marriage finally collapsed, there was little sound and less fury. As Mitchell recalls: "All the time that we were living in this duplex, the couple living beneath us was screaming and yelling. They never lowered their voice to a normal level. We never had a harsh word. We just decided it would be better to part. It wasn't the life that either of us wanted, I guess."

Greenspan and Mitchell had their marriage annulled in 1953, after just ten months together. They didn't get divorced because the legalities involved were very complicated in that era, requiring proof of something drastic such as infidelity. Annulment was the cheaper, easier option for brief marriages that simply didn't work out.

Curiously, the pair actually grew closer in certain ways after they split. Greenspan had a knack for holding on to the people in his life. Not being bound together in marriage put Greenspan at an emotional distance where he felt more comfortable with Mitchell. The two picked up where they'd left off a year before when they were dating. They were able to become good friends and discuss art, music, and literature, the things that had drawn them together in the first place.

4

RAND AND THE COLLECTIVE

It's ironic that during his marriage to Joan Mitchell, Greenspan felt disdain toward the Objectivists, because after they had split up, he did a complete turnabout and gave the philosophy a chance. He also grew to admire Ayn Rand, the woman behind the philosophy. For the next fifteen years—from Greenspan's late twenties to his early forties—objectivism played a major role in his life, and he spent countless hours in the company of Rand and her circle. The controversial writer was to wind up a very significant influence on Greenspan, falling somewhere between Arthur Burns and his own mother.

Rand was a formidable presence. Brilliant, charismatic, iconoclastic, she was logical to a fault, yet capable of outlandish displays of temper. As a writer and philosopher, she carved out a vastly ambitious territory in such classic works as *The Fountainhead* and *Atlas Shrugged*. She chose to dramatize one of history's great questions—whether authority ultimately lies with society or the individual. Rand was uniquely qualified to put this timeless question into a twentieth-century context, having fled Soviet Russia for the United States. No one explored the conflict between the individual and the state, between capitalism and communism in quite the terms that she did. It was electrifying stuff to her admirers, Greenspan among them. Among detractors, her views were considered dangerous by some, merely drivel by others.

Rand was born on February 2, 1905, in St. Petersburg. Her given name was Alisa Zinovievna Rosenbaum, the first of three children born to Zinovy and Anna Rosenbaum. During her early years, at least, her family made out pretty well. They would be considered middle class by the standards of czarist Russia. Her father was a chemist and owned a small pharmacy.

As a young child, Alisa loved to sit on the windowsill in her family's apartment and gaze out at St. Petersburg's unfolding street scenes. She would later recall being particularly fascinated by the trolley cars and flashing stoplights, perhaps presaging her lifelong love of machinery and industry. It's also one of many examples of how all the elements of Rand's life were in place early on. Upon entering school, she showed an immediate aptitude for math. From the age of nine, she knew she wanted to be a writer. Her mother introduced her to classics by authors such as Victor Hugo and Henryk Sienkiewicz, author of *Quo Vadis?* Young Alisa was drawn to the sense of grandeur and heroism portrayed in their books.

Alisa kept a diary during high school. One entry read simply: "To-day, I decided to be an atheist." It's all there: her decisiveness and trademark icy rationality, along with a certain impetuousness and flair for the dramatic.

In 1917, Russia was gripped by revolution. The czarist regime was overthrown and the Communists took power. Zinovy Rosenbaum's pharmacy was nationalized by the Bolsheviks, and as a consequence, the family was often pushed to the brink of starvation. One time, Alisa was so hungry that she begged for a single pea from her father's plate. Whenever she planned to go out in public, she had to first rub carnation oil and kerosene into her hair to ward off the typhus-bearing lice that were decimating the populace.

Throughout the early years of Russia's Communist experiment, the rules changed on an almost daily basis. Leaders were in, then out; the fates of individuals rose and fell as if on a whim. A shopkeeper's store might be seized one moment, and in the next moment, he might be encouraged to open a new one as part of some state-sponsored economic initiative. Like everyone else in Russia, the Rosenbaums watched helplessly as their lives were transformed by each change in the political winds.

In 1921, Alisa entered the University of Petrograd, planning to study philosophy and history. Two years later, students were asked to fill out forms, indicating whether their parents or even grandparents had owned businesses prior to the revolution. This was the beginning of a series of university purges, meant to give priority to proletarian students. Many of the bourgeois students were expelled, and some wound up in labor camps in Siberia. Alisa was spared, due to a bureaucratic quirk on the part of the new state, and she graduated in 1924.

But the experience left an indelible mark on her. "I knew it was evil," she would later say of the arbitrary exercise of power that accompanied the rise of communism.

Alisa fled to America. In 1925, she managed to obtain a passport, one of just a handful the Soviet government doled out to its citizenry. She was permitted a six-month stay in the United States, to be spent with relatives of her mother who lived in Chicago.

Shortly after arrival, Alisa changed her first name to Ayn, after a Finnish writer whom she admired. (Ayn rhymes with "mine" or "swine," as she was fond of saying.) The "Rand" was simply a name she liked—contrary to the oft-told tale that the inspiration came from a Remington-Rand typewriter. She knew a pseudonym was necessary, because already she was planning a literary career devoted to scathing indictments of the Soviet system. She didn't want to put her parents or sisters at risk.

Russian Alisa Rosenbaum was now Ayn Rand, and living in America. She drove her Chicago relatives to distraction, however, writing obsessively and deep into the night, filling the tiny apartment with the clatter of her typewriter and disturbing their sleep.

Rand's cousin, Sarah Lipton, was a friend of a movie distributor in Chicago, who in turn knew someone who worked in the publicity department of Cecil B. DeMille's movie studio. She managed to secure Rand a letter of introduction. In 1926, Rand obtained an extension of her visa and set out for Los Angeles. She lived in the Hollywood Studio Club, a low-rent women's hotel for aspiring starlets and others set on breaking into the film business.

Rand found work in the costume department of RKO studios and hammered out screenplays whenever she found the time. She proceeded to write one with a strong anti-Soviet bent called *Red Pawn*.

Universal expressed interest, as did Paramount, which considered casting Marlene Dietrich in the starring role with Josef von Sternberg as director. But the deals fell through and the project was shelved.

During the same period, she also wrote her first novel, *We the Living*, another attack on Soviet-style communism, and not a particularly veiled one. It was the closest to memoir of any of Rand's fictional works. She managed to sell *We the Living*, to Macmillan, but it was slow to find an audience.

Rand's first big success was actually on Broadway. One of her screenplays, *Penthouse Legend*, was a courtroom drama with a gimmick. It was open-ended, never answering the question of guilt or innocence. Instead, the verdict was supposed to come from the members of the audience, chosen to act as a jury. Rand was unable to drum up interest among movie studios. But Al Woods, a prominent New York theatrical producer, bought the play, changed the name to *Night of January 16th*, and opened it at the Ambassador Theater. It became a hit and ran for 283 performances.

Rand made just $100 in royalties on *We the Living* during the 1930s. At the height of *Night of January 16th*'s popularity, however, she was netting as much as $1,200 a week. The money helped sustain her during her next project, a marathon: writing *The Fountainhead*.

Rand submitted the book to a dozen publishers, but it was summarily rejected by each. Ultimately, she found a taker in Bobbs-Merrill, an Indianapolis-based house. It was a good fit. Archie Ogden, her editor, had rejected Dale Carnegie's *How to Win Friends and Influence People*, so he was clearly comfortable championing works that flouted convention.

The Fountainhead was published in 1943. It was a literary phenomenon, provoking powerful responses in certain readers, some of whom even credited the book with changing their lives, encouraging them to stand firm as individuals and pursue their dreams. Among the book's most passionate fans were Nathaniel Blumenthal and Barbara Weidman, a Canadian couple attending UCLA. Blumenthal had been introduced to *The Fountainhead* at age fourteen, and as a freshman psychology major, he read it for the fortieth time. He wrote an adoring fan letter to Rand, and she invited him to meet her at her home near Los Angeles. A number of sessions followed in which the teenage couple dropped in on the forty-five-year-old author to talk about philosophy deep into the night. "Nathan was the first budding genius I ever met," Rand later told the *Saturday Evening Post*.

Soon Blumenthal and Weidman began introducing other young people to the philosophies laid out in *The Fountainhead*. It so happened that Barbara Weidman's best friend when growing up in Winnipeg was Joan Mitchell. By coincidence, both women had been named Barbara Joan. As young girls they made a pact: Each dropped half of "Barbara Joan," and they became Barbara Weidman and Joan Mitchell, respectively.

Another name change was soon in the works. Weidman and Blumenthal got married and changed their last name to Branden, an impossibly heroic moniker featuring a "Rand" inserted in the middle. The Brandens and Rand moved to New York. The inner circle of *Fountainhead* devotees—those granted audience with the author herself—continued to grow. It now numbered about ten and was a diverse set that included a nurse, a concert pianist, and a stockbroker.

For a time, the group was known as the Class of '43, in honor of the year *The Fountainhead* was published. But the name that stuck was the Collective. This was intended as irony. Collectivism referred to Soviet-style groupthink, where the rights of individuals were subjugated to the needs of the state. Her young fans fancied themselves instead as a collection of free thinkers and fierce individualists.

While Greenspan was married to Joan Mitchell, he had occasional brushes with the Collective in its formative stages. He had enjoyed reading *The Fountainhead* on his own, but he didn't much care for the exclusive little reading group/admiration society that surrounded it. By all accounts, the feeling was mutual. One time, Greenspan ran into Rand and some of her acolytes as they were getting off an elevator. Rand took an instant dislike to him. He was a very somber young man, she felt, wearing a dark suit and tie that matched his demeanor. "He looks like an undertaker," she remarked.

After their marriage ended, Mitchell continually urged Greenspan to be more open toward Rand and her circle. Given his personality, she was certain that he would respond to objectivism's emphasis on rationality and individualism. It was through her that Greenspan got to know Nathaniel Branden, objectivism's chief proselytizer. Over several months in 1954, they met a number of times, sometimes in restaurants, sometimes at Branden's apartment at 165 East 35th Street.

Greenspan wasn't going to be an easy convert. He'd already been exposed to a philosophy that spoke to his rational nature, fittingly called logical positivism. It was one of the dominant movements in philosophy during the 1940s and 1950s. He'd first encountered it as a student at NYU.

Logical positivism holds that mankind can't know anything with absolute certainty. That seemed harmless enough, but it was anathema to Rand and her circle. Objectivists were suspicious of anything that smacked of relativism. The truth was the truth—otherwise you risked a situation where bourgeois students were expelled, proletarians categorically elevated. Start down that slippery slope and pretty soon night would be day, right wrong, and nothing would be known with certainty, truly. In the Objectivist view, man's brain was a glorious tool, capable of apprehending anything through rigorous logic.

Branden kept after Greenspan. At their meetings, Greenspan would say things such as: "I think that I exist. But I don't know for sure. Actually, I can't say with certainty that anything exists."

"How do you explain the fact that you're here," Branden would counter. "Do you require anything else besides the proof of your own senses?"

Back and forth they went, two young men locked in earnest debate. Among the Collective, meanwhile, Branden's pursuit of Greenspan was turning into something of a joke. Rand would periodically check on Branden's progress. "How's the undertaker," she'd sneer. "Has he figured out whether he exists or not?"

But Branden wasn't about to give up. "I thought Greenspan was very, very intelligent," he recalls. "I thought he was an unusual person. I don't know how to say it any better than this: I felt a basic goodness in him."

One day, Branden was riding in a cab with Rand. He had some surprising news and could hardly contain himself. Finally, he just blurted it out.

"Guess who exists?"

Rand was shocked.

"Don't tell me," she said, "you've won over Alan Greenspan."

"Yes, I have," he answered. "And I think you're going to change your mind about him. I think he's a really interesting man with a very unusual brain."

Branden was Rand's chief protégé. A few years hence, she would officially designate him as her "intellectual heir." She trusted his judgment implicitly. If Branden said Greenspan was all right, Greenspan was all right. So it was that Greenspan was invited to join the salon of celebrated author Ayn Rand.

The Collective met Saturday nights at Rand's apartment, at 36 East 36th Street, across from the Morgan Library. It was a two-bedroom apartment, far smaller and far more modestly appointed than one would expect for a woman so wealthy and successful. The blinds were generally drawn and the windows shut, a reminder that one of Rand's beloved cats had previously leapt out the window to its death. The apartment often felt dark and stuffy. Assorted armchairs and folding chairs were set up awaiting the guests.

People would begin showing up around 8:00 P.M. and sit around talking until the small hours of the morning. The topics were far-ranging: politics, current events, philosophy, literature, movies, and painting. In much of this Greenspan wasn't so well versed, but he followed Mitchell's lead and allowed himself to be open to the discussions. As he grew more comfortable with the Collective, he started to show them a different side of his personality. He remained highly serious—though at least he came across as less grim and dour. Rand's circle, in turn, grew more comfortable with him.

Economics was also a frequent topic for the Collective. This proved to be a big sell for Greenspan, who had recently left his job at the Conference Board and was working to build up his own consulting firm, Townsend-Greenspan.

If Burns can be credited with pushing Greenspan in a free-market direction, it's Rand who finished the job. Burns was a professor, with a typically professorial style—cautious, reasoned, equanimical. In academic circles, he had been a lone voice in the wilderness, one of the few critics of Keynes. But Rand—a self-professed "radical for capitalism"—was willing to really go out on a limb. Because of her firsthand experience with communism, she pledged allegiance to capitalism with the intensity only a convert can summon.

Rand made her case for laissez-faire vehemently, incisively, passionately. A frequent topic of discussion—irony of ironies—was the futility and destructiveness of central banks. The job of a central bank, after all, is to meddle in the economy. That can lead to all kinds of distortions and dislocations. During these discussions, the Fed was often taken to task for making mistakes that brought on the Great Depression. Errant Fed policies could also lead to inflation, in turn making citizens' money worth less. The Objectivist party line held that inflation was an insidious form of taxation.

These were curiously compelling notions, though not entirely original. As Joan Mitchell had predicted, they spoke to Greenspan. He was drawn to objectivism's logical rigor. Discussions of the primacy of free markets, meanwhile, awakened a sense of moral fervor in the onetime Detective Scout of Washington Heights. Objectivism even had its own in-speak and lingo. It was infernally addictive. Rand had a rare knack for coming up with catch phrases such as "whim worshippers" and "second handers." Had she not been an American fiction writer, she would have made a great Soviet slogan writer. Whim worshippers are people who live by the credo "If it feels good, do it." They forswear logic, relying instead on their emotions to guide them. Second handers are people with an underdeveloped notion of self. They look to society for validation and approval. Rand's terminology was bandied about at the Saturday-night sessions until it was almost as if the Collective was speaking a foreign language.

But no matter how free-flowing the conversation, the final authority lay with Rand. Despite being a small woman, she had a commanding presence, with dark piercing eyes and a vast repertoire of lacerating language. She smoked incessantly through a tapered cigarette holder. Long after it went out of style, she continued to wear her hair in a flapperish pageboy. Often she'd cut a speaker off midstream, uttering, "Check your premises." Or she might fix someone with an icy stare and ask, "Are you in focus?"

The big treat was when Rand would pass around her novel in progress, *Atlas Shrugged*. The members of the Collective would take turns reading the manuscript, and feverish discussion would invariably ensue.

Greenspan was riveted by these reading sessions.

"Alan became wildly, wildly enthusiastic about the book and about the heroic vision of business at its best the book conveyed," recalls Nathaniel Branden. "It reached him at a very deep, personal level. And the fact that it did so endeared him very, very much to Ayn Rand."

Barbara Branden—now long divorced from Nathaniel but still in possession of that heroic name—has similar recollections of Greenspan's enthusiasm. What sticks with her is his reaction to one particular scene in the book. "As I remember, one of the heroes in *Atlas*, Francisco, gives a long talk on the nature of money, that money is not the root of all evil, but the root of all good. I know I was overwhelmed by that talk and so was Alan. It was a justification of money as the way man maintains his life on earth."

Greenspan and Rand continued to grow closer. They had some real areas of commonality. Both had an aptitude for math. Near the end of her life, as a woman in her seventies, Rand studied algebra just for the fun of it.

Greenspan's particular rhetorical style also stood him in good stead with Rand. Debating was a way of life for the Collective. But where arguments between the members often took unseemly ad hominem turns, Greenspan favored a cool and dispassionate style. Of course, disagreement with Rand herself was rare. But even here, Greenspan was one of the few—with the notable exception of Nathaniel Branden—who could directly oppose her without disastrous results.

Rand had extremely idiosyncratic music tastes. She was passionate about the composers Rachmaninoff and Lehár and felt a special affinity for the traditional song "My Irish Molly-O." She disliked Beethoven, Wagner, and Elvis. But she didn't see this merely as a matter of taste. As the founder of objectivism, Rand was confident that her views on the relative merits of various pieces of music were rooted in objective truth. Barbara Branden recalls that Greenspan was about the only person who ever made any headway with her on this issue.

"Alan loves Mozart," she says, "and Ayn did not. But Alan was able to convince Ayn—and it was really quite amazing—that there was in fact value to Mozart that she wasn't aware of."

Rand valued Greenspan's opinion. She also appreciated the fact that Greenspan was a bit more seasoned than some of the other Collective members. He was in his thirties during the height of the Collective, while many members were still in their twenties. His consulting firm was doing well and he was becoming a success in business, a realm she held in high esteem.

In fact, she called upon Greenspan to help her with some of the research for *Atlas Shrugged*. Where *The Fountainhead* had dealt with architecture, her new book would take as its setting the world of heavy industry. She needed to learn all she could about railroads and oil derricks and steel mills—the very things Greenspan had doggedly analyzed while working at the Conference Board.

Greenspan was part of the inner circle now. It was a surprising turn, given that Rand had initially derided him as an undertaker in the grip of an existential crisis. Ultimately, Greenspan was to occupy a position in the Collective equal to Leonard Peikoff, a cousin of Barbara Branden's who was studying philosophy at NYU. Depending on her mood, Rand looked alternately to either Greenspan or Peikoff. The two had rather opposite personalities. Greenspan was worldly—he'd toured the country in a jazz band and was in the process of growing an economic consulting business. Rand enjoyed his input when she wanted to hear from someone who was self-possessed and of an independent mind. By contrast, Peikoff was something of an empty vessel, highly malleable, but also fiercely loyal. When Rand needed her ego stroked, Peikoff was her man.

She liked each equally, which was fair enough. But the strange thing was that she didn't like them equally at the same time. One always had to be up a notch in her estimation, one down—statuses she'd often confide privately to Nathaniel Branden. Once he asked why she couldn't accept liking both men roughly the same, but for different reasons. Rand shot back that she simply had to think hierarchically.

The hierarchy was clear. Rand was at the top, followed by Nathaniel Branden, her intellectual heir. Next came Barbara Branden. Then Greenspan and Peikoff, or Peikoff and Greenspan, depending on Rand's mood. The rest followed.

As for Rand's husband, Frank O'Connor, people couldn't help noticing that he took a very passive approach to the various goings-on. Often, he'd serve coffee, then retreat to the sidelines, where he'd sit in silence.

One thing is for certain: Collective meetings were not fun. In fact, they could be downright stressful, with the constant favor currying and the ever-present possibility that one might get rung up by Rand. These were deadly serious affairs. From that standpoint, Rand was actually rather in step with the times. As radical as some of her views were in 1950s America, the temper of Rand's intellectual movement was very much in keeping with the conformity of the Ike Age.

Being party to a group as intense as the Collective changed how Greenspan related to people from other stages in his life. Old friends noticed the change, among them Robert Kavesh, his buddy from NYU. By the mid-1950s, Kavesh was married, living in New Jersey, and had two kids. Periodically, he and Greenspan would get together for dinner and to catch up. "He would be really into objectivism," says Kavesh. "He'd be saying 'check your premises' and all this stuff. If you're raising kids it's hard to be too philosophical. You're practical."

But Kavesh also recalls that Greenspan was never overbearing about his convictions. The old friends found plenty of common ground outside objectivism. Besides, Kavesh wound up with a signed first edition of *Atlas Shrugged*.

Published in 1957, *Atlas Shrugged* had taken fourteen years to complete and had all the various Randian themes crammed into a book thick enough to derail a train. Where *The Fountainhead* assayed architecture, this one was about industrialism. But it viewed its subject through a bizarre refractory lens, one that could only exist in the eye of a mind such as Rand's.

"Alan was just so struck with the moral system presented in *Atlas*," Barbara Branden recalls.

If *The Fountainhead* had been merely ambitious, *Atlas Shrugged* was to be momentous. Rand was seeking to lay out her theory of everything: politics, economics, metaphysics, aesthetics, and sex.

Atlas Shrugged is a riff on the phenomenon of labor strikes—modest enough territory, it would seem. As long as there have been businesses, there have been strikes, with workers holding out against their employers for more money and better conditions. But Rand decided to turn the notion on its head. What would happen if it was scientists and inventors, steel titans and shipping magnates—the prime movers, as it were—who went on strike?

The book has all the trademark Randian touches. It features characters with names like Midas Mulligan and Francisco Domingo Carlos

Andres Sebastián d'Anconia, a noble copper baron. There's also a Norwegian philosopher turned pirate named Ragnar Danneskjöld. He sails the high seas, plundering ships bearing U.S. government aid and bound for the collapsing Marxist-style People's States. It's a twist on the old Robin Hood tale. Danneskjöld steals from the poor and gives to the rich. As for *evil* characters, there's Wesley Mouch, coordinator of the Bureau of Economic Planning and National Resources and Claude Slagenhop, president of the Friends of Global Progress.

At the center of it all is John Galt, an engineer, entrepreneur, and all-around Renaissance man, possessed of towering genius and a virility that's greater still. Yes, Virginia, *Atlas Shrugged* features plenty of feverishly heroic, bodice-ripping sex. It's also Galt who organizes the strike of the world's prime movers. He sets up a new society out in Colorado, devoted to unadulterated laissez-faire capitalism and christened "Galt's Gulch."

If *The Fountainhead* spoon-fed Rand's philosophy to readers, *Atlas Shrugged* delivered it up by the shovelful. Her editor at Random House—the celebrated Bennett Cerf—suggested that perhaps she should pare it down a bit. "Would you cut the Bible?" was Rand's rejoinder.

So *Atlas Shrugged* was sprung on an unsuspecting world, unabridged and 645,000 words long.

The reviews were savage. "The worst piece of fiction since *The Fountainhead*," said one critic. "Longer than life and twice as preposterous," scoffed another. One of the most scathing reviews came from the *New York Times*, penned by the critic Granville Hicks.

> Not in any literary sense a serious novel, it is an earnest one, belligerent and unremitting in its earnestness. It howls in the reader's ear and beats him about the head in order to secure his attention, and then, when it has him subdued, harangues him for page upon page. It has only two moods, the melodramatic and the didactic, and in both it knows no bounds.

Hicks was only getting warmed up. A few paragraphs later, he delivered his knockout blow: ". . . loudly as Miss Rand proclaims her love of life, it seems clear that the book is written out of hate."

Rand was stung by Hicks's review and shaken by the hostile critical reception her book garnered in general. The Collective rallied around her. Several members, including Greenspan, wrote angry letters to the *New York Times*. Greenspan's was published in the November 3, 1957, edition:

To the Editor:
Atlas Shrugged is a celebration of life and happiness. Justice is unrelenting. Creative individuals and undeviating purpose and rationality achieve joy and fulfillment. Parasites who persistently avoid either purpose or reason perish as they should. Mr. Hicks suspiciously wonders "about a person who sustains such a mood through the writing of 1,168 pages and some fourteen years of work." This reader wonders about a person who finds unrelenting justice personally disturbing.

Alan Greenspan, NY

Say this for *Atlas Shrugged*: It provoked violent reader reactions. Critics could howl, academia could harrumph, the literati could recoil in disgust, yet the book would manage to find passionate devotees in equal measure. Like *The Fountainhead*, it just kept selling and selling and selling.

The popular response enjoyed by Rand's two books sparked an idea in her intellectual heir, Nathaniel Branden. He became convinced that an untapped need existed—people were hungry to learn more about objectivism. He set himself to the task of convincing Rand that some kind of educational organization was in order offering seminars maybe, or course work. In 1958, he started the Nathaniel Branden Institute (NBI), operating first out of his apartment, then out of a small office at 120 East 34th Street.

Branden kicked off with a series of twenty lectures called "Basic Principles of Objectivism." The series was offered once in the spring, once in the fall, at a cost of $70, and featured such fare as "The Destructiveness of the Concept of God" and "Why Human Beings Repress and Drive Underground Not the Worst Within Them But the Best."

Other members of the Collective also contributed to the Basic Principles series, including Barbara Branden, Leonard Peikoff, and Greenspan. He worked up a ninety-minute lecture entitled "The Economics of a Free Society."

"I remember he was very strong on the importance of the gold standard," says Barbara Branden. "He also discussed the causes of depressions, which he was convinced, as was Ayn, were the result of government interference in the economy. His style of speaking was fairly dry, but the material was interesting to anyone even vaguely interested in economics."

John Hospers was impressed, too. Hospers, a philosophy professor at UCLA, would become the Libertarian Party's first presidential candidate in 1972. He'd receive but a single electoral college vote, cast by Roger MacBride, adopted grandson of Rand's friend and fellow author, Rose Wilder Lane. "Greenspan's lectures were very good," recalls Hospers. "He was quietly persuasive, not dramatic, but very convincing in his own way. I thought his lecture was the best thing the NBI ever did."

As the series gained in popularity, NBI created audiotaped versions of the lectures. They weren't for sale directly. One couldn't simply buy a recorded version of Greenspan's "The Economics of a Free Society." Instead, people interested in objectivism could sign up for the privilege of sitting in a hotel conference room and listening to an audiotape of the course. A moderator trained in objectivism would operate the tape player and field questions afterward.

It was a curious approach, but it worked. It allowed Branden, Greenspan, and the others to reach an audience "live" without having to give the same lecture over and over again. They were also able to reach people outside New York without having to travel. By 1965, audiotaped courses were being offered in eighty cities, including Chicago, Los Angeles, and Toronto. Branden's brainchild was becoming quite successful. In 1967, the NBI moved to new digs—8,000 square feet in the basement of the Empire State Building.

Rand and Branden next tried their hand at a newsletter. This, too, was a success and quickly grew from four pages monthly to a full-fledged magazine called the *Objectivist*. Greenspan was a frequent contributor. In one essay he questioned the wisdom of antitrust regulations; in another he lambasted consumer protection laws.

"But it is precisely the 'greed' of the businessman or, more appropriately, his profit-seeking, which is the unexcelled protector of the consumer," he wrote. "What collectivists refuse to recognize is that it is in the self-interest of every businessman to have a reputation for honest dealings and a quality product."

Probably his most incendiary essay was one entitled "Gold and Economic Freedom," published in July 1966. He argued for a pure gold standard as opposed to the mixed gold standard that prevailed at the time. That, in his estimation, was the only certain antidote to inflation. A currency needed to stand for something tangible. He criticized the Federal Reserve for creating easy credit—so-called paper reserves—not backed by the promise of gold. He also cast aspersions on his future employer's capacity for independence. "And so the Federal Reserve System was organized in 1913," he wrote. "It consisted of twelve regional Federal Reserve banks nominally owned by private bankers, but in fact government sponsored, controlled, and supported."

Greenspan's essays, along with ones by Rand and Branden, are collected in a book called *Capitalism: The Unknown Ideal*.

Lectures, a magazine, essay collections, even a service that sold Rand-inspired artworks by Joan Mitchell and others: objectivism was becoming a full-fledged movement. During the first years of the 1960s, Rand was at the zenith of her popularity. *Playboy* made her the subject of one of its famously free-flowing Q&A sections. Of all things, she also made several appearances on the Johnny Carson Show.

Rand also became much sought after as a guest speaker. She was especially popular at colleges, where audiences tended to be most receptive to her provocative ideas. She'd set the students' heads spinning, detailing her odd inverted universe in a thick Russian accent. Her standard outfit for such events was a flowing black cape and a gold brooch in the shape of a dollar sign. "The cross is the symbol of torture," she once explained to *Time* magazine. "I prefer the dollar sign, the symbol of free trade, and therefore of free minds."

These were halcyon days for the Collective, as well. NBI held regular socials in its Empire State Building offices. These were favorite events for Greenspan, who enjoyed the dancing. The Collective also fielded a pair of softball teams, dubbed the "Huns" and "Witch Doctors," after a couple of Randian archetypes of evil and hypocrisy. The teams faced off in Central Park for some epically lousy games, rife with botched plays and pulled muscles. This was a rather cerebral group of people, after all. "Alan was the best player of any of us," recalls Kathryn Eickhoff, a onetime Greenspan girlfriend and professional colleague. "He was one of the few who could hit the ball. And he could actually hit it well."

Eugene Schwartz, a fellow Objectivist, who along with Greenspan was a member of the Witch Doctors, says: "Alan had a great low-key sense of humor and easygoing nature which made him a fun team player."

But at the very moment when all seemed right in the world of the Collective, the fissures were starting to form.

Rand was becoming increasingly bitter and snappish. Even in the best of times, she'd never been the most easygoing person. But now that she'd completed her magnum opus, *Atlas Shrugged*, she had no idea what to do for an encore. Gnawing away at her, too, was this: Although the university lectures and Carson Show appearances were ego boosters, her public persona was growing rather cartoonish. Rand wanted to be taken seriously by critics and the academy, hailed as a genius, a woman ahead of her time.

The tensions Rand felt began to creep into the Collective. A couple of new terms were introduced, "emotionalists" and "social metaphysicians." Unlike "whim worshippers" and "second handers," however, these new barbs were intended not so much for the ignorant masses as for her own followers. Emotionalists are people who understand the world through feelings rather than reason; social metaphysicians are those ruled by the perceptions of others. Rand and Nathaniel Branden presided over a series of what were essentially inquisitions. Students of objectivism and even some of Rand's inner circle, the Collective, were hauled in and taken to task for errors of logic, errors that had led them down the path to one, the other, or both of these terrible new afflictions.

Greenspan managed to stay removed from this ugly new phase. He had built more of a life outside the Collective than any of the rest, with business luncheons and travel and tee times.

"Alan distanced himself," says Barbara Branden. "It was a very good idea. The rest of us discussed our personal lives with Ayn, which then meant we had to continue discussing our personal lives. Alan did not, with rare exceptions, and even then he would be sort of surface-y. It was an instinct toward privacy."

Then the other shoe fell. It was a stunning event for the Collective. In what would forever after be known in Objectivist circles as "the Break," Rand announced that she was cutting all ties with Nathaniel and Barbara Branden. She did so in the May 1968 issue of the *Objectivist*, in an eight-page letter addressed "To whom it may concern."

She presented a laundry list of grievances: The two were disorganized, fell down on their business commitments, and worst of all, exhibited various and sundry forms of illogic.

Rand's letter was followed by a kind of petition.

We the undersigned, former Associate Lecturers at Nathaniel Branden Institute, wish the following to be on record: Because Nathaniel Branden and Barbara Branden, in a series of actions, have betrayed fundamental principles of Objectivism, we condemn and repudiate these two persons irrevocably, and have terminated all association with them and with the Nathaniel Branden Institute.

It was signed by Greenspan, Peikoff, and a couple of other members of the Collective. In later years, Greenspan would say he added his name hastily, unsure in the midst of all the chaos of the charges or what was at stake.

Truth be told, nobody knew exactly what had happened. Hundreds of calls poured into the NBI from worried and puzzled students of objectivism. Renouncing the Brandens was so very serious, yet their trespasses seemed so very vague. There was widespread speculation that the Brandens had been caught embezzling. Maybe they were on drugs. But the truth was far more bizarre and sordid than anyone could have imagined. And almost no one—Greenspan included—would know the real story for many years to come.

Meanwhile, the Objectivists' world came crashing down. It was like a mini-civil war, cousins against cousins, husbands against wives. Peikoff sided with Rand and broke with his cousin, Barbara Branden. Nathaniel Branden and his cousin Allan Blumenthal, who was also in the Collective, parted ways. Presently, the Brandens got divorced.

Nathaniel was soon to leave New York and would become a prominent Los Angeles psychotherapist. He wrote a memoir chronicling his turbulent time in the Collective, titled *My Years with Ayn Rand*. Barbara Branden eventually settled down in New Mexico and wrote a book of her own, *The Passion of Ayn Rand*. It was made into a Showtime movie, starring Helen Mirren as Rand and Peter Fonda as Frank O'Connor.

Rand, meanwhile, would spend the rest of her life in a downward spiral, socially. Even before the break of 1968, she had left a long trail of broken friendships. Afterward, she was a terror. People ran for cover. Rand's vituperative attacks on Joan Mitchell's tastes in art and music grew so wearying that Mitchell finally had to simply cut her off.

Still, a handful of people managed to stand by Rand. Frank O'Connor, Rand's husband, stuck by, weary and worn but loyal to the end. Leonard Peikoff hung around as well, fawning and needy, a slightly less obsequious version of Uriah Heep. He seized the opportunity to edge ever closer to his mentor.

Greenspan also never abandoned Ayn Rand. He selected the ideal emotional distance—remaining Rand's friend but not seeing her nearly as much. In the years to come, he was to spend countless hours in Washington and in service to his consulting firm. But he would never forswear his association with Rand. In fact, he would remain ever grateful to her for opening his eyes to a moral dimension of capitalism.

5

THE FIRM

Greenspan was more protective of his privacy than the rest of the Collective. As a consequence, he always managed to maintain a healthy distance from Rand. By 1968—the time of the big Break—he'd spent fifteen years in her inner circle. But he'd also built a life of his own. Unlike some members of the Collective, he never bared his innermost feelings to Rand, never solicited her opinions on personal matters or sought her help in ridding himself of various foibles.

Neither did Greenspan devote his time in the Collective to idle philosophizing about the moral primacy of capitalism. He actually went out and accomplished something.

The entire time Greenspan was in the Collective, he was busy building an extremely successful economic consulting firm. He got started back in 1953, while still a full-time employee at the Conference Board. There, Greenspan specialized in analyzing the issues facing heavy industry. As a sideline, he started a small consultancy, serving clients in the steel business. He provided them with projections of economic growth, predictions about interest-rate swings, and other observations about the broad economy that nevertheless had crucial bearing on the demand for steel.

Greenspan wanted very badly to strike out on his own. But this was the 1950s, the golden age of corporate paternalism. A generation later, with the compact between employers and employees breaking down, people began to jump—or be pushed—en masse out of old-line companies such as IBM and AT&T. Many reinvented themselves as consul-

tants, and as their ranks swelled, consulting became a common and accepted profession.

However, this was not the case in the 1950s. In fact, the handful of
practicing consultants concentrated mostly on providing management
advice or helping corporations to streamline their industrial processes.
Economic consultants, by contrast, helped companies interpret various
measures—inflation, interest rates, housing starts—so that they could
plan for the future. Within the small and rarefied world of consulting,
economic consultants were a tiny subgroup. But their ranks just happened to include Greenspan's father, who made his living as a stockbroker and economic consultant.

Greenspan chided himself over his lack of entrepreneurialism. Although his father had never been particularly successful, at least he'd
taken the plunge. Furthermore, Herbert Greenspan had written an inscription in his book *Recovery Ahead!* urging his son to pursue "like
work of your own." But the younger Greenspan had trouble summoning the courage and confidence.

By a stroke of good luck, Greenspan's full-time work at the Conference Board put him in touch with a firm called Townsend-Skinner. It
was a tiny, bare-bones operation, but it also happened to be one of the
few economic consultancies in existence. Greenspan worked closely
with the firm, providing Conference Board data and offering his own
prognostications about the economy. In the process, he managed to
impress one of the partners, William Townsend. When Townsend decided to take on a new partner, he thought of Greenspan and asked
him to come in for an interview.

When the two met, Townsend was shocked. Up to this point, they
had talked only on the telephone. Given Greenspan's deep voice and
methodical manner of speaking, Townsend had assumed they were
both the same age. Townsend was sixty-five, Greenspan twenty-seven.
Nevertheless, young Greenspan dazzled the much older Townsend and
was handed the job.

Townsend-Skinner had originally been formed by Townsend and Dana
Skinner in the inauspicious year of 1929. The firm's primary business
was providing economic intelligence to people who managed investments. This included portfolio managers at banks, insurance companies, and pension funds as well as wealthy individuals. During the

firm's earliest days, economic data of any stripe were extremely hard to find. The country was mired in a depression, and people hungered for the slightest clue about where the economy was headed. To someone with bond holdings, for example, simply getting a read on the general trend in interest rates was service enough.

Townsend was the firm's salesman, expert at drumming up clients. Skinner was the economic guru and proved to be a master at combing for data and identifying trends. Early on, he worked directly with his contacts in the banking industry to get information about liquidity and loan-deposit ratios. Over time, this information became widely available. But Skinner always remained one step ahead. He'd simply shift his concentration to different data sets that were hard to come by, and hence of value to clients.

Skinner died in the mid-1940s, not long after the end of World War II. His daughter—also an economist by training—took his place for a while, but she left the firm to marry an Italian count. Townsend brought in his son-in-law, Bill Knowles. When Knowles left, Townsend went looking for yet another new partner.

By now, it was the 1950s. The postwar industrial machine had kicked into high gear. Oil and chemicals, steel and autos—those were businesses to keep tabs on. Per the famous adage, "What's good for General Motors is good for the nation," Townsend needed someone with expertise in the burgeoning heavy industries; Greenspan was his man. Together, they formed a new company called Townsend-Greenspan to consult on industrial issues. It coexisted with the old Townsend-Skinner, which continued to service financial clients.

In truth, the combined Townsend-Greenspan and Townsend-Skinner was hardly an empire. It consisted of five people—the two principals, two researchers, and a secretary, all crowded into a shabby office at 52 Wall Street. Greenspan would pace back and forth in the tiny common area, periodically stopping to take an imaginary golf swing, a nervous tick.

Townsend took an instant liking to his young partner. Upbeat and affable, Townsend was a born salesman, while Greenspan was considerably more reticent. As such, he reminded Townsend of his old partner, Skinner. Townsend seemed particularly pleased by the creative chaos that prevailed in Greenspan's office.

"Alan's desk was always pretty messy. Townsend's was neat as a pin. He'd regularly remark that a messy desk is a sign of genius," recalls

Bess Kaplan, who worked at Townsend-Greenspan from 1956 until 1987, when the firm closed its doors.

Greenspan dove into his new job with aplomb—analyzing heavy industry, after all, was a data-head's delight. The economy of the 1950s was a physical economy in very real and quantifiable terms: X number of men worked Y number of hours to produce Z tons of steel. It all got loaded onto so many railcars and wound up pounded into so many girders and aircraft struts and auto fins. The intervening years have seen the U.S. economy evolve, becoming increasingly high-tech and service oriented. Measuring a postindustrial economy driven by brainpower and tiny wafers of silicon has proved quite a challenge. But back in the 1950s, it was still possible to piece it all together like a giant puzzle.

Greenspan was the master. He'd get behind government data, track down the primary sources and obtain the raw numbers. Often he'd go directly to companies or trade associations. Every chance he got, he'd quiz executives and line workers to get a read on the competitive climate in their particular industries.

Bob Kavesh, Greenspan's old friend from NYU, worked as a business economist at Chase Manhattan Bank from 1956 through 1958. He remembers going to meetings of economists where Greenspan was present. "He was the ultimate anatomist of the system," says Kavesh. "He knew how the whole thing fit together. He knew the bones, muscles, blood. By the late fifties, nobody knew the numbers better than he did."

Greenspan had finally found his calling.

Of course, a number of people had helped push him in the right direction. Arthur Burns, Greenspan's onetime Columbia professor, inculcated him with a rigorous empiricism. From Conference Board cohort Sandy Parker, he learned to view the economy as an organic and interconnected whole. Parker was often lauded for his ability to see how a butterfly wing flap in one distant corner of the economy could lead to a thunderstorm in another. Ayn Rand's idiosyncratic upside-down logic also helped shape Greenspan, the economic consultant. Rand, for instance, held that there was no such thing as a contradiction. If you look closely enough, she held, the one true truth would emerge. Greenspan also used his practice as a platform to champion

Rand's vigorously laissez-faire views, though never in a strident or overly dogmatic way.

Lowell Wiltbank became acquainted with Greenspan through Objectivist circles and later joined Townsend-Greenspan, where he rose from photocopy machine operator to senior staff economist. He recalls Rand's pervasive influence on the firm. "There was an absolute rule at Townsend-Greenspan. No communication that came out of the firm should ever be interpreted to advocate any expansion of government interference in the economy. If we advocated anything in terms of government policy, it was deregulation."

While Burns, Parker, and Rand were instrumental in Greenspan's development, he was more than the sum of these influences. A command of data was a gift that came naturally to him. In a curious way, it can also be seen as a logical alternative to his failed career in music. Music involves a progression of notes marching toward a satisfying conclusion. Data, as well, are meant to be arranged in a series that tells a compelling story and achieves resolution. As Greenspan would later tell the *New York Times Magazine:* "I get the same kind of joy from solving a hard mathematical problem as I do from hearing a Haydn quartet."

Economic consulting also appealed to Greenspan's innate sense of pragmatism. He'd left Juilliard anxious to start a career in music in lieu of taking classes on music as a career. Greenspan enjoyed rolling up his sleeves and plunging into real-world detail. A case in point: Greenspan favored paperboard sales as an economic indicator during his time as a consultant. Paperboard is an incredibly pervasive material, used to package all kinds of items for shipping. If demand for paperboard was up, Greenspan took it as a signal that economic activity was on the increase. Such a prosaic indicator holds scant appeal for an academic economist. But it has the benefit of uncanny accuracy. Greenspan was forever adding to his toolbox of indicators. People who worked for him over the years were driven to distraction by the ever-increasing amount of data he would track.

Client companies looked to Townsend-Greenspan for observations about economic conditions on an industry-specific basis. This would help them to make decisions about hiring, opening new factories, or investing in equipment. Clients also looked for available data sliced and diced in new ways. One of Townsend-Greenspan's most sought-after services was monthly estimates of gross national product. The government numbers came out quarterly. Townsend-Greenspan also produced custom charts at a time—before the widespread use of computers—when charting was a rigorous and time-consuming task.

Of course, Greenspan faced the same statistical obsolescence problems that had dogged his predecessor, Skinner. Data were forever making the transition from rare to commonplace. Like Skinner, Greenspan remained forever ahead of the curve, always dreaming up new measures to benefit clients. By the late 1950s, Townsend-Greenspan had built up an impressive roster of industrial clients, including U.S. Steel, Owens Corning, Weyerhauser, and Aluminum Company of America (Alcoa).

Even while enjoying this success, Greenspan enrolled in NYU to renew his pursuit of a Ph.D. Although he'd left Columbia, feeling ambivalent about academia, short on money, and itching to get out into the real world, he also appreciated the value of an advanced degree, both as an intellectual accomplishment and as a practical credential. He once slyly referred to a Ph.D. as a "union card."

Despite having done graduate work at Columbia, the doctoral office at NYU required him to pretty much start from scratch. Very few of his course credits were allowed to transfer. Given that he was by now an established consultant, NYU didn't want to give the appearance of favoritism.

One course he took was "Current Economic and Financial Problems," taught by Kavesh, who had made the switch from the business world back to academia. It was a survey course with 250 students. "Here was this guy who knew more about the economy than anybody else," says Kavesh, "and he sat there quietly listening to lectures about what the Fed was doing and where interest rates were headed."

Greenspan got an A in the course. He would continue his doctoral quest for many years to come, taking courses when he could fit them into his busy schedule. He'd attend to his various Ph.D. requirements in a slow, piecemeal fashion.

In 1958, at age seventy, William Townsend died of a heart attack. Left alone and in charge, Greenspan—just thirty-two years old—was nervous about whether he could keep the firm going. But by this time, it was well established with a solid reputation. Business didn't falter. Presently, Greenspan set about buying stakes from Townsend's heirs until he owned the firm outright. He also absorbed the original financial services clientele into a single firm, called Townsend-Greenspan.

He maintained the name for continuity's sake and also in deference to his old partner, who had given him his big break.

As the 1950s gave way to the 1960s, a shift took place in the field of economic consulting. Computerized econometric modeling became all the rage. Larry Klein at the University of Pennsylvania's Wharton School of Business was in the vanguard of this movement. He later won a Nobel Prize for his pioneering work. "It was an exciting time," recalls Klein. "Computers were in their infancy and we were trying to harness them to learn about the general economy."

The cutting edge of econometric modeling favored a so-called black box approach. A slew of data and equations was fed into computers, which in turn spit out a detailed picture of the economy. Every variable affected every other variable. For instance, an increase in auto sales would lead to an increase in oil consumption. Various interrelationships had to be accounted for in the computer programs, which became increasingly complex, accumulating line upon line of code like so much digital silly string.

Greenspan—the economic anatomist—never entirely trusted computers. To stay on trend, Townsend-Greenspan did purchase one, an IBM 1130 which cost $100,000 but had less power than a 386 microprocessor. It was the size of a compact car and oscillating fans had to be arranged around the machine just to keep it cool. Townsend-Greenspan developed a program called MOUSE, meaning "model of the U.S. economy." A huge library of punch cards had to be maintained as well as primitive forerunners of the floppy disk, which weighed roughly five pounds apiece.

Computerized econometric modeling was always more art than science. Everyone—even a technical whiz like Klein—was forced to massage the computer's output. Greenspan, however, was especially inclined to tinker with the findings. He would often make substantial changes, certain that punch cards were no substitute for good old-fashioned observation. "Alan didn't think it was possible to adequately capture all of the economy that way," recalls Kathryn Eickhoff. "He favored analyzing the economy from the ground up. That was part and parcel of the Townsend-Greenspan approach. It didn't buy into the black-box model."

Eickhoff was first introduced to Greenspan as a recent graduate of the University of Missouri, working as a research assistant at the Wall Street brokerage house Van Alstyne, Noel and Company. The two met when her boss invited her to an American Statistical Association business luncheon where Greenspan was also present. They immediately hit it off—both professionally and personally.

Eickhoff joined Townsend-Greenspan as an economist in 1962. She also became Greenspan's girlfriend, and the two carried on a discreet interoffice romance that lasted for several years.

They enjoyed movies, theater, and concerts, the standard New York City cultural whirl. But they also indulged in domestic pleasures, sometimes simply staying home and watching TV. Greenspan even tried his hand at cooking. He had a limited repertoire at the time, but Eickhoff enjoyed his scrambled eggs. "There were a lot of things he liked to do, a lot of places he liked to go," recalls Eickhoff. "He was a very attractive person, very confident and sure of himself. That sureness may not have been there earlier in his life. He certainly could carry on a fascinating conversation. That's the part I don't think comes across in his Senate testimony as Fed chairman."

Greenspan also introduced Eickhoff to objectivism. She, too, would get to know Rand. In fact, Eickhoff's commitment to the philosophy endured beyond her time with Greenspan. "My relationship with Alan was serious," she says. "But I don't think we ever got anywhere close to talking about marriage."

After their breakup, she stayed on at the firm. Later still, when political service forced Greenspan to be an absentee manager for increasingly long periods—even years at a time—Eickhoff acted as his deputy, helping run Townsend-Greenspan.

Greenspan was an odd bird. He showed a rare aptitude for comingling his past and present, the personal and the professional, without it becoming a volatile cocktail. Apparently, his famously dispassionate temperament made it possible for him to live with situations that would be untenable for others. The cool objective style championed by Rand came naturally to Greenspan.

When Eickhoff got married, Greenspan actually employed her husband, Jim Smith, for a stint at Townsend-Greenspan. Smith was a fellow Objectivist and for many years owner of the Village Corner, a popular downtown jazz club. Economics and ex's, music and objectivism—they flow through Greenspan's life during this period with surprising harmony.

Greenspan remained close, too, to his ex-wife. In fact, the two stayed tight even after she married a fellow member of the Collective, Allan Blumenthal, Nathaniel Branden's cousin. Truly an incestuous group, the Collective: It was an intricate web of blood relations and intermarriage.

With his characteristic impassivity, Greenspan accepted that his ex-wife had a new husband and that they were all part of the same social circle. The truth, the objective truth, was that Greenspan and Allan Blumenthal—known to the Collective as A. G. and A. B., respectively—had a lot in common. Blumenthal had briefly been a doctor but had abandoned medical practice, had gone to Juilliard, and was now trying to make it in New York as a classical pianist.

Blumenthal recalls of Greenspan:

We became friends very early on. We would often talk about musical performances. We both liked similar things, particularly Mozart. But our perspective on it was totally different. I would be talking to him about this and that passage and about how Mozart was a genius. But he'd be talking about the counterpoint and hearing the inner voices, the mathematical aspects of music. It ended up the same way, but our focus was entirely different.

Greenspan and Blumenthal even formed a classical trio—Greenspan on clarinet, Blumenthal on piano, and fellow Objectivist Eugene Schwartz playing violin. They'd practice late into the night and with reckless disregard for Rand's own personal tastes, playing Bach and Beethoven, Mahler and Mozart. "Any economist who digs Mozart has to be in touch with the fundamentals of life," recalls Schwartz of his onetime trio mate.

Greenspan also frequently double-dated with Allan and Joan, now Joan Mitchell Blumenthal. But Greenspan confided to Joan that he didn't think he'd be making another trip to the altar anytime soon.

He didn't want to repeat past mistakes that weighed on him, according to Joan. He saw echoes in his own personality of the full-blown glacial remoteness he perceived in his father. In and of itself, that was not a terrible thing in Greenspan's eyes. Aloofness was aloofness, and if that was his nature, he could live with it. What he didn't want to do was go against his own nature. That was the mistake his father had made, going so far as to have a child that he was unable to take responsibility for raising.

The other woman Greenspan dated long-term during this period was Marjorie Scheffler. Scheffler was a housewife with children from a previous marriage. She was a tall redhead, and by all accounts was quite good-looking.

"Marjorie was a rather stunning woman," recalls Robert Hessen, a historian and Collective member, adding: "I thought she could have done better. It's a funny thing to say, considering the power and prestige and prominence that Alan has managed to achieve."

But Greenspan, date-deprived at NYU, was starting to have considerably more success with women. He was coming into his own, running his own business, and becoming increasingly self-possessed.

"Alan projected a great deal of strength—I don't mean physically, but morally and intellectually. He liked women, and women generally respond to that," recalls Barbara Branden.

Anyone as quirky as Greenspan was bound to be an unusual business manager. Foremost among his quirks was that he hired a number of female economists besides Eickhoff. This was nothing so sordid as Alan's Angels. Rather, it was more a matter of temperament. Greenspan had always gotten on well with strong women. A single mother had raised him, and he had figured out how to stay on the right side of Ayn Rand's outlandishly forceful personality. The same attitudes prevailed when he ran Townsend-Greenspan. During the 1950s and 1960s, at a time when men were often uncomfortable working with women as peers, Greenspan had no such qualms.

Judith Mackey, a classmate of Greenspan's at Columbia, recalls facing preposterous professional hurdles as a female economist in the 1950s. She was working for the Life Insurance Association and had been promised a promotion to assistant director of research. But meetings that were key to her advancement were routinely held at places such as New York City's University Club, open to men only. Feeling stymied, she was on the lookout for another job and ran into Greenspan at a McGraw-Hill networking party in Philadelphia.

Mackey and Greenspan retreated to the edge of the room and sat down with their backs to the wall. Mackey recalls that she let it all out, voicing her anger and frustration. Greenspan asked her to send him a résumé, and she was hired soon after as an economist for Townsend-Greenspan.

"I was very grateful," says Mackey. "He gave me an opportunity to move up to a level that was being denied me elsewhere. This was my entrée into a man's world."

But Greenspan wasn't entirely gender-blind. He paid women more than they could get elsewhere, but still less than a man would have received in a comparable job. After all, Greenspan was running a small business, trying to hold down costs. Ever the economist, he had identified a golden opportunity for arbitrage. As he once told the *New York Times:* "I always valued men and women equally, and I found that because others did not, good women economists were cheaper than men. Hiring women does two things: It gives us better quality work for less money, and it raises the market value for women."

Greenspan also proved adept at winning the confidence of corporate chieftains such as Dan Lufkin, a cofounder of Donaldson, Lufkin and Jenrette, and Sandy Weill, who ultimately became CEO of Citigroup. Something in Greenspan's quiet, no-frills demeanor grabbed them. "People responded to Alan's integrity," says Mackey. "His brilliance came through clearly. He had an ease of presentation. They wanted to hear what he had to say and keep on hearing it."

Stories began to circulate about Greenspan's epic capacity for data grubbing. One story—perhaps apocryphal, perhaps not—held that Greenspan, while attending a party, happened to notice that the host had the latest *U.S. Statistical Abstract.* He snatched it up, plunked down in the corner, and was lost to the world for the duration of the evening.

Edgar Fiedler, an economist at Bankers Trust during the 1960s, remembers a colleague saying of Greenspan: "Alan takes apart the industrial production index before breakfast just as a setting up exercise." Meanwhile, Frank Ikard, the Washington representative for the American Petroleum Institute, described Greenspan as the "kind of person who knew how many thousand flat-headed bolts were used in a 1964 Chevrolet and what it would do to the economy if you took out three of them."

Greenspan's reputation was on the rise. In 1966, he and Sandy Parker teamed up for a project that attracted considerable attention. Parker, the chief economist at *Fortune* magazine at the time, solicited

Greenspan's help in putting together an article that dissected federal budget assumptions about the Vietnam War. Sleuthing by Parker and Greenspan revealed that if the war continued at its current pace, it would cost $9 billion more than President Johnson had earmarked in the 1967 budget. *Fortune* ran the groundbreaking story as its April 1966 cover, and the fallout was immediate.

As Greenspan's reputation grew, so too did Townsend-Greenspan. By the mid-1960s, it employed about a dozen people. The firm made a couple of moves to progressively larger offices, first to 39 Broadway and later to 80 Pine Street. The spaces were far from palatial. Greenspan was a true pack rat and crammed the offices full of blue binders with such labels as "Mobile Home Sales" and "Massachusetts Department of Labor." As an aesthetic touch, though, he did hang a couple of his ex-wife's paintings. They were abstract cityscapes with a kind of heroic *Fountainhead* feel about them.

In the mid-1960s, Greenspan created a small board of directors for Townsend-Greenspan. It consisted of himself, Kathryn Eickhoff, and his mother. Meetings were held monthly, but Greenspan rarely attended. Instead, Rose Goldsmith and Kathy Eickhoff would simply have lunch at Fraunces Tavern, a historic Wall Street watering hole where George Washington held an emotional farewell dinner with his officers at the end of the Revolutionary War. Rose would also call the Townsend-Greenspan offices every single day to check on Alan. As she didn't want to bother him, she'd usually get a report from Eickhoff, Bess Kaplan, or Judith Mackey.

Greenspan's father was also involved in his life during this period, though in a very small way. Both men worked on Wall Street, just blocks apart, but they saw each other only on rare occasions. Typically, Herbert Greenspan would take his son to lunch each year on his birthday. Apparently, the cool feeling was mutual. "Alan didn't have much interest in having anything to do with his father," says Eickhoff.

Although Greenspan had truly followed in his father's career footsteps, he was very much his own man, and a successful one at that. In 1967, Greenspan bought an apartment at 860 United Nations Plaza. The complex had been constructed by Alcoa, one of Townsend-Greenspan's clients. In exchange for buying in early, Greenspan was given a good deal on an apartment. UN Plaza would prove to be a very sought-after address. Later, other apartments would be bought by the likes of Johnny Carson and Walter Cronkite.

But perhaps the most telling indicator of Greenspan's success is a pretty basic one: By the late 1960s, he was a millionaire.

Still, the general impression among people who knew Greenspan in those days was that he wasn't exactly marked for real greatness. His consulting firm was doing well. He was a success, no question. But no one expected him to rise to dizzying heights. People generally found him modest, reliable, gracious, erudite, and more than a tad introspective. None of these traits seemed to lend themselves to setting the world on fire. Even Joan Mitchell Blumenthal says she just didn't see it coming.

In retrospect, friends from this period in his life suspect that the seeds of his ambition must have been present, only buried or invisible. Perhaps the flip side of his modesty and introspection was the detachment and quiet inner drive necessary to succeed on a grand scale. At any rate, no one had so much as an inkling. His old friends were destined to watch his career unfold—Nixon adviser, Ford adviser, Fed chief, four-term Fed chief—in stunned amazement.

6

TEAM NIXON

The late 1960s found Rand's circle in full meltdown mode. But even as the world was collapsing for the Collective, a new one was opening up for Greenspan.

Three different people from disparate corners of Greenspan's past played roles in ushering in this next phase of his life: Lenny Garment, his old bandmate from the Henry Jerome swing days; Arthur Burns, his mentor and Columbia professor; and Martin Anderson, an erstwhile student of objectivism.

One day in 1968, Greenspan ran into Garment on Broad Street in lower Manhattan. The two had only stayed in the vaguest touch in the twenty-odd years since the band had broken up. While Greenspan was busy attending NYU, becoming an Objectivist, and founding a successful consulting firm, Garment had graduated from Brooklyn Law School, joined the white-shoe firm of Mudge, Stern, Williams and Tucker, gotten married, and had two children.

Due to numerous personnel changes, Garment's law firm had subsequently morphed into Nixon, Mudge, Rose, Guthrie, Alexander and Mitchell. The new lead partner was Richard Nixon, fresh from a pair of political failures. He'd lost the 1960 presidential election to John F. Kennedy and the 1962 governor's race in California to Democratic incumbent Pat Brown. Thereupon, he'd delivered his famous exit line:

"You won't have Nixon to kick around any more, because, gentlemen, this is my last press conference."

Nixon was in his "wilderness" period. After years of building a power base in the West, he had decided to move to the East. And following years of making little money as a presidential candidate, he chose to take a lucrative law job. This newfound wealth allowed him to purchase a twelve-room apartment in a Fifth Avenue building that boasted Nelson Rockefeller among its residents. The price tag in 1963: $135,000.

But by the mid-1960s, Nixon had begun to grow restless. The law firm became a power base for a fresh presidential run. Several people who played prominent roles in his campaign against Hubert Humphrey came out of the firm. Partner John Mitchell, for example, became Nixon's campaign manager and went on to serve as attorney general during his administration.

Garment also served on the campaign. While working together at the law firm, the pair had become good friends, despite Nixon's conservatism and Garment's credentials as a "birthright Democrat." Nixon handed Garment a role in the campaign that was oddly similar to that which he had held with Henry Jerome's band. Heterodox and idiosyncratic, Garment had long possessed a unique talent for bridging separate worlds. Two decades earlier, he restlessly crawled the clubs in Harlem and along 52nd Street, checking out cutting-edge acts and arranging auditions to bring fresh talent to the band. Now, Nixon had charged Garment with inviting unusual people into his campaign, people who otherwise might not have come to his attention.

It was within this context that Greenspan had his chance encounter with Garment. The two had lunch at the nearby Bankers Club and proceeded down memory lane. When Garment returned to his law firm, he suggested to Nixon that it might be worthwhile to make Greenspan's acquaintance, and a meeting between the two was arranged.

Greenspan was in rare form at his get-to-know-you session with Nixon. Not exactly shy in the presence of a presidential aspirant, Greenspan apparently waxed on about the economy in the obscuro-mystical style that has become his trademark. His lecture topic for the day was the federal budget. He dissected recent budgets and discussed how, from the raw numbers, one could extrapolate a picture of various presidents and their political styles. In Garment's recollection, it was quite a performance, but pretty technical stuff. He sat by glaze-eyed and would later describe Greenspan's verbal meanderings as "Nepal Katmandu language." But whatever he said, it piqued Nixon's interest.

"Nixon was favorably impressed with him," recalls Garment, a partner with the D.C. firm of Verner, Liipfert, Bernhard, McPherson and Hand. "It wasn't Nixon's style to say, 'Wow, he's a hell of a guy!' He said, 'That's a very intelligent man. He knows what he's talking about. Let's make sure that we get as much time out of him as we can and fold him into the troupe.'"

In addition to Garment, another political intimate of Nixon's was Arthur Burns. The pair had formed a lasting bond, thanks to a good turn Burns had done Nixon back in 1960, when Nixon was vice president under Eisenhower and Burns was serving as an economic adviser.

Burns warned Nixon that according to his calculations, a recession was percolating. This was key intelligence for Nixon, who was preparing to use the vice presidency as a launching pad for a presidential run of his own. With great urgency, he passed the news along to his boss, Eisenhower. Ike was not convinced, but sure enough, a recession kicked in during 1960, and Nixon lost the presidency to Kennedy by an incredibly thin margin.

Ever after, Nixon blamed his election loss on the recalcitrant economy and felt a debt of gratitude toward Burns. As his 1968 campaign got under way, Nixon brought him on as an economic adviser. Burns, in turn, chose Martin Anderson, a thirty-two-year-old Columbia professor and Rand devotee, as his deputy.

Anderson was something of a celebrity in conservative political circles, thanks to a book he had written called *The Federal Bulldozer*. It was a fierce critique of misguided government spending on urban renewal projects. His role in the Nixon campaign was to head up the research efforts of the policy shop, a kind of improvised think tank for developing positions on a huge range of issues. Through his involvement in Objectivist circles, meanwhile, he had an arm's-length familiarity with Greenspan. Thus, through these combined acquaintances, Greenspan had his first taste of politics as part of Anderson's policy team.

For Nixon, the 1968 run required a radical political face-lift. Thanks to his recent defeats, he was tagged with a "loser" image. Because this was his eighth campaign for public office, he faced a serious familiarity-breeds-contempt quotient. He also had a well-deserved reputation as a tricky, nasty, no-holds-barred Red-baiter.

It was in this latter role that Nixon first came to national prominence. As a young congressman from California serving on the House Un-American Activities Committee, he was a key figure in the investigation to determine whether Alger Hiss, a State Department official, had been a Soviet spy. Then there was his infamous "pink sheet." In 1950, he ran for the Senate against Helen Gahagan Douglas, a Democratic incumbent and former actress. Nixon issued a flyer—on pink paper—comparing Douglas's voting record in Congress to that of Vito Marcantonio, a congressman from New York and alleged Communist sympathizer.

By 1968, however, the country had gone through some serious changes. Vietnam occupied the national consciousness far more than the Soviet threat. On the domestic front, all hell was breaking loose. Martin Luther King Jr. was assassinated. In June, Robert Kennedy—Nixon's likely Democratic presidential challenger—was also assassinated.

Against this backdrop, Nixon adopted a very different political tack. History threatens to distill Nixon down to a single screaming footnote: Watergate. But 1968 was unquestionably Nixon at his political best, a far cry from the subsequent evil-twin Nixon of tapes and paranoia and ethnic slurs. He ran as the great conciliator, offering a soothing prescription of law and order and an end to Vietnam, aimed at what he variously termed the New Majority or the Silent Majority.

Behind the new Nixon, a massive campaign machine rattled and hummed. Along with Mitchell, H. R. Haldeman and John Ehrlichman were key players. In the days before they served hard time for their involvement in Watergate, Haldeman and Ehrlichman were a pair of hard-boiled campaign operatives for Nixon. The Nixon speech-writing team included Raymond Price, Richard Whalen, Pat Buchanan, and William Safire. The thirty-year-old Buchanan was sharp-tongued, pugnacious, proudly Catholic, and deeply conservative. In other words, he was simply a younger version of the latter-day Buchanan, the blunt-edged perennial presidential candidate. Safire had first come to Nixon's attention while working as a public-relations executive.

Nixon's media team, meanwhile, featured Harry Treleaven, Frank Shakespeare, and future spin-meister extraordinaire Roger Ailes, then twenty-seven and fresh from producing *The Mike Douglas Show*.

It was with high hopes that Greenspan joined this campaign team. Despite a distrust of politics—developed during his years with Ayn Rand—Greenspan sensed something refreshing about Nixon's 1968 effort. Anderson recalls:

We were mired in Vietnam. There were riots in the streets, and the word out was that the Republican Party was dead after [Barry] Goldwater [1964 candidate]. This brought in a number of new people who would normally stay out of politics. I think that Alan joined the campaign for the same reason a lot of people did. I think the basic common thread was that people were very concerned about what was happening and saw the election as a chance to get it right again.

Greenspan's role was to be coordinator of domestic-policy research. His job was to gather position papers, pertinent news articles, government statistics, and stray pieces of data and funnel it all to the Nixon team out on the road. He worked out of the New York City campaign headquarters, on the fifth floor of the old American Bible Society building at 57th Street and Park Avenue. Greenspan oversaw a stripped-down crew that included a couple of secretaries and Martin Anderson's wife, Annelise. This was a volunteer part-time gig, requiring just a few hours a day. Greenspan often came in during the evenings after working a full day at Townsend-Greenspan.

Position papers poured into the Bible Building headquarters from a wide variety of task forces assembled by the Nixon campaign. There were task forces on just about every conceivable topic: crime, the elderly, black capitalism, education, pornography, American Indians, campus riots, and—irony of ironies—wire tapping. The idea was for Nixon to have something to say about just about anything that could come up in the course of a presidential campaign.

The people who served on the task forces hailed from a vast network of contacts made by Nixon and his associates. George Shultz—who later served in the Nixon cabinet in several capacities—was on the labor task force. An economic advisory committee included Nixon pals Elmer Bobst, who was chairman of Warner Lambert, and Donald

Kendall, president of Pepsico. All in all, a vast spectrum of viewpoints and ideologies was represented. "There could be white papers offering up about any kind of policy," recalls Dwight Chapin, who at twenty-seven was a wunderkind aide during the 1968 effort. "Nixon was very determined to run a campaign of inclusion, with a place for someone as conservative as Buchanan or as liberal as Lenny Garment."

Of course, Greenspan was far from expert on most of the issues covered by the task forces. But almost every topic—whether it be education reform or wetlands preservation—had an economic component. Here, Greenspan could provide guidance. When he saw fit, he'd write comments in the margins, maybe thread in a pertinent statistic. He also kept careful tabs on rival-candidate Humphrey's pronouncements on economic issues and provided the Nixon campaign with refutations.

Martin Anderson typically traveled with Nixon and was there to receive the domestic policy papers on the other end. Buchanan used to carry around a fat notebook stuffed with policy papers marked with little red tabs.

Information trickled up to Nixon in a variety of ways. Often, ideas from the white papers would find their way into speeches written for him by Safire or Buchanan. But Nixon wasn't averse to wading through the policy shop's output in pretty raw form. He had a mind like a sponge and soaked up arcana and statistics with ease, and he could be counted on to retrieve them during impromptu moments in the campaign.

Nixon also enjoyed doing his own writing as a way of working out problems. He felt that a policy had a better chance of succeeding in the real world if he could work it out on paper first. As Nixon shuffled through the policy shop output, he was pleased whenever Greenspan added his two cents. "Nixon was extremely high on Alan. He had a real respect for him in terms of his judgment on a whole range of policy issues," Anderson recalled in an interview during his tenth presidential campaign, this time working in support of George W. Bush.

Not everyone was impressed with the policy shop's output, though. As election day 1968 drew near, the press began to gripe that Nixon had run an issue-lite race. Anderson called Greenspan at headquarters and suggested they rush to compile a book detailing the topics Nixon had addressed during the campaign. Greenspan scrambled to pull together the anthology of position papers. Six days later, on October 17,

1968, they introduced a 291-page testament for the benefit of the skeptical press—"Nixon on the Issues." Anderson also presented the candidate with a leather-bound copy, embossed in gold with "Nixon Socks It to 'Em."

Even if the media weren't dazzled by Nixon's grasp of issues, he managed at least to win over a decent portion of the public. Once again, it was a close race. But not as close as 1960, when Nixon lost the popular vote to Kennedy by two-tenths of 1 percent. This time Nixon won 301 electoral votes to Humphrey's 191. Running as an independent, Alabama governor George Wallace managed to tally up 46 electoral votes.

Nixon asked Greenspan to stay on during the period between his election victory and his inauguration in January 1969, in the new role of budget liaison, one of the most important jobs on a presidential transition team. Greenspan was supposed to work with Charles Zwick, Lyndon Johnson's budget director, to smooth the changeover from one administration to another.

Given the quirks of the federal government's fiscal calendar, an outgoing president actually prepares the budget that will be in effect during the first year of the incoming president's term. Johnson's fiscal 1970 budget was due on January 13, 1969, and Nixon was scheduled to take office on January 20.

As budget liaison, Greenspan was charged with giving the numbers a thorough once-over to see whether Johnson had buried any bombs that might embarrass Nixon. Having researched the landmark *Fortune* article showing that Johnson was understating the cost of the Vietnam War, Greenspan was well suited for the task.

The key budget issue was a 10-percent tax surcharge that Johnson had used to try to keep the government's books balanced and inflation in check while financing the war in Vietnam. It was an extremely unpopular measure. Johnson had the option of proposing elimination of the tax surcharge as a farewell gesture—an event that would leave Nixon with a dilemma. During his campaign, Nixon had promised an end to Vietnam, though he hadn't provided a timetable. Unless he deescalated America's involvement in an awful hurry, he was going to need those revenues and would be forced to reinstate the tax. Greenspan crunched the numbers to see what options were available.

In the end, Johnson chose not to meddle with the tax surcharge. When Nixon took office, he left it in place as well. *Newsweek* described this decision as "surely the least popular of his young administration."

Quite an outcry arose from the public and from Democrats in Congress. What followed was a wild series of somersaults, as various tax proposals were issued, altered, amended, and tabled. Right in the thick of it was Albert Gore Sr., a liberal senator from Tennessee and outspoken advocate for tax relief for the middle class and the poor. It wasn't until a full year later that Nixon gained some measure of closure on the issue when he signed the Tax Reform Act of 1969.

By that time, Greenspan was long gone from the government. He'd been offered the job of budget director in the Nixon administration but had declined. He'd also been considered for various posts in the Treasury Department and on the Council of Economic Advisers. Greenspan said no to any and all offers.

First and foremost, he was concerned about returning full time to his business. Townsend-Greenspan was a small operation and couldn't run as well without his presence. Apparently, Greenspan had also developed doubts about Nixon. He'd joined the campaign team feeling optimistic, but even in the heady days of 1968, Greenspan seems to have caught a whiff of something rotten.

As Greenspan recalled in a 1974 interview:

[Nixon] and I never really got along very well together. One of the reasons I didn't want to go to Washington was because I was terribly concerned about what type of relations I would have with him. . . . I was fairly heavily involved in the 1968 campaign, and I think I was the only person in the economic area who did not go to Washington. One of the reasons was that I felt very uncomfortable with the man, as in fact most intellectuals or people like Burns and Bryce Harlow would feel uncomfortable with him.

The reason is that he himself somehow feels intellectually insecure, which is a great irony, because I've always maintained, and I still maintain, that Richard Nixon probably had the highest IQ of any president since Woodrow Wilson. I actually saw that man do remarkable intellectual feats. Yet there was this extraordinary attitude that made it very difficult to deal with him.

If Greenspan had serious reservations about Nixon, he was thoroughly unenamored of Haldeman and Ehrlichman. He found Nixon's two most trusted aides to be tense and autocratic and assumed he'd have an extremely difficult time working with them.

Greenspan also made this curious comment to a *Business Week* reporter during the 1968 Republican National Convention in Miami: "I'm disturbed," he said. "Every single decision is governed by politics, and the narrowest kind of politics."

Burns and Garment remained in the administration. Nixon, determined to find a place for Burns, wound up nominating him as chairman of the Federal Reserve. Garment, meanwhile, was handed a couple of typically Garment-type tasks, working on civil rights issues and helping to develop a Nixon arts policy.

Even though Greenspan declined to formally join the Nixon camp, he cultivated his newfound Washington contacts by serving on a series of commissions, including the Task Force on Economic Growth and the Commission on Financial Structure and Regulation. As the names suggest, these were not landmark, change-the-fabric-of-society endeavors, with one notable exception: the Commission for an All-Volunteer Armed Forces.

Serving on this particular commission put Greenspan smack in the middle of a cultural debate that had been raging for years as U.S. involvement in Vietnam escalated. Both sides had ample support for their positions. The pro-drafters pointed to Pentagon studies showing the unfeasibility of an all-volunteer force. Opponents could count as an ally founding father Benjamin Franklin, a trenchant critic of the British navy's conscription of colonial Americans.

During a campaign flight to New York from Washington, Nixon highlighted his own position in one of his impromptu moments with the press. He told reporters: "I think we should eliminate the draft and move to an all-volunteer force."

Following the election, Martin Anderson, who had taken an active interest in the topic, was charged with selecting the members for a commission to study the divisive issue. Anderson's instincts told him that if he loaded the deck with draft opponents, the commission's findings would be suspect. Instead, he envisioned a cross-section of society with varied perspectives debating and haggling, kind of like a jury. If a diverse group of people found in favor of ending the draft, the commission's report might actually have an impact.

Of the fifteen people chosen for the commission, five were pro-draft, five were opposed, and five undecided. Not surprisingly, the draft-supporting contingent included several prominent members of the military. Thomas Gates Jr., a former secretary of defense, was named chairman of the commission, ultimately known as the Gates Commission. Also squarely in the pro-draft camp was General Alfred Gruenther, a former supreme Allied commander in Europe and Eisenhower's bridge partner.

The undecideds included Roy Wilkins, executive director of the NAACP, as well as a couple of prominent businessmen—Frederick Dent, president of Mayfair Mills, and Crawford Greenwalt, a director and former president of Du Pont.

Rounding out the commission were the anti-drafters, among them Greenspan and Stephen Herbits, a college student named to the commission to supply the youth perspective. There were also several people with University of Chicago pedigrees. They included Allen Wallis, a former professor at Chicago who had become president of the University of Rochester; and William Meckling, dean of the University of Rochester School of Business, who had done his Ph.D. work at Chicago. And then there was Milton Friedman.

Greenspan and Friedman held similar views on a number of issues. The two also shared a mentor in Arthur Burns, and both rank among the most prominent economists in history, when all is said and done. Yet the Gates Commission would prove to be the only time that the two would work together in a significant capacity.

While at Chicago, Friedman became a free-market apostle, no less fervent than Rand. He, too, saw a moral dimension to capitalism. His classic *Capitalism and Freedom*, published in 1962, won him a number of disciples, though they tended to be a bit more sophisticated—Ph.D. economists, as opposed to the earnest young searchers often drawn to Rand's work.

Friedman was a strong proponent of limited government. He favored the elimination of most federal agencies, Social Security, and the minimum wage. Better to leave such issues to unfettered markets was his standard rap. He regularly criticized the Food and Drug Administration on grounds similar to those offered by Greenspan when he attacked consumer protection laws in the *Objectivist*.

Like Greenspan during his Collective days, Friedman took serious issue with the Fed. His landmark work *A Monetary History of the United States* found a strong correlation between tight money policy by the Fed and the onset of recessions and depressions. He felt the Fed should be stripped of its control over the economy. Instead, he advocated what has come to be known as monetarism, a theory that holds that the key to a stable economy is growing the money supply at a steady rate, roughly equal to the speed at which production is increasing.

Despite strong ideological similarities, Friedman and Greenspan have always had key differences in temperament. For one, Greenspan is no ideologue. He was then and remains almost constitutionally incapable of heated argument. In fact, his very strengths stem from an ability to absorb disparate and even conflicting influences. How else to explain a onetime jazz musician and Keynes devotee turned Randite who would eventually head up the Federal Reserve?

By contrast, Friedman—a small, puckish man given to argument and brash opinion—was a revolutionary. As such, he was never able to make the accommodations with the world of politics that Greenspan eventually managed. Friedman always viewed the government with great suspicion, preferring to offer criticism and occasional advice from a perch high in academe.

It is inconceivable that someone so doctrinaire could ever hold a post, say, on the Council of Economic Advisers. Equally inconceivable is the notion of Greenspan developing controversial theories and defending them with such vehemence and conviction that he's awarded the Nobel Prize in economics, as Friedman would be in 1976.

In Friedman, the Gates Commission got a strong anti-draft voice, a leader, and a lightning rod for controversy. He viewed conscription as both immoral and contrary to sound economic principles. It was, in a nutshell, a form of taxation without representation. By employing the draft, the government forces young people to leave the workforce and join the military at a lower rate of pay. Worse still, a disproportionate number of draftees are minorities and college dropouts—in other words, the people least able to protect themselves against this insidious form of taxation.

Wallis and Meckling, Friedman's Chicago cohorts, shared his view fervently. Greenspan, however, was more of a question mark.

According to Walter Oi, a distinguished economist from the University of Rochester and a researcher on the Gates Commission, as soon as Greenspan learned more about the argument, he became a convert. "Greenspan had not been too aware of the issues," recalls Oi. "But as soon as he learned more about them, the Ayn Rand Libertarian part of him came through."

At the outset it was vital to establish that a volunteer force wouldn't be too expensive. In fact, the Pentagon had concluded in a series of studies that an all-volunteer force might cost anywhere from $5 billion to $17 billion extra per year. It was untenable and left the anti-draft contingent scrambling to come up with a lower number. But the number had to be both convincing and credible.

The research staff crunched the numbers. One of Greenspan's roles was checking their math, testing various assumptions. They wound up with an estimate that an all-volunteer force would add between $2 and $4 billion to the budget each year. That alone was a clincher because it established that ending the draft was economically feasible. From that, all the other arguments flowed.

Another concern among pro-drafters was that an all-volunteer force would mean an all-black force. An article in *Time* magazine in January 1969 suggested the following: "Conceivably, Negroes could flock to the volunteer forces for both a respectable reason, upward mobility, and a deplorable one, to form a domestic revolutionary force."

That is an alarmist sentiment, no doubt born of a militant late-1960s climate of race riots and Eldridge Cleaver's *Soul on Ice*. It also proved a cinch to dismiss on purely economic grounds. The draft already drew disproportionately on minority communities: Pay decent wages to a volunteer force and people would at least have a choice.

Such concerns were very much on the mind of General William Westmoreland, commander of the American forces in Vietnam, when he testified before the Gates Commission. The result was a dramatic confrontation that Friedman recounts in the memoir *Two Lucky People*, cowritten with his wife.

Westmoreland suggested that he didn't want to command an army of mercenaries.

To that, Friedman rejoined, "General, would you rather command an army of slaves?"

Westmoreland wasn't used to such insolence. He squared up in his seat and said, "I don't like to hear our patriotic draftees referred to as slaves."

Friedman shot back: "I don't like to hear our patriotic volunteers referred to as mercenaries."

Friedman was really rolling now.

"If they are mercenaries," he continued, "then I, sir, am a mercenary professor, and you, sir, are a mercenary general; we are served by mercenary physicians, we use a mercenary lawyer, and we get our meat from a mercenary butcher."

The flummoxed general was struck dumb.

While Friedman played bad cop, Greenspan was more inclined to be the good cop for the pro-volunteer contingent. "Milton Friedman was so cutting, so concise, that people could really get their backs up," recalls Stephen Herbits, the commission's erstwhile youth representative. "But people could listen to Alan comfortably. Alan's role, in my view, was to come in and offer reasoned argument. He was able to be a dispassionate advocate when it was important to talk quietly, intelligently, and thoughtfully in order to bring people together."

Gradually, the pro-volunteer contingent wore down and won over the pro-drafters. It may seem surprising that a handful of Libertarians and free marketers could change the minds of a group of gruff-talking generals. But the most decisive arguments from Friedman, Greenspan, and the pro-volunteer camp were the ones that appealed directly to the generals' self-interest.

This was the height of Vietnam, and the armed forces were unquestionably facing serious morale problems. They were proving to be insubordinate and given to acts of sabotage. The pro-volunteer contingent carried the day by suggesting that ending the draft would create a more satisfying environment: Recruits would train harder, work harder, and stay in the army longer.

On February 20, 1970, the Gates Commission issued its final report. It was a unanimous decision to end the draft. Of course, opposition to the draft was an issue that had been seized upon by the Left, what with draft-card burning and antiwar anthems such as Country Joe and the

Fish's "I-Feel-Like-I'm-Fixin'-To Die Rag." That arch-conservative economic theory helped push along their agenda is an odd historical twist. Conscription's official end came on January 23, 1973.

Friedman would remain proud of his work. As an emeritus professor at the University of Chicago, he pointed out that during an ensuing generation, none of the fears about an all-volunteer force have been borne out. The armed forces have been sufficiently prepared for conflict in various hot spots ranging from the Persian Gulf to Somalia to the Balkans. "I still have no doubt that the Gates Commission was one of the most successful ever," he says.

He also has warm memories of serving with Greenspan. "I think Alan was a tower of strength during the proceedings," he recalls.

The Gates Commission concluded what was certainly one of Milton Friedman's most satisfying brushes with government, whereas Alan Greenspan's term of public service was just beginning.

7

SHUTTLE DIPLOMACY

Following his stint on the Gates Commission, Greenspan threw himself into Townsend-Greenspan with renewed vigor. The firm was doing well and growing in size. By the summer of 1970, Greenspan decided to move to new offices in the recently completed Atlas-McGrath Building at One New York Plaza, a fifty-story glass-and-steel skyscraper at Broad and South Streets near the Staten Island Ferry terminal.

The building had been designed by the prominent New York City architectural concern Kahn and Jacobs. The firm's managing partner was none other than Ely Jacques Kahn, the architect with whom Ayn Rand had done a stint as an unpaid intern while researching *The Fountainhead*.

On Wednesday, August 5, 1970 just a month after Townsend-Greenspan had set up its new thirty-third-floor offices—a fire broke out at around 6 P.M. About a half dozen employees were still in the office, including Greenspan. Kathryn Eickhoff was the first to smell smoke and urged everyone to leave. Greenspan and senior economist Lucille Wu were busily preparing a forecast and didn't want to be interrupted, but Eickhoff prodded them to drop everything.

By the time they left their offices, the corridors outside were filled with smoke. It was difficult to see, so the six of them got down low and made their way to the fire stairs to walk down to the 28th floor. Feeling certain that the fire was above them, they left the stairs and got into an elevator. "Not knowing what the world knows today about elevators and fires," says Eickhoff, "we got in and traveled all the way down."

By now, the building was surrounded by fire trucks that had come from as far as Brooklyn and Queens. Even the Bellevue Hospital disaster unit was on the scene. Thousands of people milled around, gawking at the emergency.

Greenspan and Eickhoff wandered over to a little park near the ferry terminal. Clearly visible were long tongues of flame leaping out the windows on some of the higher floors. Greenspan began to methodically count floors, starting from the ground up. Sure enough, the thirty-third floor was a raging conflagration.

Eickhoff was horrified, but Greenspan remained strangely calm. He turned to her and said, "Don't worry, Kathryn, we haven't lost anything."

"What do you mean?" she asked.

Greenspan pointed to his temple, and tapped once. "It's all up here," he said.

Greenspan and Eickhoff waited—like thousands of others—and watched the disaster unfold. As it turned out, the fire had started in an electrical closet in the offices of a tenant on Townsend-Greenspan's floor. Two people wound up dead, both trapped in an elevator during the blaze. More than forty people were injured, half of them firefighters responding to the emergency.

As for Townsend-Greenspan's offices, there was abundant damage, but not as much as feared. Greenspan had not yet gotten around to hanging Joan Mitchell Blumenthal's cityscapes, so they were spared. And many of the firm's library materials hadn't been unloaded and were still stored in rolling bins. A couple of bins were incinerated, but most of the others, including one with Eickhoff's master's thesis, merely wound up waterlogged. For years afterward, certain economic abstracts used by Townsend-Greenspan had a smoky smell.

The firm did lose all its office furniture—the insurance adjuster deemed it a total loss. Right around the same time, a nearby brokerage house went belly up, so Townsend-Greenspan snatched up every piece of office furniture that the firm owned, and at rock-bottom prices.

"I think we may have come out money ahead," says Eickhoff.

Leave it to Greenspan to turn a profit on a fire.

He wasn't alone on this count, either. The image of a shiny new skyscraper spewing flames out its windows left an indelible impression. The Atlas-McGrath Building fire wound up being the inspiration for

1974's blockbuster thriller, *Towering Inferno*, starring Paul Newman and Steve McQueen, with an appearance by O. J. Simpson in a supporting role.

Greenspan's own role during the early 1970s was exhilarating. He enjoyed being able to travel between two distinct worlds. He was part Washington player, serving on various presidential committees and commissions. His consulting position with the Council of Economic Advisers gave him security clearance to visit the White House unannounced. But Greenspan also enjoyed moving in the Wall Street power circles afforded by Townsend-Greenspan. He valued his independence.

At times, he lent support to various Nixon administration initiatives. But he was just as likely to be critical, often using his firm's influential *Townsend Letter* as a vehicle.

Greenspan chose his issues without regard to politics or orthodoxy. Take, for example, the administration's official forecast that the gross national product (GNP) in 1971 would be $1.065 trillion. Greenspan thought it overly optimistic. So did Paul Samuelson, MIT professor, avowedly liberal economist, and winner of the 1970 Nobel Prize. Together, they testified before the Congressional Joint Economic Committee.

Samuelson was in rare form. He called Nixon's GNP figure "poppycock," "ludicrous," and a "comic opera" before going on to compare it to inflated projections Castro had recently made for the sugar crop in Cuba. Such attacks would ultimately earn Samuelson a place on Nixon's notorious "enemies" list.

Greenspan, being Greenspan, took a milder tack. He went before the committee and mumbled a few things about the projection being out of whack. His own forecast called for the GNP to be $20 billion lower. As it turned out, the GNP in 1971 was lower still, not even reaching $1 trillion. Greenspan was correct at least insofar as Nixon's forecast was too rosy.

On another occasion, Greenspan and Ralph Nader joined forces to fight a proposed government bailout of Lockheed. They testified along with two other economists before the Senate Banking and Currency Committee in June 1971.

Lockheed was asking for $250 million to complete development of its L-1011 Tristar, a commercial jet built to compete with McDonnell

Douglas's DC-10. Greenspan and Nader fought the rescue on the grounds that it would set a dangerous precedent. It would discourage Lockheed from getting back into shape competitively. The company might return for repeated infusions of cash and wind up on the dole. Other struggling outfits might also be expected to come out of the woodwork.

From Nader's standpoint, this would be bad for consumers. They'd be the ones stuck buying products from these flabby corporate wards of the state. Greenspan merely viewed a bailout as contrary to the principles of free enterprise. An op-ed he wrote for the *New York Times* included the following: "To place the Federal Government in a position where it can pick and choose which particular private enterprises should or should not be allowed to slip into bankruptcy must inevitably lead to subsidization of the least efficient concerns in an industry."

Greenspan and Nader lost their battle, and Lockheed got its loan. But their effort was memorable, if only because it paired a noted consumer advocate with a man who wrote a piece for the *Objectivist* urging the abolition of consumer-protection laws.

But Greenspan saved his most pointed criticism for Nixon's wage and price controls.

By 1971, inflation was creeping up into the 5-percent range. This was a mere pittance compared to the double-digit disaster lurking just around the corner. At the same time, it represented a departure from the very low inflation that had prevailed during the 1960s. In the Kennedy administration, the rate had skated along beneath 2 percent. Given this context, 5 percent was cause for alarm. Nixon had ambitious foreign-policy goals, including a planned visit to China. And a reelection race loomed in 1972. He worried that an unsound economy would put a major crimp in his plans.

On the evening of Sunday, August 15, 1971, Nixon preempted *Bonanza* to go on national television and outline his New Economic Policy. A key component—along with taking the United States off the gold standard—was an immediate ninety-day freeze on wages and prices. Wags were fond of pointing out that the appellation New Economic Policy, or NEP, had also been used by Lenin.

The government was literally stepping in and taking control of the economy. In Nixon's view, this was the only way to defang so-called cost-push inflation. Essentially, costs were creeping up on raw materials for manufacturing. As a consequence, companies were having to raise prices on final products. Workers, in turn, were demanding higher wages to keep up with rising prices. Of course, wage hikes upped a company's cost of doing business once again. Round and round, the U.S. economy was trapped in a deadly spiral. The solution: Enact a freeze, stop both wages and prices in their tracks.

The move was met with immediate criticism, especially from professional economists and others with a sophisticated view of such matters. History had not shown wage and price controls to be particularly effective. This included relatively recent American history, in which Nixon himself had played a role. As a twenty-eight-year-old attorney, Nixon had worked in the Office of Price Administration, which administered controls during World War II. After the war, the controls were relaxed and inflation immediately spiked up. Therein lay the harsh lesson of wage and price controls. Inevitably, when they were lifted, it was like a dam bursting, with pent-up wage and price pressure spilling forth. The risk was that wages and prices would soar higher than if there had never been controls in the first place.

Nixon pressed forward with his program, ignoring the precedents. The Watergate blowup was still a few years in the future. But among free-market conservatives in particular, wage and price controls would be forever remembered as an early indicator of the cynical heart of his administration.

During the 1968 campaign, in fact, Greenspan had answered a journalist's question about wage-price controls by saying they "fight the symptoms of inflation, not the causes." It was a curious echo to Nixon's own answer to a campaign question about controls: "My administration would address the fundamentals of problems, not their symptoms."

Now Nixon was going back on his word. Even so, everything went well at the outset. To the general populace, the freeze seemed like a novel approach to fighting inflation, and people responded by voluntarily complying with the wage and price guidelines. Everybody pulled together with something akin to patriotism. After ninety days, the government released statistics showing that inflation was being tamed. The price of toothpaste was creeping up at an annual rate of just 1 percent; TV sets, 0.3 percent; a man's haircut, 0.4 percent.

But then the freeze was extended through Phases II, III, and IV. Policing everything from pro football player salaries to the price of rice pudding required an increasingly Byzantine bureaucracy. The IRS printed up a blizzard of forms. Companies had to fill them out each time they wanted to make an exception to the wage-price guidelines— to grant an employee a raise, say, or increase the price of a product.

Applications for raises were considered by the official government Pay Board. Under heavy pressure, especially from unions, it often bent. Railroad signalmen managed to finagle a 46 percent pay increase, despite a guideline setting the maximum raise at 5.5 percent. There was also an official government Price Commission that looked into violations. But only a few hundred IRS agents were assigned to cover the nearly 3 million retail outlets across the country.

Violations became increasingly frequent and flagrant. Meat processors shipped beef into Canada and repackaged it so that they could "import" it back into the United States, thereby circumventing controls. As the controls broke down, a chorus of critical voices rose up.

Milton Friedman concluded that the freeze was "the worst mistake in American economic policy that has been made by an American president in the last 40 years."

Ayn Rand weighed in as well. She devoted two entire issues of the *Ayn Rand Letter* to excoriating the controls, lacerating Nixon, and lamenting the stupidity of the American people in general.

Greenspan also went on record against the controls, though as a writer, he could summon neither Friedman's bite nor the passion of Rand. In a *New York Times* op-ed, he asked: "How in little more than a decade have we moved from a political philosophy which considered economic fine tuning an inappropriate Government function to a point where the price of popcorn has become something for which the Government is ultimately responsible?"

All the while, Greenspan continued his shuttle diplomacy with the Nixon administration, making himself available for consultation about the controls. He was part of an all-star panel of economists assembled by C. Jackson Grayson, chairman of the Price Commission. It included John Kenneth Galbraith, Walter Heller, Arthur Okun, and Otto Eckstein. "I really didn't learn a lot from them," Grayson recalls, "except that they all disagreed."

Greenspan also met regularly with Donald Rumsfeld, director of the Economic Stabilization Program, the bureaucratic body that oversaw the controls. Rumsfeld recalls, "Alan's advice was that it was a mistake to get into controls, and the thing to do is figure a way to get out of it."

The Nixon administration worked to extricate itself from the situation. But it did so in stages. Some aspects of the economy were decontrolled while controls were left in place in other areas. That led to distortions in the economy, such as the notorious odd-day/even-day gas lines. Another economic distortion fostered a truly bizarre and disquieting event.

In June 1973, employees at a hatchery in Joaquin, Texas, drowned 43,000 baby chicks in barrels filled with water. Why? Because decontrolled grain feed prices were rising, while the price of chicken was still frozen. "It's cheaper to drown 'em than to put 'em down and raise 'em," explained the manager of the hatchery. The whole episode was captured on film and was covered on the evening news by stations across America. It served for many as a grotesque illustration of the folly of wage and price controls.

By April 1974, controls had been lifted on everything except domestic oil. But the damage was already done. Wage and price pressures had been bottled up; thus, relaxing the controls would be a factor in ushering in the double-digit inflation of the mid-1970s—the next challenge in Greenspan's career.

Greenspan's lukewarm attitude toward Nixon and Washington couldn't have worked better had he planned it. Stepping forward, then pulling back, serving on select committees, then criticizing the administration in the very next breath turned out to be the perfect approach. Greenspan was his own man. In the eyes of the Nixon camp, he was fiercely independent. As the Watergate scandal heated up and the economy simultaneously began to slide into shambles, that quality was precisely what they desperately needed, someone perceived as above the fray. Early in 1974, he was offered yet another post in government.

Once again, it was with the Council of Economic Advisers. But this time, the administration dangled the high-profile job of CEA chairman.

The CEA was founded as part of Congress's Employment Act of 1946. In the post–World War II period, good objective economic counsel was at a premium. Because the domestic production machine had stopped cranking out bullets and battleships, there was serious concern that the United States might slip back into a depression.

The CEA's mandate is to advise the president on economic policy. It prepares memos explaining how to interpret the reams of data churned out by various arms of the government. It also does forecasts and prepares an annual report on the state of the economy for the benefit of Congress and the president. When necessary, the CEA's staff assists the other cabinet departments in preparing or interpreting economic data. In certain cases, the CEA is also called upon to adjudicate economic-policy turf wars. If Treasury and State have conflicting perspectives on an international trade issue, for example, the CEA may be called upon to help sort it out.

By design, the CEA is a small and specialized body. It consists of three so-called members, one of whom is chairman. They tend to be economics professors, on leave from universities. Paul McCracken, for example, took a sabbatical from the University of Michigan to serve as Nixon's first CEA chairman. Along with the three members, there are ten staff economists, once again usually professors on leave from universities. The idea is for the CEA staff to provide the government with the latest economic thinking by drawing on connections within the academic world. The CEA, the Treasury, the Office of Management and Budget (OMB), and the Federal Reserve are the four agencies charged with U.S. economic policymaking. Together they make up what is known as the Quadriad.

But the job of CEA chairman carries with it a no-win aspect of the kind that only Washington can dream up. The chairman is appointed by the president, the same as is a cabinet secretary. But that's where the similarity ends. Whereas the secretary of the Treasury is expected to be a partisan political adviser, the CEA chairman must directly advise the president, yet remain impartial.

Not surprisingly, the CEA's relatively short history has also been a fractious one. Edwin Nourse, the first CEA chair, really got on President Truman's nerves with his constant displays of equanimity. Apparently, he couched every single pronouncement with, "on the one hand . . . on the other hand." As the story goes, Truman got so irked that he finally said,

"What I want most is a one-handed economist." When Nourse's tenure ended, Truman nominated Leon Keyserling, who proved to be fiercely partisan.

Keyserling suited Truman, but now Congress was annoyed by his style. It retaliated by providing the CEA with only nine months' worth of appropriations for fiscal 1953. When Eisenhower came into office, he was inclined to dissolve the troublesome council altogether. He chose Arthur Burns to serve as an informal economic adviser. Burns set himself to the task of convincing Congress that he would run a professional shop, far different from Keyserling's. Ultimately, the CEA was restored and Burns was named its chairman.

By 1974, the Nixon administration was well into its second CEA chairman, Herb Stein. Stein was a celebrated and eclectic economist. While generally conservative, his greatest renown came from convincing a skeptical postwar business community of the merits of Keynesian policy. Stein's erudition was legendary. His economic prognostications were generously peppered with Shakespeare quotes and biblical verse. He was also a great wit. "If a thing cannot go on forever, it will stop," was a favorite quip.

Stein's son, Ben, served as a Nixon speechwriter and eventually grew into a true Renaissance man. With his father, he coauthored a thriller about a worldwide financial panic. He also taught law at Pepperdine, penned a column in *New York* magazine, appeared as an actor in Clear Eyes ads, and memorably, as a phlegmatic high-school teacher in *Ferris Bueller's Day Off* as well as serving as host of Comedy Central's *Win Ben Stein's Money*.

Stein pater's CEA chairmanship was marked by the usual tumult. Among the media, there was a widely held perception that he put an overly happy face on the increasingly grim economic news of the early 1970s. Congressional Democrats thought some speeches he delivered in 1972—a campaign year—smacked of partisanship. By the spring of 1974, Stein was itching to escape the Nixon administration for a promised post at the University of Virginia.

Initially, Greenspan refused to take the job. It would mean trading an income of more than $300,000 a year for the $42,500 salary paid to a CEA chairman. It would require that he move to Washington and deal with Nixon and his cronies on a daily basis. He'd have to put his business into a blind trust and turn over operations to his deputies. It would also mean putting his graduate studies on hold one more time. With a course here, a course there, he had been working toward a Ph.D. for a quarter of a century, and the prospect of deferring his studies yet again was not pleasing.

Greenspan's contacts within the Nixon administration kept after him about accepting the chairmanship. He got a series of calls from Treasury Secretary William Simon, an acquaintance from Wall Street circles. Overtures were also made by Kenneth Rush, an economic spokesman for Nixon who had been a client of Townsend-Greenspan while president of Union Carbide. Nixon chief-of-staff Alexander Haig gave Greenspan the royal treatment, chartering a plane to fly him down to Key Biscayne for a meeting.

Greenspan had a long conversation with Haig in which he spelled out his views:

> Look, you're making a mistake. You really don't want me. I'm the type of chairman who, if he gets involved with policy and finds that he cannot agree with the policies being implemented, is likely to resign. In fact, I will guarantee it. You don't need that. I don't need that. I could not possibly stay, for example, if there were some significant moves toward wage and price controls.

Despite a steady stream of entreaties, Greenspan remained steadfast about not joining the government. It was akin to Lucius Cincinnatus's working his farm and waiting to be summoned as head of the Roman state.

It took Arthur Burns to finally break Greenspan down. Burns appealed to Greenspan's sense of patriotism and suggested that it was his duty to go to Washington and fight inflation.

"I changed my mind because some people in Washington destroyed my absolute conviction that I could do nothing to make things better," Greenspan told the *New York Times* shortly after deciding to accept the CEA job.

Discussing the same decision on a later occasion, he struck a slightly more upbeat note: "What is at stake is so large that if anyone has the possibility of making a contribution, he should. It's one of the rare instances when the issue of patriotism comes up."

Once Greenspan accepted the nomination for the CEA chair, the real fun began. A couple of FBI agents came calling on his ex-wife, Joan Mitchell Blumenthal. They sat in her living room sheepishly, fumbling to form questions. Periodically, almost like a mantra, one of them would say: "When you want to know the negatives about a person, you ask the ex-wife."

Blumenthal was puzzled. "Yes, I understand that's why you're here," she kept saying. "But I don't know what you want."

This went on—back and forth—for roughly forty-five minutes, in Blumenthal's recollection. She became increasingly frustrated. The FBI agents got more and more irritated.

Suddenly, a light bulb went on for Blumenthal.

"Oh, you're trying to find out if he's gay."

Here, after all, was a man who had last been married twenty years before, for all of ten months. If he were gay, from the FBI's perspective, that would make him vulnerable to blackmail in his new high-profile post.

"Absolutely not," Blumenthal assured them. "There's no question."

Red-faced, the two FBI agents thanked her and beat a hasty retreat out her door.

On August 8, 1974, Greenspan received a grilling of his own. He appeared before the Senate Banking Committee's Housing and Urban Affairs Committee for a nomination hearing. Among those present were Adlai Stevenson III of Illinois, John Tower of Texas, Delaware's Joseph Biden, and Wisconsin's William Proxmire.

The proceedings kicked off with the standard "So good of you to join us, Mr. Greenspan." Greenspan, in turn, offered some pieties about the dangers of inflation and the need to pursue long-term rather than short-term solutions.

Then Proxmire launched into his questioning. He had a well-earned reputation as a thorough and uncompromising inquisitor and as a master in the art of silver-tongued evisceration. In fact, Proxmire became nationally famous for his Golden Fleece Awards, handed out monthly to a project that made especially egregious waste of government funds. One recipient was a scientific study on why people fall in love. "Even if we could find out, I don't think we'd want to know," he said.

Proxmire and Greenspan would become frequent sparring partners over the years. On this day, Proxmire began with:

> Mr. Chairman, I want to alert the committee that I expect to take some time in questioning Mr. Greenspan. I apologize if my questions will seem in detail; but, as you said, he will be chairman of the Council of Economic Advisers; he will come before our Joint Economic Committee; and it's of great importance that we understand him and his views be as much as possible on the record.

At this point, John Sparkman, the committee chair, interjected: "Can you give some estimate of the amount of time?"

"I think forty minutes, and perhaps longer," Proxmire responded.

Then Proxmire let rip. He was particularly troubled by the fact that Greenspan was head of a profitable economic consulting practice that numbered some of the nation's largest businesses among its clients. Given this constituency, Proxmire questioned whether Greenspan was in a position to provide impartial counsel. He also suggested that Greenspan might funnel insider information back to his firm.

Presently, Proxmire zeroed in on Greenspan's economic philosophy. He never specifically mentioned Ayn Rand, but the questions he raised showed that he was quite familiar with Greenspan's Objectivist writings.

At one point, he said, "Now you are on record in the past as opposing consumer protection laws as being not really in the interests of the consumer."

"Yes, sir," said Greenspan, who then expounded on his view that companies already had sufficient incentive to be straight with consumers, even without protection laws: ". . . in many instances, the reason why the quality products have emerged in the forefront of the market place is that it really is in [companies'] self-interest to maintain the absolute highest quality and highest integrity."

At length, Proxmire prodded and tested and queried and cajoled Greenspan. Greenspan bore up fairly well. His own rhetorical style— unfailingly polite and remarkably dispassionate—made him better suited than most to stand up to the inquisition. Proxmire worked his way through the various philosophical issues on which he and Greenspan disagreed. Then he concluded in his inimitable style:

Well, I want to thank you very much. My problem with your nomination, Mr. Greenspan, is that it is very difficult, because you are honest, you are capable, and some of the things that you propose I enthusiastically applaud; but I have great, great difficulty with the fact that you are a free enterprise man who does not believe in antitrust, does not believe in consumer protection, does not believe in progressive income tax; and the latter may be consistent with a laissez-faire position, but you seem to be opposed to many of the social programs that we have been able to achieve.

With that, the hearing adjourned. It had lasted two and a half hours. True to his word, Proxmire had spent well more than forty minutes questioning Greenspan.

But now the members of the Senate Banking Committee needed to turn their attention elsewhere.

That very night, Nixon was scheduled to go on TV to address the nation.

8

"WHIP INFLATION NOW"

Nixon announced his resignation on August 8, 1974. The very next day, Gerald Ford was sworn in as the thirty-eighth president.

It was to be a tough tenure. Where history threatens to boil Nixon's entire political career down to Watergate, Ford's record runs the risk of being altogether obliterated. Deemed the "accidental president," he assumed the highest office in the land without the benefit of being elected. Over time, the notion has emerged that Ford was merely a caretaker of the presidency, a stopgap between the disgraced Nixon and the duly-elected Carter. Ford's lack of charisma and oratorical fire didn't help matters.

But Ford's mild manner belies a rather dogmatic streak. The fact is, he took over the presidency with quite distinct ideas about what he wanted to accomplish in the job. His political philosophy was clear-cut and fully formed, honed during decades as a congressman. He seemed to have a great deal of trouble communicating this philosophy to the public, but it was a philosophy, nonetheless. In fact, his views would prove remarkably consonant with those held by Greenspan.

Ford, thirteen years Greenspan's senior, grew up in Michigan and studied economics, government, and history at the University of Michigan. He was also a football hero, playing center for a pair of un-defeated teams, in 1932–1933. After graduation, Ford received offers to play pro football from the Detroit Lions and Green Bay Packers. He turned those down, wanting to be a lawyer instead. Ford attended Yale Law School and also served as the university's assistant football coach. One of the players he coached was William Proxmire.

During World War II, Ford served aboard the USS *Monterey*, a light-aircraft carrier. He saw enemy fire on a number of occasions and at one point was almost killed, not by the Japanese but by a typhoon in the Philippine Sea in December 1944. Nearly washed overboard, he was saved by a two-inch metal ridge designed to keep tools on deck. He grabbed it and held on for dear life.

After the war, Ford married Betty Bloomer Warren, a recent divorcée who had studied dance with Martha Graham and modeled in New York. This was also about the time Ford got into politics. Encouraged by his stepfather, who was active in local Republican circles, Ford challenged Barney Jonkman, an incumbent congressman from his district. He won and entered the House of Representatives for the first of thirteen terms.

Ford's distinguished congressional career included service on the Warren Commission, which investigated Kennedy's assassination. In 1965, he coauthored a book, *Portrait of an Assassin*, that defended the commission's finding that Lee Harvey Oswald had acted alone. He also tried to launch an inquiry into the possible impeachment of William Douglas, a liberal Supreme Court justice. Ford maintained that some of Douglas's writings advocated a "hippie-yippie-style revolution."

But Ford truly made his mark serving on the House Committee on Appropriations, where he was charged with keeping close tabs on federal spending. Ford proved a real stickler and took frequent aim at expensive social programs and other forms of big government. It was while serving on the Appropriations Committee that Ford came of age politically, as a staunch conservative of the school that favors minding the till and keeping Washington off Main Street. One of Ford's favorite sayings was: "A government big enough to give us everything we want is a government big enough to take from us everything we have."

For Congressman Ford, even becoming vice president was accidental. In 1973, he took the job over from Spiro Agnew, who had resigned in the face of a tax-evasion investigation. Thanks to the Twenty-fifth Amendment—ratified only a few years back, in 1967—Nixon was allowed to pick Agnew's replacement, and Ford was confirmed by Congress as vice president on December 6, 1973. Eight months later, he was president. First Agnew, then Nixon. At his swearing-in ceremony, Ford famously declared: "Our long national nightmare is over."

Perhaps politically. But on the economic front, Ford inherited appalling problems that had been allowed to fester throughout the Nixon administration. By the time Ford took office, inflation was running at 12 percent, double the rate at the beginning of Nixon's term. Unemployment had grown to 5.3 percent, compared to 3.4 percent in early 1969. The Dow Jones Industrial Average, which had stood at 785 when Nixon took office, was now down 17 percent.

There were abundant culprits for these economic tribulations. The relaxation of wage and price controls played a significant role. So, too, did an OPEC oil embargo in the fall of 1973, which led to an overnight quadrupling of prices, from $2.29 to $11.65 a barrel. Another guilty party was Fed chairman Arthur Burns, who in 1972 helped worsen inflation further by pursuing especially lax monetary policy.

There was no question that Burns had made a tactical error. But some critics have gone so far as to suggest that he upped the money supply specifically to help his old pal Nixon during an election year. Print loads of money and you can make people very appreciative come voting time; it's only later that inflation starts creeping in.

Burns always denied the charge. No compelling evidence was ever unearthed showing collusion between the Federal Reserve and Nixon during election year 1972. But it's a moot point—unintentional or not, the result was the same. Burns hit the gas when he should have hit the brakes.

By 1974, the economy was spinning out of control and the Ford administration was left to contend with "stagflation"—a vexing situation in which inflation and unemployment spiral upward at the same time. As if that wasn't enough, Ford's term would be marked by economic crises on what seemed like a daily basis.

Along with Nixon's economic problems, Ford also inherited his appointees. Greenspan's nomination as head of the CEA still required confirmation by the Senate, and Ford had the option of pulling the plug. Here, once again, Greenspan benefited from his stated ambivalence toward Washington. He'd been reluctant to join the Nixon administration in the first place; that proved to be a plus, as Ford struggled to recast a government that was stuffed to the gills with Nixon friends and associates.

Donald Rumsfeld, who headed Ford's transition team, has the following recollection:

Watergate still had enormous steam and momentum. Now we had a new president who had never run, never developed a campaign platform, didn't have a team of people fashioned for himself. He presided over a government deemed illegitimate by a large percentage of the American people. For Ford, it was kind of like stepping onto an airplane that's going 500 miles an hour, is at 40,000 feet, has a crew you've never met, and being asked to fly it.

It is in this context that Rumsfeld recalls Greenspan's pending nomination. "One of the first calls I got involved what we should do with nominations pending before the Senate," he says. "One was Alan Greenspan. I went in to see Gerald Ford, and remember saying to the president: 'Look, this is a wonderful situation. It's an absolute home-run ball. You couldn't pick a better person.' We embraced him, made him a Ford appointee."

Greenspan and Ford would get along extremely well. Over the next two years, the economy would go into free fall, congressional Democrats would raise hell, spats would erupt among cabinet members, and there would be ample public outcry, but never once would a cross word be exchanged between these two mild-mannered men.

Leonard Garment would also play a small role in the Ford administration. Along with Greenspan, he was one of the few who managed not to be tarnished by an association with Nixon. As the Watergate scandal heated up, Garment began serving Nixon in a new capacity, as acting legal counsel. He recommended that Nixon fire Haldeman, Ehrlichman, and White House counsel John Dean. He also asked Nixon to give him access to various tapes and documents so he could evaluate the strength of the case against the president. Nixon refused. That suggested to Garment that the case against Nixon was solid. Garment's next step was to request a meeting in Key Biscayne with the president in which he planned to urge Nixon to give consideration to the inevitable: his resignation of the presidency. Anticipating Garment's recommendation, Nixon declined to meet with him. Garment hung in until the bitter end, though, trying to act as a voice of reason.

During the Ford administration, Garment was appointed U.S. representative to the UN Human Rights Commission. Garment chronicled his strange journey from Brooklyn to swing music to presidential politics and beyond in a memoir entitled *Crazy Rhythm*.

In due course, Greenspan's nomination was submitted to the full Senate for consideration. On August 13, 1974, Proxmire sent a "Dear Colleague" letter to his fellow legislators. "I think it is essential that the members of the senate be fully informed of the controversial nature of this nomination," it read in part. With the transition from Nixon to Ford in progress, there was much chaos afoot. The Senate had plenty to consider. Thus, Proxmire failed to stir much interest in a nomination that might otherwise have invited greater scrutiny. On August 19, the Senate confirmed Greenspan as head of the CEA. It was done without a record vote; only three senators spoke.

Greenspan left his consulting firm in the hands of four female deputies—Bess Kaplan, Judith Mackey, Lucille Wu, and Kathryn Eickhoff. He placed his 99-percent stake in Townsend-Greenspan in a blind trust. Any profits generated in his absence could either be distributed to employees or to charity. As a special contingency designed to allay the concerns of his critics—Proxmire chief among them—he was strictly forbidden from communicating about business matters with members of the firm. After all, Greenspan was a consultant rather than an academic. He was in a position to profit financially from knowledge gained during his stint in government.

Although he maintained his Manhattan apartment, Greenspan also selected new Washington digs. He chose to live in the storied Watergate complex, scene of the Democratic Party headquarters break-in that was Nixon's undoing. Arthur Burns was a fellow resident.

Greenspan's particular building, Watergate East at 2500 Virginia Avenue, was the oldest, built in 1968. By 1974, an entire mini-city had grown up on the nine acres of prime D.C. real estate, directly across from the Kennedy Center and twenty blocks from Capitol Hill. Along with three residential buildings, the Watergate complex featured a hotel, two office buildings, and a health club—a deluxe amenity in those days. It also had its own mall, offering almost anything a person might need: a pharmacy, post office, dentist's office, and roughly thirty boutiques.

Greenspan's apartment was two bedrooms, with two baths, roughly 1,500 square feet, and a view of the Potomac River. He rented it on a month-by-month basis, with a cancellation clause. He was not yet convinced that Washington would be home.

On the day of Greenspan's inaugural ceremony, September 4, 1974, President Ford led a motley crew of invited guests on a tour of the White House. Ayn Rand came down from New York, her hard-drinking, long-suffering husband, Frank O'Connor, in tow. Also present was Rose Goldsmith, Alan's mother.

A brief swearing-in ceremony in the Cabinet Room followed, in which Ford made a speech that alluded to Greenspan's musical past: "But now as the ninth chairman, he has a new responsibility to try and stop playing the blues and start curing the blues." He added: "I was told the other day that being a clarinetist or musician in Washington was not necessarily bad. Len Garment was an accomplished musician and has done extremely well here in Washington."

Looking on was Rand, the cool rationalist and unapologetic atheist, as well as Greenspan's emotionally vibrant mother. It was an incredibly proud moment for both women.

A photographer snapped a picture of Rose giving her son a big hug after the swearing-in, a copy of which she carried with her everywhere and treasured as her favorite picture of Alan. Ford wrote an inscription to Greenspan in the copy of the Torah used at the swearing-in ceremony. Greenspan gave this to his mother, and it also became one of her prize possessions.

For Rand, the White House ceremony was a kind of vindication. On the one hand, she professed contempt for the compromised world of politics. But she also craved influence. That someone from her circle was assuming legitimate power was truly gratifying. "I'm very proud of Alan," she said shortly after her White House visit. "His is a heroic undertaking."

Of course, inviting Rand was a risky move. She was a best-selling author, but she courted controversy and had plenty of detractors. Among a large portion of the population, she was viewed alternately as dangerous, as a kook, and as a dangerous kook.

Greenspan handled this potential public-relations land mine with his characteristic grace. He never allowed himself to be publicly put on the defensive regarding his friendship with Rand. Whenever the media inquired about their association, he responded in ways that played up her seriousness as a thinker and his earnest debt of gratitude to her. This comment to *Newsweek* is typical: "When I met Ayn Rand, I was a free enterpriser in the Adam Smith sense, impressed with the theoretical structure and efficiency of markets. What she did was to make me see that capitalism is not only efficient and practical, but also moral."

Rand made things easier, too, by not alleging undue influence on Greenspan. "I am a philosopher, not an economist," she told *Time* magazine. "Alan doesn't seek my advice on these matters. He can tell me more than I can tell him, and knows more about the day-to-day events."

Satisfied that no Objectivist conspiracy was brewing in government, the press quickly turned its attention to other matters. Greenspan moved into the Old Executive Office Building next to the White House and got down to the very difficult job at hand.

The first order of business was a big summit on inflation planned for the fall. It was to be a televised two-day event, with participants ranging from politicians to economists, union heads, business leaders, consumer advocates, and so on. There was a sense that the old economic assumptions were breaking down. The summit was meant to foster an exchange of ideas, and maybe identify some fresh solutions.

Throughout the post–World War II period, inflation and unemployment appeared to have an inverse relationship: When inflation rose unemployment fell, and vice versa. Keynesians had long relied on the existence of this relationship to justify tinkering with the economy. A common notion among liberal economists was that the populace could tolerate a bit more inflation in the interest of bringing down unemployment.

But by fall 1974, both inflation and unemployment were out of control. The double whammy of stagflation seemed immune to the conventional remedies. Each of its components—inflation and unemployment—was frightening in its own right.

Inflation makes it difficult to plan for the future. For instance, wages had to be adjusted three times a day to keep up with the galloping inflation that gripped Hungary in 1948. Workers had to have a dedicated helper, typically a spouse, who rushed checks to the bank so they'd start earning interest immediately. Otherwise, a person's paychecks would be unable to keep pace with inflation and would be virtually worthless by the end of the day.

At its most extreme, during the collapse of Weimar Germany, inflation's effects had people pushing around wheelbarrows full of money. The Nazis soon seized power. History's gruesome lesson was that hyperinflation equals complete loss of faith in the system and leads to a breakdown of the social order. It was a terrible and frightening possibility that helped propagate inflation hawks—people who take an extremely hard line on the issue.

As of the mid-1970s, Greenspan was an inflation hawk of the first order. "If inflation continues, our system will not hold together in its present form," he said during the fall of 1974.

Always deeply conservative on economic matters, Ford shared Greenspan's concern. On more than one occasion, he dubbed inflation "our domestic public enemy number one."

Of course, unemployment is no picnic, either; but the conventional view among inflation hawks holds that price instability is the greater evil. It affects everyone, whereas unemployment rarely hurts more than a sliver of the population at any given time. During the fall of 1974, unemployment was high, but not alarmingly so. Therefore, the great summit was aimed squarely at the inflation component of stagflation.

Leading up to the inflation summit, a series of "foothill" summits were held in preparation. They covered a variety of topics, including agriculture, housing, transportation, and finance. The idea was to compile inflation-fighting proposals from experts in varying fields. Delegates from the foothill summits would then be chosen to speak at the larger summit.

Greenspan was charged with briefing the participants at each of these minisummits on the broad state of the economy. At the Health, Education, Income Security, and Social Services Summit, held on September 19, 1974, Greenspan committed what will surely go down as one of the greatest—if not the greatest—gaffe of his career.

Caspar Weinberger, secretary of the Health, Education, and Welfare Department, was chairing this particular summit. On hand to discuss inflation were representatives from a slew of advocacy groups, including the Child Welfare League, Gray Panthers, Anti-Defamation League of B'nai B'rith, American Council for the Blind, Easter Seals, and the National Association for Retarded Citizens.

The proceedings had a particularly critical tone. Often, remarks were hurled directly at Greenspan, who was there, after all, as a representative of the administration. One such comment was made by Jerry Wurf, president of the American Federation of State County and Municipal Employees. He suggested that Ford's policies favored rich bankers over poor citizens.

"Mr. Wurf," Greenspan replied, "we all have an interest in this economy. If someone believes that there is some way that someone is not hurt by inflation, we are obviously all hurt by inflation. If you really wanted to examine who percentage-wise is hurt the most in their incomes, it is the Wall Street brokers. I mean their incomes have gone down the most. So if you want to get statistical, I mean let's look at what the facts are."

This was met with booing and hooting. One participant jumped up and yelled: "That's the whole trouble with the administration!"

The fallout was fast and furious. The AFL-CIO announced that it had put Greenspan's name in the hopper for its annual "dubious distinction" award. Meanwhile, some home builders in Oregon formed a group called Save Our Brokers. (The housing industry was taking a real beating in the fall of 1974.) They mailed handkerchiefs to local stockbrokers, the better to sob into, and paper cups in the event that they could no longer afford champagne glasses.

"This may be the last time Greenspan ever tried to make unrehearsed, off-the-cuff remarks," says Murray Weidenbaum, chairman of the Center for the Study of American Business at Washington University in St. Louis and a CEA chief during the Reagan administration.

For Greenspan, it was certainly a low point. He'd put his worst foot forward—the bionic accountant, numbers-over-emotions aspect of his personality. Granted, from a literal, digit-head perspective, stockbrokers had seen their incomes fall the most, "percentage-wise." But it was a truth that was shut out by other, more visceral truths.

Greenspan was quick to apologize. "Obviously the poor are suffering more," he said before a joint session of Congress.

If there was one saving grace in the whole episode, it was that Greenspan backed down immediately. He showed contrition and it had the effect of quieting his critics.

In the end, the much-hyped summit wound up being no great shakes. Held at the Washington Hilton on September 27 and 28, 1974, it drew 800 people, including half of Congress. The proceedings were broadcast live on public television and public radio.

It kicked off with a prayer by the White House chaplain, possibly the first and probably the last invocation directly related to the consumer price index. "In spite of all the differences, may we be of one mind, possessed by one spirit, motivated by one purpose, to serve our nation with all our hearts that inflation may not only be met but managed and not only managed but mastered."

Amen.

Ford arrived late to the summit. His wife, Betty, had just been operated on for breast cancer. Looking back, people who were present recall being impressed by Ford's bravery during the family crisis. They remember that he spoke knowledgeably and eloquently about the problem at hand.

But there's one other nearly universal impression of the great summit: It wasn't of any real use.

"No new ideas, no breakthroughs, no consensus, no nothing," is the recollection of Edgar Fiedler, a retired Conference Board economist who worked for Treasury Secretary William Simon during the Ford administration.

Paul McCracken, Nixon's first CEA chief, was also present. As an emeritus professor at Michigan, age eighty-four, he remembered the summit thusly: "I think it was 50 percent just show. I think the new president wanted to show that he meant business when trying to deal with the inflation problem."

Coming out of the summit armed with a paucity of inflation-fighting ideas, Ford opted for volunteerism. He decided to literally leave it up to the American people to tackle inflation through their own efforts—shopping wisely, conserving energy, that kind of thing. He was pushed in this direction by Sylvia Porter, the noted financial columnist. Greenspan, fresh from a firestorm of criticism, kept his distance from this next phase in economic policymaking.

During a series of speeches, Ford laid out the principles of the volunteer approach. He suggested people plant gardens to grow their own vegetables. He confirmed that he and Betty were going to eat more casseroles, urging the American people to do the same. To keep energy costs low, he suggested carpooling, turning off unused lights, and keeping rooms at 68°F during wintertime. "Shop wisely, look for bargains, go for the lowest-cost item, and most importantly, brag about the fact that you're a bargain hunter. You should be proud of it," he said during an October 15 speech before the Future Farmers of America in Kansas City, Missouri.

"It was Republican nonsense," counters William Niskanen, chairman of the Cato Institute. "I remember shopping in Safeway. A nice blue-haired Republican lady whopped me with her purse because I bought too expensive a cut of meat."

But the most eminently lampoonable part of volunteerism was the WIN button. At the behest of the White House, Alvin Hample, an adman for Benton and Bowles, developed the concept. He was the man behind a successful button for Continental Airlines that read, "We Really Move Our Tail for You." For volunteer inflation-fighting, he searched for something similarly snappy. Finally, it hit him. WIN: "Whip Inflation Now." In the fall of 1974, the U.S. government printed millions of WIN buttons.

The coup de grâce was that the button was red with white lettering. Originally, it was to be a boldly patriotic red, white, and blue. But it was wisely decided that paring the button down to two colors was less inflationary than pulling out the stops with a tricolor button. WIN was the butt of endless jokes. Lester Kinsolving, a member of the White House press corps, printed up his own custom SIN button, "Stop Inflation Now."

But in a curious way, this emphasis on volunteerism was very much in keeping with Ford's overall philosophy. He had a classic conservative's faith in the common sense of Americans. The summit had produced no new ideas. Wage and price controls and other recent attempts at intervention in the economy had been disastrous. A modest program that left citizens to solve the problem themselves had a compelling logic all its own. "I plan to continue the WIN program—to Whip Inflation Now—not because it is setting the world on fire, but, frankly, because it is not," said Ford in one speech.

It was a hard message to bring home with stagflation loose in the land. Ford's advisers did what they could to dissuade him.

"Greenspan and my boss, Bill Simon, and I thought it was crazy. But we didn't know how to get Ford off the idea," says Edgar Fiedler.

Greenspan would later say of WIN: "It was an unfortunate program from the beginning, precisely what Ford did not need, and probably the low point in economic policy making in the administration."

While the administration was casting about for voluntary solutions, the economy was flailing. It appeared to be sinking into recession—a marked slowdown in business activity, often defined as two consecutive quarters of economic contraction. Warnings had been issued by congressional Democrats, labor leaders, and liberal economists, but the administration had chosen to focus on inflation as the big bugaboo. "We went dutifully to the summits. Greenspan and Burns wore their WIN buttons, even though a number of the economists present—myself included—said that the major problem for the U.S. was the developing recession rather than inflation," recalls MIT professor emeritus Paul Samuelson, age eighty-four.

The indefatigable economist and Nobel laureate was witness to many of the twentieth century's economic events, but few would rival the recession of 1974–1975 for sheer knuckle-gnawing, bottom-drops-out intensity.

Consumers and businesses wound up locked in a kind of death dance. Spooked by rising inflation, consumers began cutting back on their spending. In response to waning consumer demand, businesses were forced to cut back production. Industrial production fell nearly 10 percent during the fall of 1974, the steepest decline since 1937. As activity slowed, businesses began to lay off workers.

By year's end, three-fourths of all nonfarm businesses had cut back on personnel. General Motors laid off one-third of its 440,000 blue-collar workers. Ford Motor Company announced plans to shut down twenty-two of sixty-six U.S. plants, idling half the 155,000 workers who made up its hourly force. Black and Decker simply shut down the entire company for a week. As the New Year rolled in, the unemployment rate was pushing 8 percent, the highest since 1941. Between 1960 and 1973, unemployment had averaged 4.9 percent.

Fears of an all-out depression gripped the populace, although the percentages weren't yet supporting the panic. Unemployment hadn't tipped 10 percent—a benchmark sometimes viewed as the threshold for a depression. (Although it averaged 17.9 percent during the entire decade of the 1930s, the high-water mark was 1933 when the rate hit 24.9 percent.)

But these differences were of scant comfort to anyone who had lived through the depression, and for many who hadn't. By the end of 1974, confidence in the economy was severely shaken, and technical distinctions between recession and depression were merely academic. This was summed up neatly in a quip made by a member of the Ford administration at a press conference: "A recession is when you're out of work. A depression is when I'm out of work."

Clearly, something needed to be done. Both inside and outside of the administration, a chorus of voices began calling for a switch from fiscal restraint to stimulus.

Greenspan joined the stimulus crowd. This was a surprising turnabout for him. Upon taking the CEA job, Greenspan had urged severe budgetary austerity as a means of combating inflation. During the first days of the Ford presidency, there had been abundant talk of keeping the budget in line and the deficit in check.

Now Greenspan was urging stimulus, which could potentially ignite further price increases, this despite his decidedly inflation-hawk leanings. It's as good an example as any of Greenspan's fundamental pragmatism. Under the tutelage of both Burns and Rand, Greenspan had learned to be rigorously empirical. Sometimes that required him to adopt a position at odds with his general philosophy. In a pattern that has been repeated throughout his long Washington tenure, he showed a preference for evidence over orthodoxy.

"Everyone knows Greenspan is a Republican who doesn't think you can steer the economy with fine tuning," says David Munro, who worked in the Ford administration CEA under Greenspan. "But he was very inclined to sit back and take matters under advisement. On balance, he felt that a shot of adrenaline was needed."

Thus, Greenspan urged Ford to push for a tax decrease. During his 1975 State of the Union address, the president recommended a $16-billion cut. But the Democratic Congress gave him more than he had bargained for. In March 1975, it handed Ford a bill calling for a cut of $22.8 billion.

A bitter battle ensued among the president's advisers about whether to veto the legislation. It threatened to really blow up the budget, which might have spiked inflation even more. But there was also that second component of stagflation to consider—jobs. It was a real Gordian knot. Perhaps a tax cut would lead to an increase in consumer spending. In response, production might kick back up, and companies might rehire some of those laid-off workers. That was the theory, anyway.

Ford asked his top economic advisers to submit their opinions in writing to prevent them from having to openly clash on such a divisive issue. Fed chair Burns and Treasury Secretary Simon came down in favor of a veto. But not Greenspan. In a memo dated March 28, 1975, he wrote: "Mr. President: I recommend that the tax bill be signed."

Ultimately, Ford took Greenspan's advice. He signed the bill which provided such relief as an increase in the standard deduction and a tax credit of up to 5 percent on the purchase of a new home, intended to shore up the beleaguered housing industry. But the real Christmas-in-April component of the bill was a rebate of 1974 taxes to the tune of roughly $100 to $200 per taxpayer.

Of course, a couple of hundred dollars was no major windfall, even in 1975 terms, but all told, the rebates plowed $8.1 billion back into the economy. Whether it would be enough to spark a recovery remained an unanswered question.

One thing is certain, though: The tax-cut issue was the first real sign of the growing influence Greenspan had with President Ford. As Dick Cheney, the administration's chief of staff, once told *Fortune:* "At the end of the day, after he talked to everybody else, President Ford would say, 'Let's get Alan over here,' and then Ford would make the key decision."

While Greenspan and Ford were going great guns, dissension was growing among the staff of the CEA. The reason had everything to do with the close relationship between Greenspan and the president. It cramped his colleagues' style.

Traditionally, CEA staffers have hailed from academia. In fact, other than Greenspan, the only non-Ph.D. to head up the CEA was Leon Keyserling, who was actually a lawyer by training.

Thanks to this heavy academic influence, the CEA has tended to hew closely to the manners and mores of university life. It's usually a collegial working environment, with people sharing in the research and forecasting duties. An unwritten CEA rule is that the three people holding the most senior positions—the members—are equals, even though the chairman is the nominal leader. By design, the three members often have diverse and complementary areas of economic expertise. It makes sense to divvy up the work. One might advise the president on antitrust, another on agriculture.

Among the CEA staff, there's also a tradition of being above the fray in a professorial, ivory-tower kind of way. That's a rare luxury, not shared by career politicians who have to curry presidential favor to keep their jobs. "When you take a leave of absence from a university it gives you a great feeling of independence because you have a place to go back to. And presidents know it," says Reagan's onetime CEA chief, Murray Weidenbaum.

Greenspan turned CEA tradition on its head when he formed a close bond with the president. And he jealously guarded the most attractive and high-visibility assignments. An unnamed CEA staffer told the *New York Times* in March 1975: "With Alan spending so much time and energy on White House work, the CEA is in the position of not having a full-time chairman. I rarely see him. He rarely tells me what he's up to. And he doesn't really care all that much about what I'm up to either."

Gary Seevers, a onetime member of Greenspan's CEA, has a similar recollection: "The thing about Greenspan, he was a different chairman. He didn't go out of his way to treat the council or the staff as an important entity. I respect him a lot, but he's not a team player. He wasn't somebody who had worked at a university, where you have to lead a group."

On April Fools' Day 1975—with the United States still deep in a slump—Seevers quit, as did William Fellner, the other CEA member. Both men resented Greenspan's failure to involve them more fully in policy. Greenspan was now left alone atop the CEA.

It took several months to drum up suitable replacements. Eventually, they were found in Paul MacAvoy, an energy expert from MIT's Sloane School, and Burton Malkiel, a Princeton professor. MacAvoy described himself as an "isolated Democratic conservative micro-industrial economist." He has since gone on to teach at Yale. Malkiel returned to Princeton after his CEA stint and wrote the investment classic *A Random Walk down Wall Street*.

Upon hiring the two for CEA slots, however, Greenspan was careful to adjust their expectations. MacAvoy recalls that Greenspan took him to lunch in the West Wing basement presidential dining room. "He spelled out all the territory that was his, then said, 'Now tell me, what can you make of the job?'"

MacAvoy adds: "Greenspan had a special one-on-one relationship with Ford. Burt and I never had an advisory role to the president."

Besides short-handedness and dissension, Greenspan's CEA also suffered the consequences of a volatile economy. During the relative calm of the Kennedy years, CEA chairman Walter Heller and staff probably could have gotten away with working banker's hours. Seven-day weeks were not uncommon in the Ford administration.

By the summer of 1975, the economy was showing the first tentative signs of recovery. The trough of the recession had been reached in March, and unemployment had peaked in May at 9 percent. From there, the economy began a long slow climb.

More than anything, the economic resuscitation confirmed a view that both Greenspan and Ford shared in the primacy of a laissez-faire approach. There had been five recessions since World War II, and the economy had always come back. While some would argue that recovery was due to savvy intervention, Ford and Greenspan would counter that it was in spite of intervention. Markets are smarter than the government bureaucrats who meddle in them, or so goes the classic argument.

"One thing that we know about our economy is that it attempts to eliminate imbalances. In other words, it leans more toward some state of equilibrium," Greenspan told *U.S. News and World Report*, explaining the swing from recession to recovery. At a later date, he amplified this view: "I often come out almost ad nauseam with free market solutions not because I have an ideology, but because I believe it works. Where it doesn't, I recognize that it doesn't. But my inclination would be to presume that the system works. There are others that presume that unless you prod it all the time, it will never function."

Of course, Greenspan had urged a little prodding himself with the tax rebate. But the rebate was like baby bear's porridge, neither too hot nor too cold. It played a role in the recovery for certain, but against such a violent downturn, there's a limit to how much bang you can get even from $8.1 billion, especially when doled out in increments of $100 to $200. Essentially, it served as a shot in the arm for consumer confidence. But intervening in the economy in a serious Keynesian way might have done even more harm, at least in Greenspan's estimation.

Now there are recoveries and there are recoveries. This one proved modest, slow, and extremely fragile. Even the slightest disruption or unexpected event threatened to throw it back into a tailspin. It was in this context that the Ford administration was forced to contend with the decade's second Great Grain Robbery.

The first one had occurred in 1972 during the Nixon administration, making it yet another serious factor—along with the OPEC crisis, relaxation of wage and price controls, and Burns stepping on the gas— that contributed to stagflation. It began when the Soviet Union was hit with a horrific shortfall in its grain harvest. Trade Minister Nikolai Patolichev dispatched agents to the United States. Quietly, stealthily, they cut a series of individual deals with grain wholesalers. Before anyone quite knew what was happening, the Russians had bought up 19 million tons of wheat and corn, roughly one-fourth of the U.S. supply. By getting into the market early, the Russians got the grain at a bargain-basement price of $1.1 billion.

Now history was repeating itself, and the timing could not have been worse.

One day in the summer of 1975, a CIA operative dropped by the offices of the CEA. He had three pieces of information. First, satellite pictures revealed that the grain crop in Siberia was in terrible shape. Second, the Soviets were selling gold in Zurich. Third, they were also buying cargo space in Rotterdam.

"How do you put those things together, Mr. Greenspan?" asked the operative.

It was pretty simple. The Soviets were preparing to launch a second covert foray into the world grain market. CIA intelligence reports indicated that worse-than-normal snowfalls had decimated the winter wheat crop and that droughts had destroyed the summer plantings. Estimates put the Soviet grain harvest 25 to 30 million tons short of the 215-million-ton goal—yet the country's minister of agriculture denied that anything was amiss. They were buying time to sneak into the market again. If farmers in the United States and other countries actually knew the extent of the Soviet crop deficit, they might raise prices in anticipation of grain growing increasingly scarce.

Greenspan became heavily involved in trying to figure out what the Soviets were up to. Frantic calls were placed to foreign officials and U.S. grain wholesalers in an effort to tally up whatever sales had been made. The suspicion was that the Soviets were doing another piecemeal buying job, getting a bit of grain here, a bit there.

"The Canadian Wheat Board this morning confirmed the sale of 2.03 million metric tons of wheat to the Soviet Union. . . . The Australian Wheat Board today denied that specific wheat negotiations are underway with the Soviets," reads a July 17, 1975, memo to Greenspan from G. Edward Schuh, an agricultural economist doing a stint with the CEA while on leave from Purdue University.

Working with various estimates, the CEA tried to figure out how Soviet purchases would affect inflation in the United States. The fledgling recovery couldn't withstand a serious shock. An alarm bell was sounded by the prestigious Brookings Institution, which published a study indicating that increased grain prices were likely to push up the price of bread, which might then ripple through the food chain. The likely result was a reprise of the first Great Grain Robbery in 1972, when food costs shot up 20 percent. But Greenspan was less concerned; the CEA's official estimate was for a fairly mild inflationary impact.

Then in August, a drought threatened the U.S. corn crop. At this point, Ford announced an embargo. No new grain sales to the Soviet Union until the U.S. crop had been harvested. The Soviets simply looked to other markets in France, Argentina, and Brazil.

U.S. farmers were livid. They were being denied desperately needed sales, and all the while the Soviets were simply turning around and buying from overseas competitors. Secretary of Agriculture Earl Butz began petitioning Ford to lift the embargo. At the same time, U.S. longshoremen were threatening to not load the shipments of grain that the Soviet Union had contracted for before the embargo. Their complaint: Back in 1972, the bulk of Soviet grain purchases from the United States had been transported in foreign vessels, chartered in places such as Rotterdam. The longshoremen wanted assurances that at least 50 percent of U.S. grain sales would be carried aboard U.S. tankers. Buy American, ship American, was their view of the matter. In their corner was Labor Secretary John Dunlop. The Ford cabinet was in a complete uproar.

Through all of this, the CEA maintained a fairly consistent stance. Long term, an embargo was probably not the way to go, especially where inflation was concerned. After all, the Soviets could always make up the difference by buying elsewhere. World economies were interlinked in such a way that the inflationary effect on the United States would wind up virtually the same. "Greenspan's view was that if the Soviets want grain they're going to get it. The issue is whether they pull it out of our side of the lake or the other side," says Schuh, a regents professor at the University of Minnesota.

The CEA's advice was that grain-purchasing arrangements between the two countries should be normalized. Rather than the Soviets sneaking into the market every few years, they should agree to buy a certain amount of U.S. grain annually. They should also share information about their anticipated harvests. In other words, Communist Russia's woes had a capitalist solution—the free exchange of information. If the United States knew about Soviet shortages in advance, it could try to be adequately prepared. And the Soviets wouldn't have to resort to frantic eleventh-hour international grain speculation.

In October, Ford lifted the embargo and worked out terms largely in line with Greenspan's recommendations. The Soviets were allowed to buy 7 million tons of grain in addition to the 10.3 million tons they'd already contracted for. They also agreed to buy at least 6 million tons from the United States in each of the next five years and to give advance notice if they might need more.

It was only after the deal was sealed that the Kremlin admitted the true extent of the nation's troubles. The worst-case estimate for the 1975 harvest had been a shortfall of roughly 30 million tons, but they had actually missed their target by 78 million. This was even after the Soviets had managed to scrounge up millions of tons from foreign markets. Lack of feed grain forced Soviet farmers to slaughter one-fifth of the nation's hogs and poultry. The poorest citizens were pushed to the brink of starvation. All told, the poor harvest of 1975 was one of the harshest events the Soviet Union had faced since the German invasion in 1941.

Looking back, the grain sales to the Soviets was an issue of immense complexity, throwing various government departments together, sometimes in conflict, sometimes in improvised alliance. Besides involving the Departments of Agriculture and Labor, the CEA, the CIA, and the president, the 1975 crisis also occupied Greenspan's old schoolmate, Secretary of State Henry Kissinger.

It was remarkable that both Greenspan and Kissinger found themselves holding high posts in the administration of a U.S. president. For anyone growing up in Washington Heights during the 1930s, the horizon had looked pretty limited. Kissinger's government post was higher, of course. And he was not above pulling rank.

The imperious Kissinger made it clear that he had little interest in economics. He was an international diplomat. Relying on a deep knowledge of such nineteenth-century statesmen as Metternich and Bismarck, the onetime Harvard professor and 1973 Nobel Peace Prize recipient trotted the globe brokering agreements with hostile governments.

During the Nixon administration, Kissinger had even become something of a celebrity. It was a most unlikely turn of events. Kissinger was given to brash pronouncements delivered in a thick German accent, a vestige of having spent the first years of his life in Bavaria before fleeing the Nazis. He was also not exactly a candidate for *People*'s "50 Most Beautiful" list. Nevertheless, Kissinger became that rarest of breeds, international-relations wonk man-about-town. He was often spotted in the company of actresses, among them Marlo Thomas, Liv Ullmann, Candice Bergen, and Jill St. John. "Power is the ultimate aphrodisiac," was his famed explanation.

Kissinger saw a diplomatic opportunity in the Great Grain Robbery. He tried to link the grain arrangement to a Soviet agreement of noninterference with the United Nations regarding the recent Sinai agreement drawn up between Israel and Egypt—as if matters weren't already complicated enough.

He also envisioned a grain-for-oil linkage. In the wake of the OPEC crisis, the United States was trying to lessen its dependence on the Middle East. Meanwhile, the Soviets had oil fields, and some measure of production. What if ships could arrive at U.S. ports filled with Soviet oil and return carrying American grain? But the details never coalesced.

One unintended consequence of the grain crisis was that Greenspan and Kissinger managed to form an acquaintance. "I had very high regard for Alan," recalls Kissinger. "His great strength was strict professionalism. He always stuck to his subject and never played politics."

Both men were valued advisers to Ford. Their paths would cross frequently in the future, and their relationship would grow closer over the years.

The economic crises just kept coming, fast and furious. First, the Great Grain Robbery, and then—in the fall of 1975—the Big Apple Blowup.

Thanks to astoundingly poor budgetary practices, New York City was on the brink of bankruptcy. If the city went down, it might set off a chain reaction, wreaking financial havoc in other municipalities, in New York state, on Wall Street, and ultimately within the nation's banking system.

Once again, the fledgling economic recovery was at risk. On this particular issue, Greenspan's loyalties were divided quite neatly. He'd grown up in Manhattan, maintained family and other ties there, and still kept his apartment there. At the same time, he was not partial to the idea of the federal government meddling in a local problem.

The origins of the city's current distress stretched back many years. In simplest terms, it grew out of boundless and unrealistic largesse. By 1975, New York City had a giant army of civil servants on its payroll—338,000, or nearly one in twenty-three city residents. One out of eight residents was on welfare, which carried an annual tab of more than $2 billion. The city's costs were enormous.

Meanwhile, the tax base was fast eroding, as many of the more affluent residents were fleeing to the suburbs. Businesses were moving out as well. Throughout the 1960s, the number of *Fortune* 500 companies headquartered in New York City had hovered around 150. By 1974, the number had fallen to 98.

As a consequence, the city's balance sheet was way out of whack. Expenditures were growing at a rate of 15 percent a year, while tax revenues were increasing just 8 percent.

To stay afloat, New York City resorted to accounting gimmicks—similar to the little tricks employed by anyone impatient to balance a checkbook, but on a grand municipal scale. It became common practice, for example, to shore up one year's budget with the next year's revenues. For fiscal 1974, the budget included eighteen months' worth of revenues from the public water works. The only problem was that fiscal year 1975 would be left with only six months to draw on.

Then there was the city's pension, underfunded by nearly $2 billion between 1967 and 1975. Why? Because funding was based on actuarial assumptions from the period 1908–1914, when people didn't live nearly as long. Municipal bean counters had conveniently never bothered to update the city's tables.

Given this penchant for creative bookkeeping, it's only natural that questions began to crop up about whether New York could make good on its bond obligations. That put a vital source of funds in jeopardy. The city had always been very savvy about selling bonds, even going into foreign markets. But in March 1975, Moody's and Standard and Poor's, two major bond-grading outfits, dropped New York City's rating to unsalable.

The roller-coaster ride began.

The city's next move was to create something called the Municipal Assistance Corporation. It was headed up by Felix Rohatyn, a dapper Vienna-born investment banker and member of the board of governors of the New York Stock Exchange. The idea was to restore investor confidence by introducing a new type of New York City bond. Instead of being issued by the city, these so-called MAC bonds were issued by investment houses such as Lazard Frères, Rohatyn's firm. The bonds were to be backed by monies that had been segregated from the city's general coffers. That way, no accounting tricks could threaten their solvency.

A giant sales drive was launched, with the goal of selling $3 billion worth of MAC bonds. But recession-racked 1975 was not the ideal time to introduce a new and untested financial instrument. What's more, in recent years a number of other cities such as Houston and Los Angeles had elbowed in on New York's leadership in the bond market. The competition was getting tighter.

Not surprisingly, it proved difficult to drum up enough customers to buy $3 billion worth of MAC bonds. Meanwhile, each and every week the city faced a desperate struggle just to pull together enough money for payroll. Matters were growing dire. If the city couldn't raise enough money, the only option left would be to start cutting costs.

As a first step, forty-three public schools were closed. Then came the announcement that 60,000 part-time and full-time city workers were to be laid off. Those lucky enough to keep their jobs faced the prospect of reduced benefits and pay cuts.

Angry sanitation workers went on strike, and from July 1–3, 20,000 tons of rubbish piled up under the hot summer sun. Laid-off policemen gathered in the city's various transportation terminuses—Penn Station, La Guardia airport, and Port Authority bus depot—and proceeded to hand out pamphlets entitled "Fear City." The conceit of "Fear City" was that visitors were about to enter a place so bereft of services such as policing and medical emergency help that they were taking their lives into their hands. Tourists were understandably unnerved.

New York City sank so low that summer that it was unable to even replace police horses as they died off. This sad fact came to the attention of an eccentric, but still relatively unknown multimillionaire named Ross Perot, who donated twenty Tennessee Walkers to the NYPD.

Summer turned to autumn, and New York kept lurching along. With each passing day, the prospect of bankruptcy grew more terrifying and more real. Assorted delegations began to descend on Washington, hats in hand, begging the federal government to ante up money for a bailout. On October 9, Greenspan met with New York's deputy mayor James Cavanaugh and Paul O'Dwyer, the City Council president. The meeting was arranged by Ed Koch, the future mayor, who at the time was a state congressman representing the Greenwich Village section of Manhattan. Coming out of the meeting, Greenspan summed up the proceedings in a single word: "Despairing."

A terrible dilemma was shaping up. Standing by and watching New York City go bust was a pretty sorry option. But bailing out New York City carried what economists term a "moral hazard." It might set a dangerous precedent. If you help New York you have to help Cleveland, Newark, Detroit—and where does it ever end?

Best to give New York some tough love was the prevailing view in the administration. Ford and Greenspan both felt that handing the city money would simply turn it into a giant welfare recipient. But refusing to give in to New York's demands might actually force the city to get its act together. Ron Nessen, Ford's press secretary, drew the analogy between New York City and a wayward daughter addicted to heroine. "You don't give her $100 a day to support her habit," he said. "You make her go cold turkey."

Toughest among the tough-love set was Bill Simon. By nature, secretaries of the Treasury have to be zealots on the issue of fiscal responsibility; it's requisite to holding the job. But Simon had an additional qualification. Before joining the government, he had been an investment banker for Salomon Brothers in New York in the municipal and government bond department. He knew the business, and he had no patience for the city's irresponsibility.

"I would say Greenspan tended to be less of a hard-liner," recalls L. William Seidman, who served as an economic adviser to Ford. "He was a little more sympathetic to New York than some others. But we all said, 'Clean up your act before you get any help.' The basic attitude was that no one can help you until you help yourself."

Desperate, New York governor Hugh Carey and Mayor Abraham Beame continued to plead for aid. The administration continued to rebuff them. In late October 1975, Ford delivered a speech at the National Press Club. He promised that he would veto any legislation designed to bail out New York. "Ford to City: Drop Dead," screamed a famous *Daily News* front-page headline.

It was getting ugly. Frightening studies began to circulate, attempting to estimate the size and scope of economic disaster should New York City go bankrupt. The CEA did its own analysis and found fault with the doomsayers' projections. In a memo, Greenspan wrote: "Despite a number of scare stories, largely out of New York, a default of the City can be contained without serious economic consequences for the rest of the country."

The CEA also began to field anxious phone calls from comparable government economic agencies in other countries such as France, Great Britain, and Japan. What would happen if New York City went bankrupt? That was the question on the minds of foreign economists. CEA staffers did their best to point up the separations inherent in a federal system, the standard line being that local and state governments keep their own books. A meltdown in a single city—even one as big and important as New York—did not have to spill over to the rest of the nation.

David Munro, then a senior economist in the CEA, remembers talking with a French economic official who called up to express alarm.

"If Paris is broke, it's obvious the French government is broke," said the official.

"Such is not the case here, thank you very much," responded Munro, who then launched into his stock lecture on federalism.

In November, Governor Carey and Felix Rohatyn drew up a list of vital expenditures. The exercise was akin to that old grade-school exercise in which kids are asked to choose the five items they'd like to have with them if stranded on a desert island. Topping Carey and Rohatyn's list was food and medication for prisoners. Without that, they reasoned, all hell might break loose and the most dire predictions of the "Fear City" pamphlets would be realized. Also high on the list were police salaries and welfare checks for women with children.

It was hard to believe. New York City was about to go belly up.

At the eleventh hour, with seconds to spare, a compromise was reached. No, the federal government would not simply hand the mayor of New York a chunk of change. But it would provide a loan, to be paid back with interest. The city would receive installments of $2.3 billion annually until 1978. The loan would need to be paid back at an interest rate of roughly 8 percent, 1 percent higher than the U.S. Treasury borrowing rate at the time.

"Alan Greenspan to a significant degree was the architect of that plan," recalled Ford during a 1999 telephone interview from his home in Rancho Mirage, California. "What the mayor wanted was just a bailout of cash money, without taking any corrective action to straighten out New York City's pension program or its wage program. Alan was helpful in developing an overall program to solve the problem without a bailout."

New York did manage to pay back its loan in full. But the lingering effects of the 1975 crisis were to be felt for decades to come. Even at the turn of the twentieth century, New York was still fixing up roads and bridges that had been left in a state of disrepair since the 1970s. But perhaps most of all, the effect of the 1975 crisis can be seen in the city's pathological fear of abandonment when it comes to businesses. New York has witnessed firsthand the effect of a diminished tax base. Out of that has grown a sense that the city can't afford to lose even one more business. Throughout the 1990s, Mayor Rudolph Giuliani was willing to give generous tax abatements to businesses that agreed not to vacate New York.

With crisis following hot upon crisis, Greenspan's first months as CEA chairman were fraught with difficulty. But the period also proved significant from a career standpoint. In the course of handling grain robberies and municipal emergencies, Greenspan demonstrated an unexpected flair for the political arena. It wasn't long before others in Washington began to take notice.

9

THE INSIDER

Greenspan's clout was growing. Members of Congress as diverse in their political leanings as George Bush and Hubert Humphrey solicited his views on the economy. Vernon Jordan—destined to play a future role as President Clinton's man-behind-the-scenes—called on him to discuss an upcoming black economic summit. Greenspan grew so close to Frank Zarb, the federal energy administrator, that the two did their Christmas shopping together. Mr. Disturbed-by-the-Ways-of-Washington was turning into a real power broker.

It was a surprising development. Given his personality, old friends never expected he'd show such an aptitude in the political realm. Then again, Greenspan's mentor, Arthur Burns, was one of the masters. Burns was an economist, with an economist's personality, but he managed a brilliant Washington career.

Burns and Greenspan remained good friends during the Ford administration. Lenny Garment has one especially vivid recollection of the two together.

"Arthur was a lovely man, a dear man and very, very wise," says Garment. "He and Greenspan were very close, teacher and student, professional colleagues. They shared rather basic similar views on government, how to keep it fiscally sound.

"I have one memory of them that stands out . . . Arthur was puffing smoke rings through his pipe, very quiet, very wise—owl-like. He looked like a wonderful gray-haired owl with glasses. He was sitting with Alan Greenspan, looking owlish also. The two owls!"

Many who served in the Ford administration saw marked similarities between Fed chairman Burns and CEA chairman Greenspan—not only in a shared and uncanny resemblance to Woodsy but also in their political styles. "There was a great deal of respect for Burns up on Capitol Hill. He knew how to really move around D.C.," says Donald Rumsfeld. "Greenspan developed that ability as well. He's confidential, he's measured, and he learned how to manage a relatively low-profile external persona."

That last part—maintaining a relatively low-profile external persona—is key. If there's one mistake the council chairman can make, it's politicizing the CEA. To avoid this requires a delicate balancing act. The line is drawn between advising the president and actively advocating the president's policies. As to which side of the line a given CEA chairman occupies, it's a matter of perception on the part of the press and other members of the government. The penalty bell is sounded when the CEA is viewed as acting as a cheerleader for an administration's economic programs.

There's no doubt that Greenspan was partisan. There's no doubt he had a special relationship with Ford. But he was perceived as a behind-the-scenes adviser as distinct from a get-the-message-to-the-masses advocate. Greenspan cut back the number of press briefings. He restored a measure of professionalism to the CEA, which had seen its image tarnished along with so many other institutions during the Nixon administration.

CEA chiefs hold sway over presidents to varying degrees, of course. As chairman of the CEA under John F. Kennedy, Walter Heller was intimately involved with policy decisions. By contrast, Arthur Okun had very little influence over Lyndon Johnson, who expected to wage war in Vietnam, fight poverty at home, and launch numerous social programs, all without raising taxes.

A major determinant on any given CEA chief's influence is whether the president he advises is even interested in economic issues. Many have not been. Presidents tend to be drawn to broader areas of expertise such as leadership and diplomacy. A foreign policy triumph is likely to pack a lot more wallop with voters than enacting a tariff, after all. Faced with an economic crisis, Warren Harding apparently said, "There must be someone in this administration who could explain it to me, but I probably wouldn't understand it. There must be a book I could read, but I probably couldn't understand that either."

Nixon was notoriously unreceptive to economic issues. "I don't give a shit about the lira," he uttered when informed that speculators were beating down the Italian currency. The comment was captured on the infamous June 23, 1972, "smoking gun" tape and for many seemed to sum up his attitude toward economic policy. On another occasion, Nixon was called upon to discuss the state of the U.S. economy with a group of businesspeople who were visiting the White House. "He had all the enthusiasm of a third-grade boy having to speak a piece," says his onetime CEA chief Paul McCracken. "On foreign policy, he'd get all wound up. Ford, by contrast, seemed to find economic policy intellectually interesting."

Ford had become a master at understanding budgets during his time in Congress. "Politics is the art of the possible," goes the old saw. He understood that what was possible was dictated by the government's revenues. He firmly aligned himself with what might be called the Eisenhower internationalist wing of the Republican Party, which advocated large-scale defense spending to contain communism. At the same time, Ford took a very hard line on domestic spending. He voted against almost every single piece of social legislation offered up by Kennedy and Johnson, including model cities and the War on Poverty. Of course, during his presidency, Ford concentrated on the economy out of sheer necessity. The economy is something presidents hope will just hum along. That makes it possible to attend to more glamorous issues. But if the economy is ailing, it cannot be ignored.

Things were truly a mess in 1974–1975. In fact, Ford convened an Economic Policy Board (EPB) to coordinate the far-flung corners of the administration—the Agriculture Department, Transportation, and the Budget Office—in the battle against stagflation. The EPB was a formidable collection of individuals including Greenspan, Treasury Secretary William Simon, Labor Secretary Jim Lynn, and Bill Seidman. They met in the Roosevelt Room of the White House almost every day and briefed Ford once a week.

Others such as Burns and Chief of Staff Dick Cheney sat in on meetings when appropriate. As Fed chairman, however, Burns had to maintain a degree of independence from the president and often wasn't in attendance. That left Greenspan as the only economist present at most meetings of the EPB. Thus, he was able to weigh in with a special authority.

Along with his economics training, several other attributes gave Greenspan an edge with Ford. One was his very dry and serious demeanor. Herb Stein, Greenspan's predecessor at the CEA, had been accused of wringing cheer out of gloomy statistics. Ford didn't have to worry about any such charges being leveled against Greenspan, champion of logic and empiricism. The economic news was grim, and Greenspan didn't attempt to put a happy face on it. When he went before Congress or faced the press, he was suitably dour—he was the perfect messenger for hard times.

While Greenspan struck the correctly somber public pose, privately he had a superb rapport with Ford. Therein lies one of the secrets of Greenspan's success in the political realm. In Washington, you have to always be aware of your ultimate constituent. It was Ford who upheld Greenspan's nomination, and it was to Ford that he reported. Here, Greenspan's consulting experience placed him in good stead.

As a private economic consultant, Greenspan had learned to walk a fine line. On the one hand, he was called upon to render painful verdicts to CEOs of client companies. He couldn't simply tell them what they wanted to hear or he'd cease to be useful as a consultant. By necessity, he developed an aptitude for delivering bad news, while at the same time being properly attentive and deferential to the client.

Many who rubbed shoulders with Greenspan during the Ford administration saw remarkable similarities between Greenspan the consultant and Greenspan the CEA chairman. "Greenspan treated the president like his best client," recalls Paul MacAvoy, his colleague on the CEA.

In the final analysis, however, Ford and Greenspan were simply philosophically and temperamentally well disposed toward one another. They felt mutual admiration.

"He is unquestionably a secure man, with fewer psychological hangups than almost everybody I've ever met," Greenspan would later recall of Ford. "As a consequence, you never got negative emotional vibrations from the man, except when he was mad for reasons that

(Courtesy of Brooks/Glogau Studio.)

Alan Greenspan as a baby, circa 1926, and as a teenager (age 14) with his mother, Rose Goldsmith.

Nathan and Anna Goldsmith, the grandparents with whom Greenspan lived while growing up in Washington Heights.

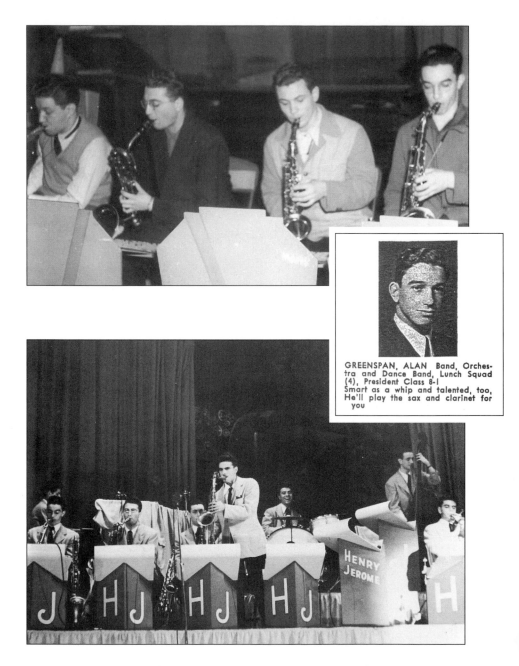

GREENSPAN, ALAN Band, Orchestra and Dance Band, Lunch Squad
(4), President Class 8-1
Smart as a whip and talented, too,
He'll play the sax and clarinet for
you

Greenspan's yearbook photo (inset)—George Washington High School class of '43. At Nola's rehearsal studios (top), Greenspan is on one end of the sax section, Leonard Garment on the other. During a live performance with Henry Jerome and His Orchestra (bottom), Greenspan is pictured at the left-edge of the photo. (Courtesy of Henry Jerome.)

*Greenspan in 1953, the year he married
Joan Mitchell, inset. (Courtesy of Joan
Mitchell Blumenthal.)*

A gathering of Rand's Collective in 1955. Left to right: Joan Mitchell, Alan Greenspan, Nathaniel and Barbara Branden, Leonard Peikoff, Elayne and Harry Kalberman (bride and groom), Ayn Rand, Frank O'Connor, and Allan Blumenthal. (Courtesy of Joan Mitchell Blumenthal.)

Central Park, 1964: The Objectivists fielded a pair of softball teams. The Witch Doctors (top) included Greenspan (third from left standing). Beside him to the right are Nathaniel Branden and Robert Hessen. Eugene Schwartz is on the far right. The Huns (bottom) featured erstwhile Greenspan paramours, Kathy Eickhoff and Marjorie Scheffler (front row left to right). The woman wearing sunglasses is Barbara Branden. (Courtesy of Eugene Schwartz.)

Alan Greenspan solo on clarinet and in a trio—circa 1965—featuring fellow Objectivists Allan Blumenthal on piano and Eugene Schwartz on violin. (Courtesy of Eugene Schwartz.)

Nixon with Greenspan. Nixon held Greenspan in high regard, but Greenspan had his doubts about the president. (Copyright © Bettmann/Corbis.)

With Ford, at his swearing-in ceremony as chairman of the Council of Economic Advisers on September 4, 1974. His mother, Rose, looks on. (Courtesy of Gerald R. Ford Library.)

Greenspan's guests at his swearing-in ceremony as CEA chairman included Rose, Ayn Rand, and Rand's husband, Frank O'Connor. (Courtesy of Gerald R. Ford Library.)

(Top) Aboard Air Force One with Henry Kissinger and President Ford's dog, Liberty. (Bottom) Talking with his mentor, Arthur Burns, chairman of the Fed at the time. The man with his back turned is economic adviser, L. William Seidman. (Courtesy of Gerald R. Ford Library.)

Greenspan shakes hands with Reagan—standing beside him is outgoing Fed chairman Paul Volcker. (Below) Greenspan and Bush in happier times—they had a notoriously poor rapport. (Top courtesy of Ronald Reagan Library, bottom courtesy of George Bush Presidential Library.)

Greenspan in the Oval Office, on April 24, 1990. Treasury Secretary Nicholas Brady sits on the right, on the left is John Sununu, Bush's chief of staff. (Courtesy of George Bush Presidential Library.)

With Clinton as Gore looks on. And, below, in the hot seat: Greenspan was dismayed when he was seated between Hillary Clinton and Tipper Gore for a State of the Union address on February 17, 1993. (Top: Courtesy of the White House. Bottom: AP/Wide World Photos.)

Greenspan and Andrea Mitchell at their wedding, held in Washington, Virginia, on April 6, 1997.

(top, *OLIPHANT* © *Universal Press Syndicate. Reprinted with permission. All rights reserved;* middle left, *reprinted with special permission of King Features Syndication;* middle right, *Sandy Campbell,* The Tennessean; bottom, *The New Yorker Collection 2000 Lee Lorenz from cartoonbank.com.)*

were absolutely objective; there weren't any subtle or subterranean motives."

Greenspan added: "Since my view was in most respects fairly consonant with his, it became rather easy for me to function."

Ford, in turn, recalls, "I was lucky to have someone as capable, who I had as much faith in, as Alan Greenspan, to give me advice and counsel. I endorsed his view and apparently he had confidence in my decisionmaking. We had a superb working relationship."

Thus, the one-time Eagle Scout and the cofounder of the Detective Scouts of Washington Heights got along famously. As CEA chairman, he had a voice in a large range of policy issues, in everything from beer excise taxes to the inefficiency of the U.S. postal system. He regularly shot off memos to Ford, commenting on the relevance and accuracy of various statistics such as housing starts or wholesale prices.

In much of his correspondence, Greenspan adopted a kind of plain-folk tutorial style. "Observe that the British economy appears to be at the point where they must accelerate the amount of governmental fiscal stimulus just to stand still," reads one memo. Obviously, one has to have a comfortable relationship to urge the president of the United States to "observe" anything.

Indeed, the consensus is that Ford and Greenspan had the best president–CEA chair relationship ever, with Kennedy and Heller running a distant second.

The pair even socialized together, watching sporting events in the White House on Sunday afternoons and playing golf in Vail, Colorado, during some of Ford's working vacations. The two attended an Army-Navy football game at one point, and Greenspan was pleased and flattered whenever the president asked after his mother.

Greenspan also showed a rare aptitude for handling Congress. This was a stellar accomplishment for an avowed conservative during the mid-1970s, when Democrats held the majority in Congress. In the wake of Watergate, voters had sent to Washington seventy-five freshman Democrats, a liberal and reform-minded group. They were itching to intervene in the economy in an effort to reduce unemployment and would come to blows with President Ford over the speed of the recovery.

In dealing with Congress, Greenspan's fundamental politeness and humility proved to be an asset. He had always been a person of strongly held convictions. At the same time, he was comfortable with people rather different from himself—Kavesh, a self-described "Franklin Roosevelt liberal," among them. While Greenspan's notorious stockbroker "percentage-wise" comment is the dark side of his mega-rational personality, this would seem to be the bright side. Empiricism dictated that he consider other points of view.

Certainly he never allowed himself to get emotional during a public discussion, which is a prerequisite in dealing with Congress. After all, the convention on members of Congress is that they engage in finger-pointing and name sullying for the benefit of constituents, then retire to a local watering hole and laugh it up together. The attacks are all in a day's work, never to be taken personally.

Joan Mitchell Blumenthal has vivid and telling recollections from the Ford years. Even after Greenspan went to Washington, the pair remained close. Often they'd talk by telephone, and the topic would frequently turn to politics. Blumenthal says:

> He knew I had a particular dislike for Ted Kennedy. Yet he had a cordial relationship with Kennedy . . . . He also knew that I had qualms about Hubert Humphrey. He got along very well with Hubert Humphrey. He got along well on a one-to-one level with a lot of these people. . . . I think he wants to do his job as best as he can and he sees all that as a part of it. He's quite conciliatory. It's not that he gives ground on the issues that matter to him. But he believes in discussion, without bringing anger into things.

"I've never seen him angry," she adds. "That's an interesting kind of person."

It was during these years, too, that Greenspan first learned to equivocate before Congress, a skill he has since mastered. Various individuals in government are summoned before Congress periodically to account for themselves. Most would agree, getting that call can be aggravating. Congress, after all, is a public forum where a senator might decide to toss out a zinger of a question, hoping to look good for the voters at home. Or members of Congress might start delving into the business of agencies they scarcely understand.

One solution, some would say, is forthright honesty; but that can backfire on the Hill.

Another solution is to equivocate, to say something without saying anything—to deftly dodge, evade, or sidestep the query. Greenspan, in fact, would practice in front of the CEA staff before appearing before Congress. "To prepare for public appearances, he used to try and say something and make it take the longest possible way to parse it out," says MacAvoy, adding, "He was about half as good [then] as he is now."

As Schuh recalls: "The staff would love to go up and hear him talk on the Hill. He's great at obfuscating. He'd do it in such a way that he'd say his piece and they wouldn't ask any questions. You don't want Congress mucking around in your business. There are days you need them and days you'd just as soon they'd go away."

In his early years of public office, Greenspan was well ahead of the curve. By handling a delicate job in a difficult time, Greenspan actually became something of a celebrity. He was even featured on the cover of *Newsweek*—unprecedented for an economist. Fellow 1975 cover subjects included Bruce Springsteen, Nolan Ryan, Patty Hearst, Mel Brooks, Christina Onassis, and Jimmy Hoffa. The economy was a big story that year, though, and Greenspan was right out of central casting—thick glasses, rumpled clothes, introspective, a bit professorial. He was Woody Allen with math skills, and the public was starting to take notice.

In the wake of his *Newsweek* cover, Greenspan was besieged with various and sundry requests. Numerous autograph seekers sent in copies of the magazine for him to sign. *Penthouse* asked if he'd submit to an interview. Greenspan declined.

Then there was the request from a psychology professor at Stanford, asking him to take part in a study on shyness. "I appreciate your interest," Greenspan wrote back. "I do not believe, however, that by any objective set of criteria I would be described as shy."

Dozens of letters also poured in from Ayn Rand acolytes from all over the country. Some simply wanted to claim Greenspan as one of their own and bask vicariously in the glory of a Randian who had risen so high. Others were concerned. Was Greenspan still an Objectivist? Considering that one of the philosophy's most enduring symbols is a fictional architect who blows up a building because it deviates from his original design, this was not a surprising question.

If Greenspan was anything like *The Fountainhead*'s rugged Howard Roark, how could he tolerate the grotesque compromises of politics? If he was a true Objectivist, when would he reveal himself? Would he perhaps do so with a spectacular immolation of America's mixed economic system?

"What has happened to you?" implored one 1975 letter. "Why are you not speaking out? . . . Have you changed your position? If not, what is your strategy?"

"Dear Mr. Greenspan," read another. "I have read your articles in Ayn Rand's *Capitalism: The Unknown Ideal* and, from them, gathered that you are an advocate of laissez-faire capitalism—as am I. Have you modified your views? Or, is it a matter of realities which prevent your convictions from becoming administration policy?"

Greenspan's response: "I tend to change my views when credible evidence forces a change. I can't say I have seen any lately."

Somewhere, in the midst of all the various crises and congressional testimony, Greenspan managed to find time to break into the rarefied Washington party circuit. This was truly unexpected. If people from his past were surprised by his political acumen, then this was a development that bordered on the absurd. Greenspan was turning into something even more unusual than Kissinger's international-relations wonk man-about-town. He was becoming an economist man-about-town.

Former Nixon counselor Bryce Harlow and his wife Betty threw a party in 1975 with a guest list composed of Washington's A-list. Greenspan was there. Tom Brokaw attended a formal dinner for radio and television correspondents. He took Greenspan as his personal guest. Many a night, Greenspan would leave the CEA at around 7 P.M., attend a glamorous reception or black-tie affair, then return to the office around 10 P.M., prepared to work well into the night.

Of course, the press had fun with the idea of Greenspan hitting the party circuit. Henry Mitchell of the *Washington Post* dubbed him a "social creeper." Mitchell painted a compelling portrait—Greenspan wending his way through crowded parties, making stilted attempts to crack the various conversational islands. But it wasn't really accurate. Anyone who actually knows the man will tell a different story. His onetime CEA deputy David Munro describes him as follows: "Here's a guy, very bright, listens intently, looks at you with owlish spectacles, often not saying a word. That can be spooky to people. He can seem to be a coldish person. But he's a guy who likes social evenings. He's a very knowledgeable discussant about things other than economics."

In another sense, however, Greenspan did find his whirlwind social life painful. Suspect health had landed him a 4-F, allowing him to avoid military duty, and he'd forever been plagued with other physical problems, particularly a bad back. During late-night meetings in the White House, Rumsfeld remembers Greenspan lying on the floor, the better to ease his lumbar pain. By contrast, Burns—another rare economist man-about-town—was known for phenomenal physical stamina. He could work a long day, hit a gala event or two, work some more, and seemingly be none the worse for it healthwise.

It was during the 1970s that Greenspan began the practice of taking a hot bath first thing in the morning to ease his aching back. Often, he would read or do work in the bathtub. He became fond of telling friends that his IQ was twenty points higher at 6 A.M. than at 6 P.M.

It was also during the Ford administration that Greenspan managed his first significant social coup. He began dating television personality Barbara Walters. The pair met at a party thrown by vice president Nelson Rockefeller.

Observers of the relationship between Greenspan and Walters did not exactly see the romantic sparks flying. There was a sense that the pair were social escorts and not passionate lovers.

"It was apparently an arrangement or a convenience," says Bill Seidman. "Both were single and needed company to go to the parties."

Seidman recalls that Greenspan didn't always have the stamina to keep up with Walters on the dance floor. As a consequence, Seidman often danced with Walters in his colleague's place.

But Greenspan and Walters certainly created a buzz. The pair were photographed at a Palm Springs party and the *New York Times* called Greenspan to confirm that they were dating. A story about Greenspan and Ford that ran in the *Pittsburgh Post Gazette* carried the headline: "Barbara's Friend, Betty's Husband."

This was an interesting turn of events, given that Greenspan had made an effort to restore credibility to the CEA by keeping his distance from the media. By dating Barbara Walters, he was courting the press—literally.

That relationship marked the beginning of a pattern in which Greenspan would pursue women involved in broadcast journalism. During the 1980s, Greenspan went out with Susan Mills, a producer for the *MacNeil-Lehrer Newshour*. When he remarried in 1997, it was to Andrea Mitchell, a political correspondent for NBC.

Theories on Greenspan's female-journalist fetish abound. Some take a distinctly Freudian tack, looking to Greenspan's relationship with his mother as the source of his curious level of comfort with strong and unconventional women. This seems apt enough, especially in light of his associations with Ayn Rand as well as the four female economists he left in charge of his consulting practice when he went off to Washington.

There are those, too, who say Greenspan's predilections grow out of the lure of the exotic other. The CEA chairmanship and more particularly the Fed chairmanship are jobs that require extreme, total, unfailing circumspection. Drop an offhand comment and the market goes haywire. Meanwhile, there's a cadre of people gunning for just such an occasion. The Washington media corps makes its living coaxing juicy comments out of the unwary. The result is a real tension. Being right in the thick of it, perhaps, left Greenspan with a highly developed sense of the power of the press, and a strong attraction to women who can have such impact on political fortunes.

There are other mundane but no less plausible notions, such as the dating-pool theory. Obviously, Washington power players are rather isolated. Members of the media are part of the limited circle of people they meet, thereby providing a ready pool of dating candidates.

Greenspan and Walters were to remain friends long after the Ford administration. In fact—as with Joan Mitchell Blumenthal—they remained close after she married entertainment mogul Merv Adelson in 1986.

"He's a lovely, soft-spoken, quiet man," Walters would later say of Greenspan. "He laughs at himself. I've never heard him sharply cut anyone off. I don't think he has such a thing as a personal enemy."

Walters gave Greenspan special credit for helping her through a difficult transition in 1976, when she moved from NBC to ABC. It was "almost like having an analyst," she told the *New York Times Magazine*.

Despite making a social splash by night, Greenspan was kept plenty busy by the daily demands of his post as CEA chairman. The economic recovery continued into 1976, albeit with great fragility. The Dow began to climb again, at least, and by early in the year was on the verge of 1,000. Meanwhile, corporate profits rebounded from a disastrous 1975. They were up nearly 45 percent year-over-year in the first quarter of 1976.

To Greenspan, such developments counted as evidence—evidence of the fundamental soundness of the economy and of the folly of government intervention. It so happened that 1976 was also the year of America's Bicentennial. Here, Greenspan perceived a real opportunity. The administration had been regularly accused of do-nothingism and lack of imagination. Its economic policies had never been an easy sell with the public or the Democratic Congress. Perhaps the Bicentennial was the proper time, it occurred to Greenspan, to draw an intellectual link between present-day policy and cherished values that had existed throughout America's history.

Greenspan sat in on a series of meetings devoted to developing themes for Ford's State of the Union address. Caught up in the spirit of '76, the ordinarily sedate Greenspan actually grew animated and excited. Greenspan suggested that the writings of the founding fathers were eerily applicable to present-day policy debates.

"Freeing individuals is a fairly profound concept," he suggested at one point. "It involves reducing the size of government, reducing regulations, and enhancing the status of individuals. A bicentennial theme for the State of the Union could be the third century—the century of the individual."

The evening before the State of the Union was to be delivered, Greenspan stayed up well into the night, working with the speechwriters and making last-minute revisions. It went through nine drafts. When Ford delivered the State of the Union address on January 19, 1976, Greenspan's fingerprints were clearly visible. Ford referred to "common sense" repeatedly, an echo of the classic work by founding father Thomas Paine. At one point, the president stated that "the truly revolutionary concept of 1776 . . . holds that in a free society the making of public policy and successful problem solving involves much more than government."

The fledgling economic recovery gained momentum through the spring, and Greenspan continued to sound his small-government, non-interventionist theme. During an appearance on the TV show *Issues and Answers,* he said, "It is often presumed that to do something, to take action, to be activist is good, whereas to simmer things down, to pull away and let the private economy, let private institutions, let private individuals do something, is somehow bad."

But no matter how often Ford and Greenspan flogged their pet theme, it remained terribly subtle and difficult to articulate. It didn't speak to a substantial percentage of the population. From a strictly technical standpoint, the economy was in recovery, that is, it was growing again. But stagflation was far from conquered. Unemployment stood at roughly 7.5 percent during the spring of 1976, and inflation was still growing at an annual rate of nearly 4 percent.

People were growing impatient. Merely waiting for an unfettered economy to work out its imbalances didn't seem sufficient to many. In certain pockets of the nation, serious problems remained. Unemployment among blacks was near 14 percent. "We are now eight feet under water instead of sixteen feet under water, but we're still underwater" was the way Arthur Okun, a onetime CEA chief in the Johnson administration, described it to the *New York Times Magazine.*

It was a Bicentennial year, a frustrating year—and an election year. Georgia governor Jimmy Carter seized on the issue of the slow recovery. With the August convention a few months away, Carter was fast emerging as the Democratic front-runner. If elected president, he promised to focus his energy on reducing unemployment and take his chances with inflation. He suggested that his "key tools" for restoring the economy would include public-works projects, expanded job counseling, and formation of an organization similar to the depression-era Civilian Conservation Corps.

On economic issues, Carter managed to quickly position himself as an alternative to Ford. He advocated a munificent government that would seek imaginative solutions to the ills that gripped the nation. By contrast, Ford stood for "spend less, do less, think small," as one Carter campaign aide sniped.

Carter's advisers included Larry Klein, the Nobel Prize–winning economist from the University of Pennsylvania and pioneer in computer-based econometric modeling; Lester Thurow, a liberal economist from MIT who had counseled George McGovern during his 1972 presidential run; and Al Sommers, Greenspan's old friend from the Conference Board.

The Democratic Congress also weighed in on the economy. A relief bill was introduced, sponsored by Hubert Humphrey and Augustus Hawkins, a congressman from Southern California. Serving as Hawkins's adviser was Leon Keyserling, Truman's onetime CEA chairman, now a private consultant.

The so-called Humphrey-Hawkins Bill was intended as an extension of the Employment Act of 1946, which, among other things, created the CEA. But where the original legislation broadly called upon the government to "provide maximum employment, production and purchasing power," the new bill spelled out the wheres and wherefores. Humphrey-Hawkins offered up a menu of old-style government stimulus and jobs programs, with the stated goal of dropping unemployment to 3 percent within three years.

The legislation would end up passing, despite Greenspan and Ford's strong objections. The programs would prove difficult to enact and would be abandoned over time. But one element remains to this day. Humphrey and Hawkins demanded greater accountability from the government bodies that make economic policy, particularly the Fed. As a result, all Fed chairmen are required to appear before Congress twice a year to offer Humphrey-Hawkins testimony.

As the election drew nearer, the Ford administration received disconcerting news. The unemployment rate was inching back up. It had been 7.3 percent in May. By August, it was up to 7.9 percent. The administration was forced to admit that it was unlikely that unemployment would fall below 7 percent during 1976.

Greenspan pointed out that this was part of the normal pattern of recoveries. Rather than moving up out of recession in a smooth, straight line, the economy tends to dip, then shoot upward, then dip again.

Greenspan described the current phase of the recovery as a "pause." The term was picked up by the press, which proceeded to run with it for all it was worth. It's just another example of Greenspan's preternatural knack for uttering phrases that capture the popular imagination—a

gift that's doubly unusual for a soft-spoken man given to circumlocu-
tion. Two words uttered as Fed chairman—"irrational exuberance"—
are a likely candidate for his epitaph. But a single word, "pause," set off
a frenzy of head scratching, finger wagging, and rampant speculation
by the media in 1976.

It was on everyone's lips. To Greenspan fell the task of delivering a
troubling prediction to President Ford. By the CEA's calculations, the
much-ballyhooed pause would last through the fall and end around
December. This was most unsettling, given a November election date.

Kissinger was present when Greenspan delivered the news. For years
afterward, he would do an impression of the event. First, he would im-
personate Greenspan, standing before Ford, mumbling into his shoes
about "spurts" and "pauses" and other economic esoterica. Then he
would revert to being Kissinger. He'd turn to an imaginary Ford,
throw up his hands, and say, "What's he doing to us?"

It was looking bleak. Despite being the incumbent, Ford barely won
his own party's nomination at the national convention, held in Kansas
City in August. By a razor-thin vote of 1,187 to 1,070, he fended off
his main challenger—California's charismatic governor, Ronald Reagan. Ford selected Kansas senator Bob Dole as his running mate and
hobbled toward the general election.

More bad news came down the pike in October—the Commerce
Department's latest reading of the leading economic indicators showed
a 0.7 percent decline. This was the very last piece of economic news
that would be released before the election. The Carter camp jumped all
over it as fresh evidence that the economy was deep in the doldrums.

On October 31, Greenspan and Klein, chief economic advisers to the
respective candidates, squared off on *Face the Nation*.

"I think, first of all," said Klein, "it's quite important that the public
authorities recognize the full significance of the lull that's taking place.
It's much more serious, in my opinion, than is being admitted, certainly in the heat of the campaign." Klein went on to recommend a
program of stimulus to restore the economy.

Greenspan countered with: "I think that the best way to get unemployment down as quickly as possible is to remove inflationary imbalances, and uncertainties in our system, and allow the private sector to
rapidly create jobs."

There it was, the difference between the two candidates spelled out in giant letters across the sky. *Leave the economy alone* versus *intervene*. Now it was left to the voters to make their choice.

On November 2, 1976, Carter won, tallying up 297 Electoral College ballots to Ford's 240, capturing an edge of roughly 2 million in the popular vote.

Ford's chances had been damaged irreparably by the depth of the 1974–1975 recession and the sluggishness of the subsequent recovery. Throughout his term, he'd also been dogged by a controversial decision made just one month into his tenure as president—to pardon Nixon of all federal crimes he may have committed while in office. Ford could never quite shake Nixon's legacy, politically or economically. Carter promised a fresh approach from government, and he carried the day.

Looking back, Greenspan deserves mixed reviews for his tenure as CEA chairman. By one measure, he was a rollicking success. Greenspan demonstrated himself to be a natural at navigating the fun-house maze that is Washington. He was an astonishingly quick study. One, two, three—he figured out how to balance the conflicting demands of various constituents and make himself indispensable to the president, and he proved himself to be an able operator in high-powered social settings. The connections Greenspan forged during the Ford administration were lasting and would significantly influence the future direction of his career.

More difficult to assess is his record as an economic policy adviser. CEA chairman is an unusual job, at once broader in scope and infinitely less powerful than Fed chairman. After all, the CEA chair is involved in every single corner of the economy, but in a strictly advisory role. The Fed chairman has just a handful of levers to push, but he makes all the difference as to whether the populace wears new shoes or eats old ones.

As CEA chairman, Greenspan weighed in on everything from New York City's near meltdown to a New Deal–style jobs bill. With the notable exception of a miniscule tax rebate in the spring of 1975, his counsel was almost numbing in its consistency—don't intervene, don't intervene, don't intervene. Granted, doing nothing was rooted in firmly held philosophical convictions that he shared with the president, but some would argue it was a fairly uninspired turn. As an adviser, why not throw out some fresh ideas, especially given the unique challenges posed by stagflation?

Then again, there are those who argue that Greenspan was merely ahead of his time. A generation later, in 1994, Republicans came sweeping into power during a mid-term congressional election. This time around, the idea of smaller, more restricted government had the force of revolution. It would become one of the guiding principles of the 1990s and would ultimately be co-opted by Clinton and other Democrats.

Laissez-faire was coronated as the new king in the 1990s. Greenspan, one of its leading subjects, was by this time installed as Fed chairman. In this new role, he had more latitude to put his principles into play. Certainly, he raised interest rates when events called for it. But he was also inclined to leave the economy on a looser leash than any of his predecessors. This leads to at least one conclusion: CEA chairman was an excellent stepping stone, but Federal Reserve chairman was the job for which Greenspan was ideally suited.

Near the end of Ford's term, Greenspan received a note from his mentor, Arthur Burns. It read in part: "I have enjoyed our association in this city and have benefited greatly from it. As I think you know, I regard you not only as a good friend but as a gifted economist whose judgment I value highly. In short, I will miss you."

Carter was sworn in on January 20, 1977. That very day, Greenspan was on the noon shuttle back to New York.

10

WILDERNESS YEARS

Upon returning to New York, Greenspan entered into what might be termed his "wilderness period." He didn't slip into the kind of lugubrious self-assessment that characterized Nixon's time in exile from public life. Rather, he simply had trouble figuring out what to do next.

He'd flown aboard Air Force One with the president, rubbed shoulders with Kissinger, been on the cover of *Newsweek*. Now what? Ford had promised that if he won the election, he would hand Greenspan a plum role in his administration, probably secretary of the Treasury. But there was certainly no place for Greenspan in the Carter White House.

"I think there was a little disappointment," says Judith Mackey, his old Columbia classmate and longtime Townsend-Greenspan employee. "But Alan is not one to say 'what if . . .' or 'I wish that . . .' He tackles what is."

Most ex-CEA chairs returned to comfortable tenured posts in academia. Arthur Burns had actually managed to parlay the position into a grand one—chairman of the Federal Reserve. Of course, he'd traveled down a few career eddies in the interim. But Burns had undoubtedly achieved the greatest prominence of any CEA chair before him.

Greenspan returned to the same consulting firm he'd run for the past twenty-three years. The offices were now firmly ensconced at One New York Plaza, the great fire a distant memory. He settled into a new workspace of his own idiosyncratic design. It was essentially an office within an office, like a Chinese box. This design provided him with a discrete work area in which he could indulge his penchant for clutter.

But when important clients visited, Greenspan would greet them in his "display" office—spacious, elegantly appointed, and most of all, neat.

Employees got a kick out of this arrangement. It was possible to glance through the front door of Greenspan's office and not know whether he was present. One had to also check the little cul-de-sac where he did his actual work. "You had to walk into his office and make a U-turn to see if he was in there," recalls David Rowe, a long-time employee.

Greenspan was a data junkie, as always. Once he found a number he liked, he never let it go. The firm even bought a Prime 300 minicomputer, a replacement for the old IBM 1130, and hooked it up to a series of dumb terminals that could be used by individual employees. While CEA chair, Greenspan had been exposed to some cutting-edge econometric modeling techniques. As a result, he was able to pump up Townsend-Greenspan's approach, enlarging the number of variables that were taken into consideration in modeling.

In 1977, Greenspan received his Ph.D. from NYU—at long last. But he never actually completed his dissertation. Instead, the degree was awarded on the basis of articles he had published in a variety of scholarly journals and popular magazines going back to 1959.

One, entitled "A Model of Capital Expenditures and Internal Rates of Return for the U.S. Economy," appeared in the May 1971 issue of *Business Economics.* Another, "The Quiet Revolution," was published in the May 1977 issue of *Across the Board,* the Conference Board's magazine. He even included a document he had prepared as CEA chairman, an *Economic Report of the U.S. President.*

The collection totaled 176 pages, and Greenspan gave it the prosaic title: "Papers on Economic Theory and Policy." Although the content was undoubtedly solid, this was not exactly groundbreaking academic-level material, nor did the collection match the size or scope of the usual dissertation.

For years after, Greenspan's Ph.D. would remain steeped in a mild controversy. Critics questioned whether his work was sufficiently meritorious. And Greenspan didn't help matters by requesting that NYU withhold from public view the collection of articles that comprised his Ph.D. work. A tradition of scholarly openness dictates that anyone can walk into a university and read the dissertation of any person who has been awarded a Ph.D.

At the same time, earning a Ph.D. on the basis of published papers is a common practice. Besides, between Columbia and NYU, Greenspan had completed more than his share of graduate-level courses.

Barbara Walters threw a small party for Greenspan at her apartment in Manhattan to toast his accomplishment. Arthur and Helen Burns were there, along with Robert and Ruth Kavesh. Also present were Greenspan's mother and Frank Zarb, a friend from the Ford administration. After the meal, Walters passed out Cuban cigars that she had received directly from the source—Fidel Castro—during an interview.

Greenspan was now Dr. Greenspan. Otherwise, it was pretty much business as usual at Townsend-Greenspan. Except now the clock was ticking; he knew he had to find a way to capitalize on the profile he'd achieved as CEA chairman, and in a hurry. In typical fashion, he even projected a time frame. The public would lose interest in a sub-cabinet-rank government figure, he calculated, within a year.

Greenspan managed to gain representation from the powerful Harry Walker Agency, which today represents speakers such as John Glenn, Mario Cuomo, and naturalist Jane Goodall. Reportedly, Greenspan commanded anywhere from $10,000 to $40,000 per speech at venues that included corporate luncheons, trade association shindigs, and meetings of organizations such as the Business Roundtable. This was great money at the time—and would still be, for that matter. But more than money, Greenspan craved influence. Immediately following his departure from the CEA, he made about a speech a week, hoping to stay in the public eye and elevate his profile.

Greenspan also began to court the press more assiduously. "You never had any problem reaching him if you needed to get a statement," recalls Bill Franklin, who was an editor at *Business Week* during the 1970s. "No matter what he was doing, you could get him instantly."

Greenspan was invited to join *Time* magazine's "board of economists." Once per quarter, an assortment of dismal-science practitioners was convened at Time-Life's corporate headquarters in midtown Manhattan. The participants varied, but regulars included Walter Heller and Arthur Okun, liberal economists who had been CEA chairmen under Kennedy and Johnson, respectively; Beryl Sprinkel, a prominent monetarist and disciple of Milton Friedman; and Murray Weidenbaum, then director of the Center for Study of American Business at Washington University in St. Louis.

Marshall Loeb, an editor at *Time* who later founded *Money* magazine, acted as moderator. The idea was to throw together an eclectic group of economists and goad them into passionate debate. The highlights of these exchanges were published in the magazine. "Alan was always very insightful," recalls Weidenbaum. "He talked with great flair about the numbers. We tended to complement one another as free-market-oriented conservatives."

The added exposure began to do the trick. Townsend-Greenspan took on quite a few new clients. During the late 1970s, Greenspan was invited to join the boards of a number of companies, including Alcoa, Mobil, and General Foods. He was even tapped for a directorship by the venerable J. P. Morgan and Company, an honor that *Fortune* magazine described as the "New York financial world's equivalent of knighthood." But far more than accolades from the corporate world, Greenspan pined to return to politics.

When 1980 rolled around, hope sprang anew for Greenspan. It was an election year, and he was yearning to get back into the game. He missed the grand scope of the political arena, where one is involved in decisions that affect millions of lives, and he also missed being a public servant. At its best, Greenspan had discovered, Washington was a place where it was possible to be influential and make a difference on a grand scale.

Surprisingly, the very first person who requested his services was Massachusetts senator Ted Kennedy. Planning a presidential run, Kennedy wanted to be certain to avoid a key mistake made by another ultraliberal, George McGovern, during the 1972 race.

The South Dakota senator's economic platform—laughingly dismissed as "McGovernomics" by critics—included proposals to tax excess corporate profits and overhaul welfare. His views were seen as so radical that even prominent Wall Street Democrats, such as William Salomon of Salomon Brothers, withheld their fund-raising support. That played a crucial role in his loss to Nixon.

Greenspan organized a breakfast for Ted Kennedy and invited a number of financial-world heavyweights. "Kennedy wanted a dialogue," recalls Townsend-Greenspan's David Rowe. "He wanted to give people on Wall Street a sense that he wasn't crazy. For his part, Alan was always able to communicate across the broad political spectrum. He's fundamentally a rationalist. He doesn't become viscerally or emotionally involved in things."

Greenspan's next political offer came from what is most decidedly the other end of the spectrum. He was asked to serve as an economic adviser during Ronald Reagan's 1980 run. Greenspan had met Reagan on several previous occasions, including a dinner party hosted by George Shultz in the summer of 1978. But the decisive meeting was brokered by Martin Anderson.

Anderson—instrumental in bringing Greenspan onto the Nixon team in 1968—was now acting as a point man in Reagan's campaign operation. He arranged a luncheon meeting between Greenspan and the candidate at the Stanford Faculty Club.

"Reagan basically asked Greenspan a lot of policy questions," recalls Anderson. "The way with Reagan is that he would always talk very casually, but he'd be trying to get at key points. He was impressed with Greenspan. He indicated to me immediately afterwards that he wanted Greenspan on his team."

Greenspan joined a campaign lineup that included Arthur Burns, William Simon, Paul McCracken, Richard Allen, and Dick Whalen—all old Nixon hands.

Due to a strange twist, however, Greenspan's most notable contribution to Reagan's 1980 run was actually in the service of Gerald Ford, in what is viewed as one of the oddest events in the recent history of U.S. electoral politics.

On June 5, 1980, Reagan visited Ford at his home in Rancho Mirage for a private meeting. The ostensible purpose was to bury the hatchet prior to the Republican National Convention, which was to be held in Detroit in July. For the sake of party unity, it was crucial that a presidential aspirant and a former president at least appear to be on good terms. Ever since the 1976 election, the relationship between the two had been tense. Reagan had run a tough primary and had very nearly stolen the Republican nomination away from the incumbent Ford.

The meeting in Rancho Mirage was a success. When the Detroit convention rolled around, one month later, any past differences between the two seemed to have been smoothed over. Ford took a suite on the seventieth floor of the Plaza Hotel in Detroit's Renaissance Center. Reagan took a suite on the sixty-ninth floor. The two paid one another a series of courtesy visits. One such visit—on July 14, 1980—

happened to fall on Ford's sixty-seventh birthday. Ronald and Nancy Reagan toasted Jerry and Betty Ford with champagne and Perrier. Reagan gave Ford a pipe and tobacco pouch fashioned in the nineteenth century by Crow Indians from Montana.

But a visit the following day had a far more serious tone. Reagan still hadn't warmed to the idea of selecting George Bush as his running mate. In the course of an hourlong discussion, Reagan dropped a bombshell, reportedly saying to Ford: "I would like you to serve on the ticket with me to run against and hopefully defeat Carter."

"I don't think it will work," was Ford's immediate response.

There were a huge number of concerns, not the least of which is the provision in the Twelfth Amendment specifying that if the presidential and vice-presidential candidates are from the same state, electors can't vote for both. Reagan and Ford were both California residents—so one of them would have to move elsewhere. Beyond that, there were countless questions about how a new president and former president could work productively as a team.

Ford left the meeting doubtful. But he did not close the door on the idea.

Within hours, a group of Reagan campaign staffers and other assorted political operatives sat down and began trying to hammer out the details. They quickly formed two teams, a Ford team and a Reagan team. The Ford team consisted of Greenspan, Kissinger, and Robert Barrett, the ex-president's chief of staff.

Of course, Greenspan was officially a Reagan economic adviser. But because he had worked closely with Ford, it made perfect sense for him to represent the former president's interests in the complicated negotiations that lay ahead.

The Reagan team included campaign director William Casey, Chief of Staff Ed Meese, and pollster Richard Wirthlin.

Late that night, the Ford team convened with the ex-president. At one point, Kissinger and Ford huddled privately for about forty-five minutes. Kissinger appealed to Ford's sense of patriotism and suggested that Carter's misguided policies had created a "national emergency."

"Henry, I don't think it will work," said Ford.

The meeting broke up, and everyone finally went to bed.

The following morning began in a mood of high drama that would become dizzying by day's end.

During a breakfast meeting, the two teams attempted to clarify their vision of a Reagan and Ford "dream ticket." It was agreed that Ford would have to be given an enhanced role as vice president, but the exact parameters were difficult to define. For each bright idea, there were a dozen possible pitfalls. Someone suggested that Ford could take part in making cabinet appointments. But wouldn't Reagan want to make all his own selections?

The two sides drew up a hastily assembled memo called "Draft Talking Points." Only a page and a half long and double-spaced, it attempted to address a vast array of practical, logistical, political, and constitutional questions. One talking point: Maybe the vice president could be put in charge of the budget. Another: Maybe there could be a single combined White House staff serving both men.

The two teams proceeded to shuttle back and forth, meeting with Ford and Reagan, reconvening, meeting with Ford and Reagan again. The frenzy was growing.

At one point, Greenspan urged Ford to run as "a matter of duty." Ford said to Greenspan: "Look, for God's sake, if I'm going to do this, would you be willing to come in and help me out on the economic side?"

Greenspan responded, "If I'm sitting here and strongly suggesting that the vice presidency isn't a bad idea, I have no choice but to say 'yes.'"

Maybe Greenspan would be Treasury secretary after all.

But the cracks were beginning to show, especially among the Reagan camp. By necessity, an enhanced vice presidency meant a diminished presidency. There was also scuttlebutt that Ford would try to reinstall Kissinger as secretary of state. Reagan did not like that idea one bit. He felt that Kissinger carried "baggage."

That evening, Ford had a couple of television interviews scheduled, with CBS's Walter Cronkite and ABC's Barbara Walters. Talk of a "dream ticket" had leaked out, of course, and the convention floor at Joe Louis Arena was abuzz. Naturally, the topic came up in the interviews. Ford responded with his typical candor, suggesting that a vice-presidential run was possible but unlikely—first a huge number of details would have to be worked out to his satisfaction. This added to Reagan's growing frustration. It was a breach of confidence, he felt, for Ford to even entertain the topic.

As the evening wore on, Ford's doubts grew as well. At 11:00 P.M., he walked down to Reagan's suite and declined. By now, the feeling was pretty much mutual. The strange dalliance had blossomed and died within the span of thirty-six hours. The two talked cordially for about ten minutes, and then Ford returned to his room.

A few minutes later—at 11:37 P.M. on July 16, 1980, to be exact— Ronald Reagan called George Bush and asked him to be his running mate.

For his role in this little drama, Greenspan received a certain amount of criticism, as did Kissinger. Some felt that in urging Ford on, the two were driven by their own selfish motives—to recapture some of their former glory. Others merely felt that they showed a surprising naïveté for people usually possessed of such fine political instincts.

"Neither Greenspan nor I were pushing it," says Kissinger. "We were analyzing how it might work if the Reagan people absolutely wanted it to work. We thought it was important for the Carter administration to be replaced."

Donald Rumsfeld, who tends to be very complimentary about Greenspan, does not recall the 1980 convention as his finest hour.

"I don't know what Greenspan and Kissinger were thinking," he says. "Picking a former president as vice president had to be the dumbest idea I ever heard. Personally, I think they were well meaning, but wrong—flat wrong. You don't want four hands on the steering wheel. It would have weakened Reagan and made him look like he was not a full president. People don't want a president who isn't president."

Following the convention, Greenspan settled back into his role as economic adviser to Reagan. But he continued to be dogged by mild controversies, such as one stirred up by Jude Wanniski.

Wanniski was an economic consultant and fellow adviser to Reagan. He was also a zealous disciple of University of Chicago professor Arthur Laffer, famed for the Laffer Curve, which provides the theoretical underpinning for supply-side economics. His theory holds that it is possible to increase government revenues by lowering taxes. Essentially, supply-side economics is predicated on reducing people's tax burden, thereby creating an incentive for them to work harder and earn more money. That, in turn, leads to increased tax receipts for the government.

Wanniski served as the primary source for an article that ran in the April 7, 1980, edition of the *Village Voice*, written by Alexander Cockburn and James Ridgeway, entitled "Worlds in Collision: The Battle for Reagan's Mind." The basic premise was that Reagan's economic advisers were divided into two camps. On one side were supply-siders such as Wanniski, Laffer, and Congressman Jack Kemp; on the other side were traditionalists such as Burns, Shultz, and Greenspan.

Among the members of Reagan's campaign team, Wanniski's assertions were viewed as an act of self-aggrandizement, an attempt to position himself as a supply-side defender in contrast to the crusty old-school economists. Reagan immediately dropped Wanniski, but the press was all over the story. The notion of a "battle for Reagan's mind" was just too good to resist.

Even following the Republican convention in July, the belief persisted that Reagan's advisers were divided into two camps. Greenspan would forever afterward be viewed as a supply-side skeptic, someone who doubted the efficacy of the controversial theory. But this was simply a lingering—and erroneous—perception, rooted in Wanniski's incautious interview with the *Village Voice*.

The fact is, Greenspan had no special beef with supply-side economics as a theory. In the course of the campaign, he often questioned specific assumptions that he thought overly optimistic. But he also worked and reworked various projections in an effort to get the numbers to jibe. "Greenspan was instrumental in saying, 'yes, you can have these numbers.' He helped develop realistic projections," says Annelise Anderson, Martin Anderson's wife and a fellow Reagan campaign adviser.

In the general election, Reagan won decisively, tallying up 50.7 percent of the popular vote versus Carter's 41 percent and picking up 489 electoral college votes to Carter's 49.

Greenspan continued to work with President Reagan, adopting a role similar to the one he'd had during the Nixon administration. He became what is jokingly referred to as an "out-house" adviser—as opposed to an in-house adviser. He remained in New York, heading up Townsend-Greenspan, but he was available to the administration for consultation on economic issues. He also participated in assorted working groups and committees, mostly negligible in their impact—with one notable exception.

Facing an imminent crisis, the Reagan administration convened the National Commission on Social Security Reform, a.k.a. the Greenspan Commission.

Social Security is a pay-as-you-go system, meaning tax dollars paid by the current workforce flow directly to current retirees. Social Security benefits are also indexed to inflation, and have been since 1972. These two factors spelled disaster during the stagflation of the Ford and Carter years. Between 1977 and 1981, for example, inflation rose a cumulative 60 percent. But wages actually fell 6.9 percent in real terms. Basically, current workers' salaries were failing to keep pace with current retirees' inflation-adjusted benefits.

In May 1981, the Reagan administration proposed a number of measures intended to shore up the Social Security system, all involving benefit cutbacks in one way or another. The administration suggested, for example, that benefits could be pared back for people who retire before age sixty-five. As it stood, and still stands, people who retire at sixty-two are eligible for 80 percent of their benefits. Reagan's recommendation: Cut the amount back to 55 percent. The outcry was immediate.

Organized labor and the AARP went berserk. Members of Congress on both sides of the aisle rose up in protest, and on May 20, 1981, a resolution condemning the proposal passed in the Senate, 96-0. Not for nothing is Social Security called the "third rail" of politics.

Reagan faced a public-relations nightmare. On September 24, 1981, he announced a plan to convene a bipartisan commission to look into ways to clean up the Social Security mess. One-third of its fifteen members would be chosen by House Speaker Tip O'Neill, one-third by Senate Majority Leader Howard Baker, and Reagan would choose the remainder. The selections were announced on December 16, 1981, and included Senator Bob Dole (Republican, Kansas); Senator Daniel Patrick Moynihan (Democrat, New York); AFL-CIO chairman Lane Kirkland; Alexander Trowbridge, president of the National Association of Manufacturers; and Robert Ball, representing the Social Security Administration. The commission's membership was split politically, with eight Republicans and seven Democrats.

Greenspan was picked as chair. "He was chosen to head the commission because he was very well regarded in economic circles," recalls James Baker, Reagan's chief of staff at the time. "He was highly regarded in political circles, as well, as a former chairman of the CEA, and as someone with a reputation for being bipartisan."

The commission worked throughout 1982, trying to come up with a solution that would be acceptable to Congress and the American people. This was urgent—the system literally slid $20,000 deeper into the red every single second. The Social Security Administration announced that by July 1983, its funds would be so depleted that it would no longer be able to cut full-benefit checks.

Under the threat of imminent disaster, the commission's participants scrambled to come up with a solution that would be less painful than Reagan's original proposal. Ultimately, they pieced together a package of various benefit cuts and tax hikes. Short of a huge and unexpected windfall in government tax receipts, those were really the only choices. Among the Greenspan Commission's recommendations: Increase the payroll tax for Social Security, increase the level of taxable earnings, and tax Social Security itself.

The recommendations were submitted to Congress, which bypassed its typical protracted deliberations. (If Social Security payments were missed, no one wanted to feel the wrath of 36 million angry recipients.) The Greenspan Commission's recommendations passed quickly, and Reagan signed the bill on April 20, 1983.

Viewed in retrospect, the commission's solution was something of a Band-Aid. The problems inherent in a pay-as-you-go system remained. How to fix Social Security continues to be one of the nation's greatest challenges. As of the year 2000, the ratio of workers to retirees stood at 3.25:1. But by 2030, the ratio is projected to have fallen to 2:1. As aging baby boomers swell the retiree ranks, there will be a larger pool of Social Security recipients supported by a relatively smaller worker force. No doubt this is fodder for many future commissions.

Still, Greenspan won recognition for presiding over a commission that averted a disaster in the short haul. Afterward, he remained an out-house adviser, but one who was very much on the mind of President Reagan.

Meanwhile, back in New York, it was more of the same for Greenspan—except for a surprising fact that he learned about Ayn Rand.

He gained this piece of intelligence during a visit Barbara Branden paid him at his apartment in UN Plaza. The big Break of 1968 was

by this time ancient history. Greenspan—bastion of bipartisanship—
had managed to maintain friendships on both sides of the rift. He
was still friends with Rand on one side, and also with Joan Mitchell
Blumenthal on the other. Although he'd hastily signed the oath de-
nouncing the Brandens, he'd managed to patch things up with Barbara
Branden.

The two were busy catching up on old times, when Branden told
him that she had a rather startling revelation.

"Alan, this is going to shock you," she said.

"I'm not easily shocked," he replied.

Branden proceeded to tell him about the affair that her husband and
Rand had carried on. Being good Objectivists—not wanting to sneak
around—the pair had first sought permission from their spouses, Barbara and Frank O'Connor, who had reluctantly agreed, hoping the affair would be short-lived. But it lasted from 1954 until 1968. Along
the way, Nathaniel Branden had launched into a second extramarital affair with Patrecia Gullison, a fashion model and student of objectivism,
whom he'd met during one of his lectures. For New Year's Eve 1967,
Greenspan had actually been set up on a date with Patrecia's twin sister, Leisha. Like the rest of the Collective, he knew nothing about the
assorted extramarital hijinks.

When Rand found out about Patrecia, she was furious with
Nathaniel, of course. She was also angry that Barbara had known but
had not informed her. So she cut them both off.

Branden explained to Greenspan that it was this sequence of
events—rather than embezzling, drug use, illogical thinking, or any
other transgression—that actually caused the Break.

"He was dumbfounded," recalls Branden. "It all came together for
him. It made sense out of what he'd observed, but not been able to
make sense of."

Meanwhile, Rand herself was in failing health by the early 1980s.
Throughout her adult life, she had smoked heavily and with a certain
amount of glee. Perhaps the strangest among her views held that people should smoke because it represented man's taming of fire and was a
symbol, therefore, of human industriousness. In fact, the publishing
party for *Atlas Shrugged* had featured custom cigarettes embossed with
little gold-leaf dollar signs.

During the 1970s, Rand was diagnosed with lung cancer. She did her damnedest to greet the news with clear-eyed rationality. She had lived and now she would die. Rand proceeded as best she could.

In November 1981, she was invited to speak in New Orleans at a conference of the National Committee for Monetary Reform, an organization devoted to free enterprise and a return to the gold standard. The group arranged for a private railcar to transport her from New York to New Orleans. There are memorable railroad scenes in *Atlas Shrugged*, and it seemed like a fitting tribute for a champion of heavy industry.

Other speakers at the convention included Louis Rukeyser, Paul Erdman, and Adam Smith, but Rand was the big draw. There were 4,000 people in attendance. Rand ended her speech with a quote from John Galt, hero of *Atlas Shrugged*:

> The world you desired can be won, it exists, it is real, it is possible, it's yours. But to win it requires your total dedication and a total break with the world of your past, with the doctrine that man is a sacrificial animal who exists for the pleasure of others. Fight for the value of your person. Fight for the virtue of your pride. Fight for the essence of that which is man: for his sovereign rational mind. Fight with the radiant certainty and absolute rectitude of knowing that yours is the Morality of Life and that yours is the battle for any achievement, any value, any grandeur, any goodness, any joy that has ever existed on earth.

The crowd burst to its feet in a standing ovation.

Rand boarded her private train and traveled back to New York. She arrived victorious but exhausted. Shortly afterward, she checked into the hospital, and on March 6, 1982, Rand died at the age of seventy-seven.

Two days later, a memorial service was held at the Frank E. Campbell funeral home on Manhattan's Upper East Side. Rand was laid out in an open casket, beside which stood a six-foot-high dollar sign. The room was packed with flowers and filled with the strains of the song "It's a Long Way to Tipperary."

Greenspan showed up to pay his last respects to the author, as did Leonard Peikoff. So too did nearly 800 other people, a few of them friends, but mostly fans.

The following day, a small private ceremony was held at a cemetery in Valhalla, New York. Rand was buried beside her husband, Frank O'Connor. Nearby was the grave of her favorite composer, Rachmaninoff.

Of course, there are a couple of codas to Rand's particular and peculiar tale.

The date of her death—March 6—is also Greenspan's birthday.

She left her entire estate to Leonard Peikoff. It amounted to $550,000, a surprisingly small sum for a woman who had sold millions of books. The truth is that until very late in life, capitalism's great champion had been hesitant about delving into the world of stocks and investing. By that time, inflation had eaten up much of the proceeds from her book sales.

The mid-1980s found Greenspan still hungry to get to the next level. He remained on excellent terms with the Reagan camp. But an opportunity was yet to materialize in the political world. So he turned his attention to trying to further raise his profile as a consultant.

In 1985, Greenspan—never exactly a technophile—appeared as a pitchman in magazine ads for the Apple IIc. The ads carried the tag line "How to Avoid Paying Your Bills" and held as their conceit that "famous economic adviser" Greenspan relied on the computer to organize his finances.

He also tried his hand at a couple of Townsend-Greenspan joint ventures. For example, he teamed up with Roderick "Rory" O'Neil, a high-ranking executive from Travelers Corporation, and took a stab at getting into the money management business. Marvin Josephson, the well-known talent scout, provided $3 million in backing.

For the new venture, Greenspan was called upon only to lend his name and reputation—O'Neil was supposed to furnish the contacts and expertise. But money management is a very tricky business. Greenspan O'Neil Associates was started as a service for pension funds and other large institutional investors, but it hit a wall on the marketing end and was never able to accumulate sufficient funds under management. Thus, the firm earned scant fee income and closed down after a little more than a year in operation.

During this period, Greenspan and Kissinger also talked about a joint venture. Kissinger had launched a consulting business in 1982, specializing in foreign-policy issues. He and Greenspan had remained in touch since the Ford administration and had grown to be friends. In fact, Greenspan was a frequent weekend guest at Kissinger's home in Kent, Connecticut. The two enjoyed far-ranging discussions that invariably delved into their respective areas of expertise.

"I would tell him how I interpreted the foreign-policy situation," recalls Kissinger. "He'd give me his analysis of current economic conditions—extremely brilliant."

The two started to feel they would make a good team professionally. Their consulting specialties—economics and foreign policy—were enticingly complementary. Often they would refer clients to one another. Still, there were just too many details to work out, and the proposed venture never got beyond the idea stage. "I think that if Alan had not gone to the Fed, the odds are that we would have merged," says Kissinger.

It's intriguing to contemplate the kind of powerhouse consultancy the two could have assembled. Would it have been Greenspan-Kissinger Associates or Kissinger-Greenspan Associates? No matter—this and a thousand other questions are destined to forever remain in the realm of mere conjecture. Greenspan's wilderness period was about to come to an end, and in spectacular fashion.

11

CHAIRMAN GREENSPAN

In the summer of 1987, Greenspan received a call from President Ronald Reagan that would change his life. He was offered the chairmanship of the Federal Reserve, a monumentally demanding job that is often deemed the second most powerful post in the land. Some would even argue that at certain times, under certain circumstances, it's the most powerful. The Fed chairman controls levers that can literally speed up the economy or grind it to a halt.

Caution, judiciousness, and impartiality are the requisite job requirements. A Fed chairman has to be able to work with the president and Congress, yet remain above the political fray. This is a delicate balancing act. A Fed chairman also has to eat, sleep, and breathe data—and love it.

Above all, the chairman of Fed has to be Tevlar-skinned. Criticism—tons of criticism—comes with the territory. It's like being a baseball umpire, times one thousand.

Congress originally created the Federal Reserve so that a separate authority would hold a large measure of responsibility for the functioning of the economy, but traditionally, the Fed's power has not come with an equal measure of glory. During boom times, Congress and the administration vie for the credit. Only when the economy slumps does attention tend to focus on the Fed. At such times, the chairman of the

Federal Reserve is a magnet for reproach. Greenspan's cool, impassive style made him well suited on this score.

In many ways, Greenspan had spent his entire life preparing for the job of Fed chair. His mentor, Arthur Burns, had made the same progression: CEA chair, Washington insider, chairman of the Federal Reserve. Nevertheless, a person cannot really campaign actively for the job. The president nominates the Fed chairman, after close consultation with advisers and with an eye toward how Wall Street will react.

As a Reagan insider, Greenspan had been on the shortlist of possible candidates. The fact that he had never worked at the Federal Reserve was neither a drawback nor an advantage. There's a tradition of picking chairmen from outside the organization. During the Fed's entire history, the second in command—the vice chairman—has never once managed to move into the top spot. Even as a leading candidate, however, Greenspan found it impossible to feel confident that he would get the nod. There were just too many vagaries.

When Reagan finally called to offer him the post, Greenspan was at a doctor's appointment, ministering to his bad back.

"There's no telling what they're doing to that man," Reagan quipped.

Twenty minutes passed before Greenspan could be located. Once the White House had tracked him down, he accepted the job immediately. Back in 1974, it had required a whole series of people to prevail on Greenspan to come to Washington, but this time around, the decision required "milliseconds," as Greenspan later recalled.

The next day—June 2, 1987—Reagan made it public that Greenspan was his nominee. Now it was the market's turn to react. Within minutes of Reagan's announcement, the Dow dropped twenty-two points, though it quickly recovered. This sent a clear signal that Greenspan was viewed as a worthy successor to outgoing Fed chairman Paul Volcker, at least in some quarters of the financial markets. The foreign-exchange market was a different matter. The value of the dollar sank sharply against the Japanese yen and various European currencies.

Volcker had a worldwide reputation. During two terms as Fed chairman, he had built up a network of foreign central bankers that reached from Bonn to Beijing. If Greenspan had any area of conspicuous deficiency, it was in the international arena. A lightning-fast verdict had been rendered: The domestic market was comfortable with Greenspan, but he was an unknown quantity overseas.

The next step on the road to becoming Fed chairman was an appearance before the Senate Banking Committee. This body would decide whether to pass along Greenspan's name for final confirmation by the Senate at large. The nomination raised some serious concerns. Were it to pass, Reagan would achieve a presidential first—appointment of the entire seven-member board of the Federal Reserve. Martha Seger, a 1983 Reagan appointee, actually had the greatest seniority of any Fed governor. Among the members of the Senate Banking Committee, the worry was that the Fed was becoming unduly beholden to the administration and its vaunted independence might therefore be compromised.

In simplest terms, the Fed is in the driver's seat when it comes to the economy, the goal being to steer it along at a safe and steady pace. Presidents always want the economy to grow faster, faster, faster. If the Fed ever caved in entirely to presidential wishes, there would be a boom to end all booms—mortgages with 2-percent interest rates, the stock market spiking into the stratosphere. Of course, this car—careening along at 120 miles an hour—would eventually lose control.

As the hearings got underway, Donald Riegle, a Democrat from Michigan, honed right in: "If some person in the administration tried to muscle the decisions of the Federal Reserve System some time next year in advance of the election, what would be your response to that?"

"I certainly don't anticipate that happening," responded Greenspan, "but were it to happen, I obviously would reject it."

William Proxmire, the Wisconsin Democrat and old Greenspan sparring partner, was now chairman of the Senate Banking Committee. He had a litany of concerns, of which Fed independence was just one. As he had when presiding over Greenspan's CEA appointment, he again kicked off with the promise that he would be thorough. "Dr. Greenspan," said Proxmire, "I'm going to take a little longer than I've ever taken before in a preliminary statement because I think this is such an absolutely critical appointment."

Proxmire chided Greenspan for what he termed his "dismal forecasting record" as an economist. He expressed concern, too, about Greenspan's views on antitrust, because the Federal Reserve is called upon to weigh in on certain bank mergers. Proxmire pointed out that

Greenspan had written an essay that appeared in Ayn Rand's *Capitalism: The Unknown Ideal*, revealing his "philosophical objections to antitrust laws." Proxmire also worried about the fact that Greenspan was once retained by Sears to help the retailer expand more aggressively into financial services, a sector in which it faced regulatory restrictions.

Greenspan simply acquiesced on the issue of his deficiency as a forecaster. There was no arguing with the record. Townsend-Greenspan had overstated its inflation projections by between 1.2 percent and 2.4 percent each year from 1982 to 1986. Greenspan had always been more of an anatomist, able to dissect the economy and locate the first faint sign of slowing growth or accelerating inflation. Casting forward and actually assigning a number was not his strong suit. In fact, a study by the Federal Reserve itself had ranked Townsend-Greenspan dead last among eight firms in terms of inflation forecasting.

On antitrust, Greenspan did one of his patented verbal dances. "I am, as you point out, philosophically opposed to the Sherman Act. I have been and continue to be. But I understand it, and I understand the legal criteria which are involved in applying it and, hopefully, I am able to separate my own personal views from what is legally required."

Proxmire's response: "That is both very discomforting and very comforting, if you know what I mean."

Ultimately, Greenspan was grilled for three and a half hours. The Banking Committee voted to pass his name on to the Senate. Greenspan, in turn, provided assurances that he would attend to a couple of their strongest concerns.

He was required to sever all ties with Townsend-Greenspan. A buyer or new partner would have to be found for the firm, which had grown to roughly thirty employees. Greenspan and his associates scrambled to make some kind of arrangement, but the deadline pressure proved too intense. On July 31, 1987, Townsend-Greenspan closed its doors.

"It was a sad day," recalls Bess Kaplan.

She had been with Townsend-Greenspan since 1954 and took the opportunity to simply retire. Kathryn Eickhoff—Greenspan's trusted deputy—started her own consulting firm, Eickhoff Economics.

Greenspan had to rearrange his financial assets in order to avoid any conflict of interest. Filings show that he had $2.9 million worth of investments, including stock in Alcoa, Cap Cities/ABC, and J. P. Morgan, along with a portfolio of treasuries and a sizable chunk of New

York state transportation bonds. Greenspan agreed to unload his holdings of companies that had banking interests, such as J. P. Morgan. The rest he placed in two blind trusts. With typical Greenspanian logic, he pointed out that two blind trusts would keep him better diversified than one.

A few days after the close of his firm, Greenspan's nomination went before the Senate. The matter was given swift attention and received little debate. Sufficient prying and prodding had already been done by the Banking Committee, after all. Greenspan was confirmed by a vote of 91 to 2.

One of the dissenters was Bill Bradley, Democrat from New Jersey. The senator voiced his concern that Greenspan would "move rapidly toward deregulation, rather than showing the same caution as Chairman Volcker." He added, "I also believe we need a chairman with wider international experience at this time."

The other "nay" did not come from Proxmire but rather from Kent Conrad of North Dakota. When Greenspan had been up for the post of CEA chairman, Proxmire had voted against him. Not this time.

"Prox often voted for people he thought capable of doing the job, even if he disagreed with them," says Howard Shuman, his former chief of staff. "For instance, he also supported William Rehnquist for the Supreme Court on the grounds that you couldn't say he wasn't qualified."

The swearing-in ceremony was set for August 11, 1987. That day, Greenspan invited Wesley and Carolyn Halpert—his cousin and his cousin's wife—to lunch at the Federal Reserve's private dining room. Greenspan's date was Susan Mills, a producer for the *MacNeil-Lehrer Newshour*, yet another in his line of women in the media. Carolyn Halpert did not get the sense that Greenspan and Mills were particularly serious. She also found Greenspan surprisingly dour on his big day. "I think I was more excited than he was," she says. "He seemed very quiet."

The ceremony was held in the East Room of the White House. A number of dignitaries were present, among them Secretary of State George Shultz and Defense Secretary Caspar Weinberger. Outgoing chairman Volcker and the six remaining members of the Fed's Board of Governors were there as well. Greenspan's mother, Rose, could not attend because her health was failing seriously. But Cousin Wesley brought along the copy of the Torah used at Greenspan's CEA swearing-in that was signed by Gerald Ford. Rose had kept it on the coffee table in her living room as one of her prize possessions.

The oath of office was administered by Vice President Bush, while the president stood by. Reagan said a few words, praising Greenspan as an "economist's economist." Greenspan spoke briefly and attempted a joke. "Perhaps I should also thank in advance the creators of all those events that will make the next four years easy going: inflation which always stays put, a stock market which is always a bull, a dollar which is always stable, interest rates which stay low, and employment which stays high. But, most assuredly, I would be thankful to those who have the capability of repealing the laws of arithmetic which would make the foregoing possible."

No one laughed. Perhaps people weren't as attuned to his peculiar style as they would be after his umpteenth Humphrey-Hawkins testimony before Congress.

Greenspan also sounded a more serious note.

"I am particularly saddened, however, that Dr. Arthur F. Burns, former Council of Economic Advisers and Federal Reserve Board Chairman, and my mentor for thirty-five years through graduate school and thereafter, is not able to be with us today."

Burns had died earlier in the summer, at age eighty-three, from complications following triple-bypass surgery. In latter years, Burns had capped an impressive Washington career by serving as U.S. ambassador to West Germany. He was also founding chairman of the Committee to Fight Inflation, a group of prominent economists who had spent their careers in public service. In what would be a fitting epitaph, Burns once said, "I devoted a good part of my life to trying to awaken the country to the dangers of inflation."

The job of chief inflation fighter had now been handed down to the thirteenth chairman of the Federal Reserve, Burns's onetime student.

In every way, his tenure was to be a challenging one. Ahead lay stock-market crashes and global meltdowns. He'd battle Congress, battle the press, battle presidents. He'd be caricatured and lampooned, at times even demonized. Yet he'd also manage to rise above all the rabble for a spell, catching a wave of cultural zeitgeist to become an American first—a celebrity Fed chairman.

But through it all—the ups and downs, crises and calms—one thing would remain constant: A mere 0.2 percent of the population can explain just exactly what the man does.

Truly, the Fed's fearsome power is matched only by a profound capacity for engendering misunderstanding. This is partially due to the fact that managing the economy is an extremely esoteric discipline. The Fed's functions are accursedly hard to understand.

But the confusion is also partly by design. The Fed is positioned smack in the center of some of the major conflicts that run through American history: big government versus local control, elite banking interests versus agrarian interests. Therefore, muddle and mystification are hallowed Fed strategies for keeping critics at bay.

The Federal Reserve is the nation's central bank. Decisions it makes affect how much money is in circulation, how easily it can be borrowed, and at what terms. This is known as monetary policy. It is distinct from fiscal policy, which involves government budget decisions, taxation, and public expenditures. In a deliberate division of power, the Fed controls monetary policy while Congress and the administration oversee fiscal policy.

The Fed's power over monetary policy stems from its ability to control the supply of reserves. Commercial banks, savings and loans, and other deposit-taking institutions have to maintain a percentage of their holdings in reserve. They keep these reserves either as cash in their own vaults or in accounts set up with the Fed.

The Fed dictates reserve levels, usually somewhere in the neighborhood of 10 percent of deposits. Of course, banks are perpetually taking in new deposits and lending the same money out. They have to rectify their accounts frequently and make sure they are meeting reserve requirements. If they fall short of the requirements, they face substantial penalties levied by the Fed. To avoid such penalties, it's still possible to borrow from another bank to shore up reserves.

On a daily basis, billions of dollars' worth of such interbank lending occurs. And the Fed exercises its most powerful tool in this arena. The Fed sets what's known as the funds rate, the rate on interbank lending. If the Fed raises the funds rate, it becomes more expensive for banks to borrow from one another. The increased costs get passed along to corporate borrowers and individuals.

Changes in the Fed's funds rate ripple out into the economy, serving to slow things down or speed them up. Lowering the funds rate, for example, will help accelerate the economy. Money becomes cheaper to borrow, leading to increased mortgage underwriting, factory expansions, and so forth. But such monetary easing also carries a risk: If the money supply grows faster than the supply of goods and services, inflation will begin to creep into the economy. In response, the Fed may hike the funds rate, making borrowing more expensive, slowing everything down. A smooth-running economy is the goal, and the Fed regularly tinkers with the funds rate in response to inflationary or recessionary forces.

The way the Fed actually controls the funds rate is extremely complex and extraordinarily counterintuitive. It doesn't simply set the rate per se, at X percent or Y percent. Rather, it pegs the rate by engaging in what are known as open-market operations.

The Fed maintains a huge multibillion-dollar portfolio of U.S. government securities. This is considered an extremely liquid investment vehicle; there's always a market to buy and sell Treasury notes. Thus, the Fed can add to its portfolio at any time by purchasing securities. To do so, the Fed goes into the bond market and buys directly from a network of about thirty primary dealers. The Fed can snap up millions of dollars' worth of securities at a moment's notice. Payment is credited to the reserve accounts of the primary dealers' banks. Voilà! Now the banks have extra money—above their reserve requirements—that they can lend out.

In this fashion, the Fed expands the money supply. Money becomes more plentiful, hence cheaper to borrow. The funds rate falls. To raise the funds rate, the Fed does just the opposite. It sells securities to the network of primary bond dealers. Say the Fed sells $100 million worth of securities; that means $100 million less money in circulation. Because money is tighter, the funds rate rises.

By adjusting its vast portfolio—buying and selling securities in the open market—the Fed can alter the funds rate with great precision. When there's an announcement that the Fed plans to change interest rates—for instance, lowering them from 6 percent to 5.75—what it really means is that the Fed plans to engage in open-market operations that will result in the desired funds rate.

The Fed exerts enormous control over the U.S. economy by means of this single lever. But the Fed also has several other tools at its disposal. It can simply change the reserve levels. Requiring banks to hold 9 percent rather than 10 percent in reserve, for instance, would serve to free up that much more money. But this is considered a blunt tool, one that can't be as precisely calibrated as the funds rate, and as a consequence, reserve levels are adjusted infrequently.

There's also the discount rate, the only interest rate the Fed actually sets. The discount rate is what depository institutions pay when they borrow directly from the Fed. Moves in the discount rate tend to be made in tandem with moves of the funds rate. Changes send a powerful signal about how the Fed views the health of the economy.

In recent years, use of the so-called discount window has tapered off. The option is always available. Because the Fed acts as lender of last resort, money borrowed at the discount rate can be a lifeline in an emergency. With this in mind, banks often shy away from using the discount window unless it's absolutely necessary. There's a fear that it sends a signal that a bank is in trouble.

Certainly, banks don't wish to invite undue scrutiny from regulators. That's yet another hat worn by the Fed, one of several outside the strict realm of monetary policy. The Fed oversees a portion of the nation's banks, scrutinizing the quality of loans and approving mergers. But it doesn't regulate every decision by every bank. While all deposit-taking institutions are subject to the Fed's reserve requirements, some banks are regulated by the Comptroller of Currency, others by the Federal Deposit Insurance Corporation (FDIC).

The Fed also acts as the government's bank. Agencies such as the IRS maintain accounts with the Fed. Come tax time, when people mail in checks, a portion of the money winds up deposited in the IRS's account with the Fed. The Fed acts as a check clearinghouse, as well. It sorts checks en route from one bank to another. Roughly one-third of all checks wind up being sorted by the Fed. But the bulk of this work is done in the private sector, by large banks such as Chase Manhattan.

The Fed receives no funding from outside sources. It meets its operating expenses through investment income and also through fees it charges for services such as check clearing. Most of the remaining profits are handed over to the Treasury.

The Fed is not America's first experiment in central banking. At the country's very inception, the question of whether the United States should have a central bank—and how much power to vest in it—was a topic met with extreme rancor.

The issue precipitated the first great constitutional debate. The document itself makes no mention of banking. But Alexander Hamilton, Treasury secretary and leader of the Federalist Party, believed in a strong central government. He was born on the island of Nevis in the West Indies—the only founding father born outside of colonial America. As such, he tended to see the United States as a single entity rather than a collection of states.

A strong central bank, Hamilton believed, would help the fledgling nation to expand westward and facilitate the development of overseas trade. He submitted a central banking bill to Congress in 1790. It passed both houses. But it also encountered fierce opposition from Hamilton's personal and political enemy, Thomas Jefferson, leader of the Democratic-Republican Party. Jefferson—an eloquent champion of decentralization—urged George Washington to veto the bill on grounds that it was unconstitutional.

Hamilton mounted a vigorous defense, arguing that the Constitution carried certain implicit powers such as setting up military academies. So why not a national bank? Washington was won over by Hamilton's arguments and on February 25, 1791, he signed the bill into law. The first Bank of the United States was born and granted a twenty-year charter.

The First Bank bore scant resemblance to the current Fed. It didn't set reserve requirements for other banks. Nor did it act as a lender of last resort. In essence, the First Bank was simply a very large bank that could act as a repository of the Treasury Department's funds and engage in foreign-exchange transactions. The First Bank also accepted deposits from ordinary citizens. By doing so, it competed very effectively with the smaller state banks, forcing them to be more selective in their lending. Not surprisingly, farmers and small businesspeople felt the brunt of more stringent credit terms.

The battle lines were drawn: Jeffersonian yeoman farmers despised the First Bank, well-connected Eastern merchants found it valuable. When the charter came up for renewal in 1811, the vote in Congress was very close. The bank lost by one vote in the House. A tie in the

Senate was broken, with a deciding vote cast against the bank by Vice President George Clinton.

For the next several years, the United States was without a central bank. Following the War of 1812, the country's finances were a mess. To finance the war, the government had been forced to go begging to rich citizens. Bank lending, in the meantime, had gotten loose and sloppy. Inflation was rising at more than 10 percent a year.

The situation grew dire enough that President James Madison, a sworn enemy of the First Bank, began pushing for a second one. He was joined in his efforts by Albert Gallatin, former Treasury secretary and later a founder of Greenspan's alma mater, New York University. A second Bank of the United States was approved by Congress and also given a twenty-year charter. But it met with the same concerns. On two separate occasions, constitutional challenges made it all the way to the Supreme Court. Both times, the court ruled in favor of the Second Bank. In an opinion written in 1819, Chief Justice James Marshall employed Hamilton's arguments to Washington almost verbatim.

In 1832, several supporters of the Second Bank—including Daniel Webster and Henry Clay—decided to put the charter up for renewal, even though it wasn't due to expire for another four years. It passed through Congress. When the bill reached the desk of President Andrew Jackson, he vetoed it. Rugged and homespun, hailing from Tennessee, Jackson was the embodiment of the frontier spirit. In his July 10, 1832, veto message, Jackson declared himself "deeply impressed with the belief that some of the powers and privileges possessed by the existing bank are unauthorized by the Constitution, subversive to the rights of the States, and dangerous to the liberties of the people."

Congress couldn't summon the votes necessary to override the veto. During the bitter 1832 presidential race that followed, Jackson made the Second Bank's callousness toward the little guy a major campaign theme. He trounced his opponent, Henry Clay of the Whig Party. The election results—in Jackson's view—were a mandate. The American people had spoken, and they neither wanted nor needed a central bank.

The country entered into what's known as the "free banking" era. During this period, many states became extremely lax about handing out banking charters. Banks cropped up all over the place, each issuing its own competing currency. Traveling across the country, one could expect to encounter a bewildering array of notes, courtesy of the Trust

Company of Georgia or the Pawtuckaway Bank in Epping, New Hampshire. It was hell on shopkeepers.

Merchants got into the practice of discounting currency. As a general rule, the further away the issuing bank, the greater the discount. A merchant in Albany, New York, might deem a $20 note from a Buffalo bank as worth $19.80. A $20 note from a Pennsylvania bank might only be worth $19.60.

The Civil War brought an end to the free banking era. In 1863, the North passed a banking act, meant to create a network of national banks that could issue a common currency and help finance the conflict. Thus began the Greenback Era, so deemed because both the U.S. Treasury and national banks printed up notes using cheap green ink. The government also slapped a tax on the notes issued by the state banks, hoping to drive them out of the currency-origination business. But the state banks discovered a loophole. Rather than issuing notes, they printed checks. This is the point at which that modern convenience—the checking account—began to come into vogue.

Following the Civil War, the country continued to feel its way along without a central bank. The network of national banks proved to be no substitute. Banking remained an extremely localized business. As a consequence, the nation's money supply was extremely inelastic, creating all kinds of distortions. For example, banks could often provide no more currency during the Christmas buying season than any other time of year. Frequently, credit was tightest during the spring, when farmers needed loans for seeds and plows. In large cities, meanwhile, credit was tight in the autumn, when money left town to pay farmers for their crops. That's why market crashes traditionally happened in September and October.

Adding to the uncertainty was the way in which the nation's currency was backed. Sometimes banks adhered to a gold standard, promising to redeem notes for a set amount of gold. Other times, banks were on a combined gold-and-silver standard. Changes were determined by fairly arbitrary factors: silver coming in from Mexico or gold discovered in Alaska. In 1873, the government announced that silver was being demonetized. Bankers tended to be all for this decision. A currency backed by gold only—not silver—would by necessity mean less money in circulation. That would cut down the inflation that was eating into the proceeds from loans.

Once again, less money in circulation was a bane for farmers and small-time merchants. The government's decision came to be known as the "crime of '73." It became a huge political issue and was taken up by William Jennings Bryan, an imposing, fiery-eyed populist reformer known as the Great Commoner. On three separate occasions, Bryan ran for president on a free-silver platform—as a Silver Republican, as the National Silver Party's candidate, and as a Democrat. At the 1896 Democratic convention, Bryan delivered his famous "Cross of Gold" speech: "You shall not press down upon the brow of labor this crown of thorns, you shall not crucify mankind upon a cross of gold."

Bryan lost the election to William McKinley. A staunch traditionalist and religious zealot, Bryan would later gain notoriety as a participant in the famous Scopes trial, which centered on an anti-evolution law passed in Tennessee.

America's banking system remained in shambles. The money supply was uneven, unreliable, and inelastic. As a consequence, the economy was subject to this maddening cycle: boom gives way to bust slides into panic. There were panics in 1837, 1857, 1873, 1884, and 1893.

The last straw was the Panic of 1907. Massive insurance payouts following the San Francisco earthquake in 1906 had sent tremors through the financial system. Banks were besieged by long lines of depositors, desperate to get their money out. Trust magnate J. P. Morgan had to step in and act as a quasi-central banker, offering to provide loans to help banks that were in danger of going under.

Following the Panic of 1907, a National Monetary Commission was convened to see what could be done to stave off these panics. The commission conducted an exhaustive study of the world's banking systems. The United States—it was pointed out—was among the last developed nations without a central bank. But the old concerns died hard. Charles Lindbergh, a Republican congressman from Minnesota and father of the famous aviator, was one of many who spoke out, voicing fears that banking reform would put too much control in the hands of remote and unaccountable forces. He worried about the "money trust" in the Northeast.

So it was that the Federal Reserve was born in 1913 out of extreme compromise. President Woodrow Wilson, Virginia congressman Carter Glass, Oklahoma senator Robert Owen, as well as Attorney Louis Brandeis, countless bankers, and even William Jennings Bryan met for a series of exhaustive sessions to hash out a workable plan. What they dreamed up was a true hybrid, a "decentralized" central bank. The Fed would nominally be headquartered in Washington. There would be a seven-member board, appointed by the president and confirmed by the Senate. But twelve regional Federal Reserve banks would also be created, scattered about the country. All would report to Washington. But the boards of the regional Feds would consist of area bankers, businesspeople and community leaders, assuring local representation. Wilson signed the Federal Reserve Act into law on December 23, 1913.

In short order, the U.S. had a new national currency: the Federal Reserve Note, which is the formal name written across the top of every bill, $1, $5, or otherwise.

Next came the process of selecting sites for the twelve regional banks. Geographic diversity was key, but the cities chosen also had to be thriving commercial centers. The twelve original banks still exist, in their original locations. The sites chosen provide a good snapshot of America right before World War I. There's a regional Fed in Richmond, Virginia, for example. The state of Missouri has two—in St. Louis and in Kansas City. Meanwhile, responsibility for the entire region west of Colorado was handed to the San Francisco Fed. Back then, it made sense to represent that whole vast area with a single regional bank.

During those first years, the Fed was a mere shadow of the modern institution. Formal headquarters in Washington were yet to be built. The board and staff alternately worked out of rented office space or in quarters provided by the Treasury Department. At the time, the Fed was something of a poor relation to the Treasury Department. The Treasury secretary was ex-officio Fed chairman; the Comptroller of Currency was ex-officio vice chairman.

The Fed's monetary policy arsenal was limited, too. The value of open-market operations had not yet been discovered. Mostly, the Fed tinkered with the discount rate. Otherwise, it was little more than a "debating society of seven benevolent men," to quote one of the era's board members.

As a result, the Fed was hardly prepared for its first great challenge, the stock market crash in 1929. Historians agree that the Fed should have flooded the market with liquidity. That might have stemmed the panic by sending a powerful signal that there was money for the lending. But the Fed did just the opposite, clamping down hard on the money supply.

"The Fed flunked the test. The Great Depression might not have been so bad had the central bank acted like a central bank," says Richard Sylla, an NYU business school professor who specializes in financial history.

During the 1930s, steps were taken to try to bulk up the Fed. President Franklin Roosevelt wanted to attract some flintier personalities to the institution. His first choice was Marriner Eccles. Eccles was a Mormon banker from Utah. His reserve was legendary. Apparently the only time he showed even an ounce of levity was while duck hunting or eating a bag of salted peanuts. Eccles had impressed FDR by keeping the banks he owned up and running during the depression without losing so much as a cent of depositors' money. He agreed to join the Fed, but only if some changes were made.

At Eccles's urging, a series of reforms was undertaken. For example, the role of the Federal Open Market Committee (FOMC) was codified. The FOMC is the body that meets eight times per year to decide whether to alter interest rates. Changes in its composition during the 1930s insured that the Fed could truly meet its mandate as a "decentralized" central bank. It was agreed that the twelve-member committee would consist of seven Fed governors and five regional Fed presidents. That tilted the balance of power toward Washington but also insured that local interests would get a say in monetary policy.

In another reform, the Treasury secretary and comptroller were removed from the Board of Governors. That cut a tie between the presidential cabinet and the Fed, paving the way for a strong Fed chairman.

Eccles was a firm believer in government spending for public-works projects. Even before Keynes had written his famous treatise, Eccles was urging Keynesian-style pump priming. As Fed chairman, he worked closely with FDR, loosening the money supply to complement the president's New Deal programs. Thus began a tradition of the Fed chairman using monetary policy to either bolster or counter a president's fiscal policies.

During Eccles's tenure, the Fed finally got its own building. Completed in 1937, it is spartanly classical in style, made of Georgia white marble, and faces Constitution Avenue, directly across from the Washington Monument. The architect was Paul Philippe Cret, a Frenchman who designed several other notable buildings around the capitol city, including the Folger Shakespeare Library. Today, it's known as the Marriner Eccles Building.

Another formidable Fed chairman was William McChesney Martin Jr. Known as the "boy wonder of Wall Street," at age thirty-one Martin became the first salaried president of the New York Stock Exchange. In 1951, he was named Fed chairman, a post he held for nineteen years and through five presidencies—those of Truman, Eisenhower, Kennedy, Johnson, and Nixon. He was considered fiercely independent. One time, LBJ invited Martin down to his ranch in Texas and, in an inspired plea for easy money, proceeded to drive the Fed chairman at tremendous speed along unpaved back roads in a Lincoln convertible. Rates didn't drop.

Martin takes the prize for the most concise description ever offered of the Fed: "The Fed's job is to act as chaperone, taking away the punch bowl when the party gets too wild."

He died in 1998 at the age of ninety-one.

Eccles and Martin—though they didn't exactly achieve star status with the public at large, they shone brightly in the Fed's own institutional firmament as men who had paved the way and set the standards. Anyone following in their footsteps was bound to come up lacking. Arthur Burns had a good run (1970–1978), but he could never quite shake the rumors that he had caved in to Nixon during the 1972 election year and provided easy money. G. William Miller was a disaster. Appointed by Carter in 1978, he lasted just seventeen months. Miller seriously botched monetary policy, helping to unleash a round of inflation that peaked at 14 percent in early 1980.

Enter Paul Volcker—a notoriously brusque fly-fishing aficionado who stood 6'7" tall. Volcker was a lifelong Democrat; like Miller, he was appointed by Carter. He was basically charged with cleaning up the mess. As a first step, he slowed the money supply to a trickle. The Fed funds rate shot up to 19 percent in 1981. It had been 6 percent as recently as 1977. Other rates rose in kind. The prime rate—the rate banks charge their most valued customers—hit 21.5 percent in December of 1980, a record.

Volcker's bitter medicine helped push the country into a deep recession during the early 1980s. The unemployment rate rose to 10 percent in 1982, worse than at any point during the mid-1970s recession.

Of course, the Reagan administration screamed bloody murder. Farmers on tractors circled the Eccles Building on Constitution Avenue in angry protest. But Volcker remained unbowed. Basically, he clamped down hard until he had squeezed the inflationary imbalances out of the system. One way of looking at it was this: So little money became available that people had to make careful purchasing decisions, and businesses were forced to become lean and efficient if they hoped to survive.

Volcker succeeded in breaking inflation's back. The consumer price index's annual rate of change fell to 3.2 percent in 1983 and never rose above 5 percent for the duration of his tenure. Of course, few warm fuzzies came in Volcker's direction from farmers or from administration officials. But he did become a hero in certain circles—among bond traders and his colleagues at the Fed, most certainly. Volcker was assumed into the pantheon, taking his place alongside Eccles and Martin. According to one ranking—and there probably is only one—as Fed chairman, Volcker merits a grade of 93, a notch beneath Eccles at 95. Martin receives a 90.

Volcker was up for renomination in 1983. Even at this early juncture, Greenspan's name was bandied about—though never seriously—as a possible replacement.

Volcker continued on as Fed chairman, though he never managed an easy rapport with the Reagan administration. As his second term neared completion in 1987, he indicated that he wasn't interested in being renominated. He pointed to personal health concerns and to the fact that his wife had been living in New York the entire time that he'd been in Washington. By all accounts, Volcker's protestations were something of a dance. A prideful man, Volcker was willing to serve another term, but only with strong backing from Reagan.

Reagan had his own concerns. Volcker was Carter's appointee, not his own, and he'd shown a remarkable capacity for independence. With an election coming up in 1988, there was no guarantee that he wouldn't clamp down on the money supply once again. That could seriously dampen Bush's presidential hopes.

When Volcker and Reagan sat down on June 1, 1987, it was the first time the two had met in person for nearly three years. Volcker handed Reagan a typewritten letter spelling out his intention not to seek reappointment. Reagan made no effort to change Volcker's mind. Instead, he accepted the letter, saying, "I've got a policy that I never try to talk anyone out of leaving government for personal reasons."

Regardless of any conflicting feelings Volcker may have harbored about his decision to step down, his resignation was now a reality. Attention quickly turned to finding a suitable replacement. One possible candidate was John Whitehead, an assistant Treasury secretary who had extensive international experience. But Greenspan soon emerged as the top choice.

Reagan was certainly drawn to the idea. Although a Fed chief's political affiliation isn't supposed to matter, replacing a Democrat with a Republican couldn't hurt. Besides, Greenspan was a known quantity.

"It's not easy to change out a Fed chairman. You have to think very carefully about the impact on the markets," recalls former Treasury secretary James Baker. "Volcker was very highly regarded by the financial markets, as he should have been. Greenspan was probably the only person in the country who could have served as a suitable new Fed chairman."

Apparently, Greenspan had Volcker's blessing as well. "Here was a person who could do the job and do it well," says Wayne Angell, a former Fed governor. "My assumption is that Volcker said, 'You better get Greenspan.'"

12

THE CRASH OF '87

Tall Paul was a tough act to follow. Greenspan—a mere six feet, 180 pounds—took office on August 11, 1987, with much to learn and more to prove. A few days into his new job, Greenspan told a colleague that he felt like a VCR on fast forward. At the rate he was moving, he joked on another occasion, he'd finish out his term in "one year, eight months, and forty-seven minutes."

Parachuting into the top job at the Federal Reserve is preposterously difficult. Greenspan scrambled to make sense of the Fed's awesome capabilities.

One thing that he quickly grew to love was the massive research machine now at his disposal. At Townsend-Greenspan, only a handful of people had been available to assist him. The Fed had hundreds of Ph.D. economists in Washington alone—one of the largest concentrations anywhere in the world—and many more were scattered among the twelve regional banks. Greenspan was able to satisfy his hunger for all types of data: scrap-metal prices, freight-car loadings, and orders for "class-eight trucks"—an especially heavy type of eighteen-wheeler. On his first day at the job, the research staff presented him with an econometric model that looked ahead all the way to 2001. It was the perfect welcome gift for an incoming Fed chairman.

Although hardly one to walk in and shake things up, Greenspan took some initial steps to change the Fed's notoriously rigid culture. For one thing, he loosened up the stingy expense-account policy enforced during the Volcker era. As befits an inflation fighter, Volcker was legendary for his frugality. He wore off-the-rack suits and lived in a sparely furnished $500-a-month Washington apartment. He once reportedly issued a dictum that a group of Fed officials could have either a salad or vegetable with dinner, not both. Greenspan upped the wine budget by $1 a bottle. He also allowed the Fed to have its own flag—the FDIC and State Department had flags, why not the Fed?

On more fundamental issues, however, Greenspan didn't diverge from the established Fed mission of fighting inflation.

He was quick to turn his attention to this issue. Only a few weeks into his tenure, Greenspan began to see mounting signs that the economy was overheating. America was in the fifty-sixth month of an economic expansion. The Dow had recently broken 2,000 for the first time, and, on August 25, 1987, stood at a record 2,747. As often happens late in an expansion, the economy was starting to grow wobbly and imbalanced. Greenspan worried that a new round of inflation was in the offing.

On September 4—just twenty-four days into his term—Greenspan raised the discount rate fifty basis points to 6 percent. Some Fed watchers took this as a very clear indication that Greenspan was proving his mettle, putting the markets on notice that he was prepared to fight inflation as vigorously as Volcker.

Bad economic omens continued to pile up.

A Commerce Department report showed that the U.S. trade deficit stood at a record $15.7 billion for the month of August. Treasury Secretary Baker, meanwhile, engaged in a pitched battle with West Germany over economic policy that was stymieing American imports. None of these events spelled disaster, but they were taken as clues by the hypersensitive markets that U.S. economic policy was halting and confused. The colossal federal budget deficit was another lingering concern and helped drive the yield on thirty-year Treasuries into 10-percent territory for the first time in two years. The yield had stood at 8.8 percent when Greenspan took office.

Fear begets fear: A psychology of dread was starting to grip traders.

The week beginning Monday, October 12, 1987, was a terrible one. The market dropped a cumulative 235 points, erasing $300 billion worth of value from corporate stocks. Friday featured a single-day 108-point drop, ending the week on a sour note. At the closing bell on the floor of the American Stock Exchange, a trader shouted, "It's the end of the world!"

With markets closed for the weekend, traders had forty-eight hours to fret over their losses and nurture their growing concern that Monday could only be worse.

Black Monday—October 19, 1987—came on with the force of a tempest. Even before the opening bell sounded on Wall Street, sharp declines had already been registered in the Tokyo and London markets. Selling pressure washed over the New York exchanges like a tidal wave. The market was in free fall.

Greenspan conducted a midday telephone conference, patching together the Fed governors in Washington and the presidents of the regional banks. He was scheduled to fly to Dallas to deliver a speech before an American Bankers Association convention, his first public address since becoming Fed chairman.

Greenspan felt strongly that he should go to Dallas. His colleagues agreed. Canceling the address might send an unsettling signal to the markets. As a student of economic history, with twenty-plus years in grad school and countless hours debating the topic with Rand's Collective, Greenspan knew the value of appearing blasé in the face of a mounting financial crisis.

When the Panic of 1907 broke, J. P. Morgan had been at a convention of Episcopalians in Richmond, Virginia. He remained there as long as possible, knowing that his early departure would be picked up by the press. A considerable portion of market behavior is driven by human psychology—react too soon and the threat of a crisis can become self fulfilling.

When Greenspan left for Dallas at 1:45 P.M., the Dow was down 200 points. He arrived at 5:45.

"How did the market close?" was Greenspan's very first question for the Fed official who greeted him at the airport.

"Down five-oh-eight."

Greenspan was relieved—for roughly two milliseconds. He realized immediately that he had misunderstood, thinking the market had recovered during his flight to finish down 5.08. The actual number was 508.

Now it was a full-blown crisis.

Although unsettling economic signs had been accumulating for weeks, the actual event came as a shock. As always, the clues took on a weight of inevitability only when viewed in retrospect. "Crashes always come as a surprise," says former Fed governor Robert Heller. "Otherwise, they wouldn't be crashes." As grim testimony, the issue of *Fortune* that graced the stands on October 19, 1987, featured a cover story about the new Fed chairman: "Why Greenspan Is Bullish."

The Dow had plunged 22.6 percent, its worst single-session decline ever. By comparison, the exchange had fallen 11.7 percent on Black Tuesday, October 29, 1929.

The Crash of '87—as it would come to be known—had been a thorough bloodbath. Declining issues outnumbered gainers 50:1. The Amex fell 12.7 percent. The upstart Nasdaq fell 11.4 percent.

The carnage was exacerbated by a practice known as computer-program trading, employed by pension funds and other large institutional investors. As stock prices fell throughout the day, certain trigger points were reached. In response, computers automatically pursued complicated investment strategies meant to protect the institutional investors against further losses. Wave upon wave of program trades overwhelmed the system, adding to the selling frenzy.

Tensions soared. Ashen-faced traders slunk off in steady streams to vomit in the rest rooms. Tempers exploded, and a couple of fistfights broke out in the trading pits. One man was spotted slumped on the floor, glassy-eyed and near catatonic, clutching a handful of useless trading slips. The morbid, the mad, and the merely curious began to converge in the gallery overlooking the New York Stock Exchange floor. A voice came over a loudspeaker to announce: "Please clear the gallery. You will see nothing exceptional."

But by any measure, it was quite a day. At the close of trading, American investors had lost $500 billion on paper, an amount roughly equal to the GNP of France. Warren Buffett lost $347 million; Bill Gates, $255 million. The extended family of Sam Walton, founder of Wal-Mart, was out $1.75 billion. Reportedly, the value of Greenspan's blind-trust portfolio dropped by $200,000.

The moment he arrived at his Dallas hotel room, Greenspan phoned his deputies at the Fed. The question on everyone's mind: Now what? Faced with a market meltdown, the Fed has surprisingly limited power. Although its tools certainly influence the stock market, they have a more direct effect on credit markets.

But Greenspan and company had far larger concerns. The market can fall 208, or 508, or 1,008 points, and it's not a certain disaster.

People simply lose a lot of money, some of it on paper—but the market can always bounce back.

The real trouble starts if the credit markets seize up, if banks stop lending for fear that they won't get their money back. Such behavior can serve to bring on a panic. Lending grows indiscriminate, with credit withheld from risks both bad and good. Failed businesses start to pile up like so much roadkill. This is the process—not stock market crashes per se—that causes economies to slide into the dumper.

The Fed had made precisely this mistake back in 1929. The crash was a disaster, no question. But the lasting damage occurred when the Fed raised interest rates, stanching the flow of credit. Bad decisions by a series of brief-tenured Fed chairmen in the early 1930s—Roy Young, Eugene Meyer, and Eugene Black—helped push a stock-market crash into a full-scale economic depression.

Greenspan and company were well aware of this precedent as they talked things over on the night of Monday, October 19. The discussion centered on whether the Fed should issue a statement, promising to provide needed liquidity to the markets. Some said no, fearing that it might further heighten the crisis. Others said yes, but argued for a long, highly technical document. Greenspan weighed in decisively; he felt that a statement was absolutely necessary. Striking a rare blow for brevity, he also insisted that it should be concise and to the point.

Back in Washington, a crisis team convened in the office of the Fed vice chairman, Manuel Johnson. They monitored the overseas markets all night long, and the results were disconcerting. The Paris bourse fell 6 percent. London fell 12 percent. Tokyo was down 15 percent, its biggest drop in thirty years. It looked as if Tuesday was going to be another bumpy ride in the U.S. markets.

Greenspan went to bed at around 1 A.M. and slept soundly for five hours.

People who dealt with him during this crisis were awestruck—a bit spooked even—by his calm. Here he was, just weeks into his tenure, and the stock market had imploded. Although his reaction seemed odd, it was typical Greenspan. Calm and cautious are his natural states—bolstered in this instance by his age, his experience, and his knowledge of economic history.

A senior Fed official who met with Greenspan in Dallas during the 1987 crisis offers the following observation:

If you've been around for years, as Greenspan had, the issue is how do you absorb information. You don't absorb it with tension. A layperson thinks, "What does this mean to me? Am I going to have to defer my retirement another year?" Greenspan doesn't get rattled in these situations. He was in a watchful mode. He was simply trying to understand the dynamics.

Former Treasury secretary James Baker puts it succinctly: "I just don't think Alan gets nervous."

Faced with a growing crisis, Greenspan did, however, decide to cancel his speech in Dallas. He flew back Tuesday morning aboard a Gulfstream jet provided by the U.S. Air Force.

Also on Tuesday morning, nearly an hour before the markets were set to open, the statement drafted by Greenspan and his confreres went out over the wires: "The Federal Reserve, consistent with its responsibilities as the Nation's central bank, affirmed today its readiness to serve as a source of liquidity to support the economic and financial system."

The Fed was signaling to banks that the pipeline was open and that it was prepared to pump in extra money. In theory, that would increase the amount of loans available to brokerage houses and other businesses that had taken a hit during Monday's 508-point plunge. This would help them stay afloat until the market bounced back.

Promising liquidity is one thing, getting the banks to make loans quite another. That task fell largely to E. Gerald Corrigan, president of the New York Fed at the time of the crash. Among the twelve regional banks, the New York Fed occupies a special position of power. By dint of location, it's ideally suited to take the temperature of Wall Street. In fact, the New York Fed carries out open-market operations from a trading desk on the ninth floor of its building at 33 Liberty Street. Because so many banks have offices in Manhattan, the New York Fed is also in a good position to gauge the mood of the banking community.

Corrigan, a protégé of Volcker, was an experienced crisis manager. He'd cut his teeth on a couple of serious financial shocks: the near collapse of Continental Bank in 1984, and a 1980 attempt to corner the silver market courtesy of the Hunt brothers of Texas. Corrigan gathered several of his most trusted aides in his office and set to work putting out calls to his network of highly placed banking executives. Soon all eight lines on Corrigan's phone were flashing. As Corrigan talked to bank official after bank official, he urged them to keep the credit rolling, but he did so with great care and delicacy.

Corrigan explains:

> There's a real art to this. You never want to be in the position of saying to a bank, "You ought to loan money to such and so securities company." You never do that. Instead, you start out, "This is your credit decision. Let me give you a little perspective about how to go about thinking about the decisions you have to make." It's all in code. Bankers all know the code.

The Fed was delivering a one-two punch. First, it issued a statement about flooding the markets with liquidity. Then, Corrigan followed up with the banks, did a bit of canny arm twisting, made sure they actually made the loans available.

Meanwhile, down in Washington, Greenspan was working on a third front. He huddled with Baker at the Treasury offices. Their topic: how to prevail on Reagan to show more decisive leadership. Following Monday's 508-point drop, Reagan had dismissed reporters' questions with a simple "the underlying economy remains sound." Savvy observers couldn't help noticing the parallels between this statement and comments made by Herbert Hoover following the 1929 crash.

Greenspan and Baker were joined by several other administration officials including Chief of Staff Howard Baker and Beryl Sprinkel, then chairman of the CEA. All present agreed that Reagan could help restore calm in the markets by meeting with Congress to discuss the bloated federal budget.

When the government runs large deficits, inflation is the inevitable byproduct. It was fears of inflation, in fact, that had driven thirty-year Treasury yields above 10 percent. Investors—ever on the lookout for better returns—were lured out of the stock market and into bonds. Undoubtedly, this was a factor contributing to the crash.

Late on Tuesday, Greenspan, the two Bakers, Sprinkel, and the rest met with Reagan in the West Wing sitting room of the White House.

Treasury Secretary Baker led off, proposing to Reagan that he should arrange a budget summit with Congress. Greenspan also weighed in, adopting with the president his firmest and most direct consultant's tone. Going way back—to the Ford administration and before—Greenspan had argued for controlling the federal budget. He'd been a deficit hawk when deficit hawks weren't in vogue. Now he told Reagan that something had to be done about the budget impasse, otherwise the markets might continue to slide.

Reagan agreed to hold a summit with Congress. Following the Tuesday meeting, Reagan held a press conference in which he sounded a less Hooveresque note. He stated that he was "willing to look at whatever proposal" congressional leaders put forth. He also vowed to aggressively seek budget cuts, putting "everything except Social Security on the table." Going forward, neither Reagan nor Congress would make headway on the budget. In the short term, however, Reagan's comments helped buoy the markets.

On Wednesday, the Dow shot up 186 points, registering what was then its largest ever single-day gain. Thursday it was down again, by 77 points. Up, down, up, down, the market continued to yo-yo in the ensuing days. But the crisis was starting to stabilize.

The Fed continued to provide liquidity. Every day, at around 11:30 A.M., the New York Fed's open-market trading desk called primary dealers to either buy or sell securities. This is known as "Fed time." (Nowadays, because of changes to the market for Treasuries, Fed time is closer to 9:30 A.M.) If the Fed calls early, it means something is up—perhaps there's a plan to buy or sell more securities than usual. The Fed repeatedly called early during the days following the crash, sometimes as early as 10 A.M. The orders it placed were huge. During the late 1980s, the Fed would often buy as much as $2 billion worth of securities in a day. Following the crash, its daily purchases were three times that.

All of these carefully considered actions succeeded. The Fed funds rate fell and banks lowered their prime rates in kind. By week's end, for example, Citicorp had dropped its prime rate from 9.25 percent to 9 percent.

Markets remained jittery. Roughly fifty small brokerage houses went under, but no lasting damage was inflicted on the economy. Within just two weeks of Black Monday, things were almost back to normal.

For his handling of the crash, Greenspan received a great deal of credit, mixed with a small measure of criticism. Some cited his early September discount-rate hike as part of the mélange of factors that unsettled the markets in the first place. But mostly, Greenspan received praise for reacting quickly and decisively. By issuing its liquidity statement and backing it up by encouraging banks to lend, the Fed had insured that 1987 did not become another 1929.

"The crisis established Greenspan as a worthy Fed chairman," says Edward Boehne, president of the Philadelphia Fed. "I think this was his real swearing-in."

Greenspan's first days in office weren't given over entirely to crisis control. Despite the market mayhem, he managed to be out and about socially in Washington. While serving in the Ford administration, neither grain robberies nor double-digit inflation nor fear of New York City going under had prevented him from squiring Barbara Walters around town. Similarly, during the nervous days following the crash, Greenspan was to be found in the company of another poised, attractive newswoman. Her name was Andrea Mitchell.

When the two appeared together at a White House state dinner in October 1987, it marked their debut as a Washington couple. But they had actually been dating casually for several years. Both had failed first marriages, and neither was in a hurry to commit in a serious way. In fact, Greenspan had invited a different woman—Susan Mills of the *MacNeil-Lehrer Newshour*—to his swearing-in ceremony.

Mitchell was a veteran reporter at NBC—talented, tough, and highly respected. She had worked her way up through the ranks, first doing a stint covering local politics on radio and TV in Philadelphia, later as a national energy correspondent, covering the Three Mile Island nuclear debacle in 1979. Twenty years Greenspan's junior, Mitchell was a 1967 graduate of the University of Pennsylvania. She had also been an English literature major, placing her far afield from the kind of high-flown mathematics that Greenspan employs in his analysis of the economy.

But like Greenspan, Mitchell had been born in New York City—the Bronx, in her case. She grew up in suburban Westchester County. Her father owned a home-furnishings company that manufactured housewares, and her mother was a school administrator.

Greenspan and Mitchell first met in 1983 while she was working at NBC's Washington bureau, covering the administration's budgetary and economic policies. One of her sources, White House aide David Gergen, suggested that she should talk to one of Reagan's outside economic advisers.

"Why don't you call Alan Greenspan," he said. "He's the smartest person I know on the economy."

At the time, Greenspan was living in New York, running his consulting practice. Mitchell began regularly interviewing him by phone, and he became one of her most trusted sources. Then one day, out of the blue, he asked her out. Mitchell was completely surprised. The two had never met in person, but they'd enjoyed their telephone correspondence. So Mitchell agreed to meet him in December 1984, while she was in New York to tape a segment on the *Today Show*. That became the occasion of their first date.

They had dinner at Le Perigord, a French restaurant near Sutton Place in Manhattan. The two hit it off immediately. "My impression of Alan from the very start was that he was extraordinarily smart and funny and sweet," says Mitchell. "We talked about our childhoods, about music, and about baseball."

It was a lovely, crisp winter's night. After dinner, Greenspan went and picked up his car, and the pair took a drive through Central Park.

From the beginning, Joan Mitchell Blumenthal had an inkling that Andrea Mitchell was better suited for Greenspan than other women he had dated over the years. One evening in 1985, the two couples went out to dinner together. When Mitchell left the table briefly, Blumenthal took the opportunity to render her verdict.

"I probably shouldn't be saying this," she told Greenspan. "It will probably be the kiss of death if I mention it. But she seems like a wonderful person for you."

Still, it wasn't until Greenspan moved to Washington to assume duties as Fed chairman that he and Mitchell began to grow more serious.

In time, the pair found they had plenty in common. Both loved classical music—Greenspan had gone to Juilliard, Mitchell had taken violin lessons growing up. They shared a taste for Mozart, Brahms, and Vivaldi, though they parted ways on Rachmaninoff, a Greenspan favorite. The two became regulars at the Kennedy Center, often using President Reagan's box.

In Mitchell, Greenspan found someone equally rabid about baseball. She grew up rooting for the Yankees of Mickey Mantle vintage. After moving to Washington, she switched her allegiance to the Orioles. Greenspan grew up a Dodgers fan, but like so many New Yorkers, felt abandoned when they moved to LA in 1958, and the Mets became his replacement team. A few years in Washington, a few years with Mitchell, and Greenspan would also become an Orioles fan.

Most of all, Greenspan and Mitchell shared a passion for politics, though they approached it from different sides of the camera. She reported on the topic. He was the topic. Even so, dating Greenspan didn't land Mitchell any scoops. Fed chairmen are legally barred from discussing the most sensitive aspects of economic policy with anyone outside the organization. But the two loved trading observations on the political process in general, and on the inner workings of Washington.

Despite his reputation for soporific congressional testimony, Mitchell found Greenspan to be a fascinating conversationalist. It's a sentiment shared by many other women over the years. "He didn't think in predictable ways," she says. "He was always open to new ideas. That made him innovative as an economist, but also made him a charming dinner companion. He was the most interesting man I'd ever met."

Thus did their relationship begin in earnest as Greenspan cut his teeth as Fed chairman, during one of the most volatile stretches in stock-market history.

Thanks to decisive action by the Fed, the Crash of '87 wound up being mostly a speed bump. No lasting damage was done. The stock market bounced back in a hurry, and things returned to normal in astonishingly short order. So soon into his tenure, Greenspan had met and mastered a very serious challenge. Had he failed to heed the lessons of the Fed's own history, he might have repeated classic mistakes and thrown the economy into a deep recession, or worse. "Greenspan could have gone down in history as an unlucky man like Herbert Hoover," says Paul Samuelson.

Instead, Greenspan was called upon to quickly turn his attention back to fears of an overheating economy. Now that the threat of recession was receding, Greenspan became more worried about inflation. The Fed—as punch-bowl chaperone—always has to weave a delicate balance. If GDP growth slows too much, if it turns negative, then the economy starts to contract and slide into a recession. But too much growth poses threats all its own.

The perils of too much growth may seem odd at first blush. But here's the problem: As economic activity heats up, companies tend to step up their hiring. The pool of available workers shrinks and labor markets tighten. Competition for workers grows fierce and companies start offering outsized pay packages. Workers sense their leverage and begin demanding larger raises. The wage increases get passed along, as companies simply increase the price of their goods and services. Wham! You've got inflation.

High inflation, in turn, makes it difficult to plan for the future. People may hold off on purchases, uncertain about whether it makes more sense to buy that day or a year from then. Companies—worried about the return on their capital outlays—may forgo opening new plants or developing new products. Eventually, business activity slows down and the economy contracts. Bam! You're in a recession.

Basically, the Fed is like a ship that seeks to navigate a narrow pass with the threat of recession on either side. If monetary policy is too tight, the economy slides into a recession. But overlax monetary policy beats a path to the same door. It can spur the economy to grow too fast, leading to inflation followed by recession.

Not long after the crash had been contained, Greenspan began to sense the first distant rumblings of this very process. Because the Fed can't afford to wait for the release of official government economic statistics, he based his analysis very heavily on anecdotal information. Fed chairmen always do. For example, Greenspan received reports from some of the regional Fed presidents that companies in their districts were expanding at a breakneck pace. This served as anecdotal evidence that the economy was starting to overheat.

When the official government statistics were finally released, Greenspan's concerns were borne out. Real gross domestic product growth was 7.2 percent in the fourth quarter of 1987. During good times, GDP growth had often been more like 3 percent. Meanwhile, unemployment was on the way down, spelling a possible tightening in the labor markets. By year's end in 1987, unemployment stood at 5.7 percent, but it would be down around 5 percent within a matter of months.

Greenspan swiveled his stance 180 degrees. By early 1988, the Fed had reverted to a tightening mode. The aim was to navigate a soft landing by steering the economy neatly between the threats posed by too much or too little growth. A soft landing is the Holy Grail of Fed policy. It's also an extremely delicate operation, one that must be conducted with great care, so as not to confuse the markets.

After all, Greenspan had kicked off his tenure with a discount-rate hike, a signal to the markets that he'd be Volcker's equal as an inflation fighter. A few weeks later, he had loosened monetary policy in response to the stock-market crash. Now he was in a tightening mode once again. "Adaptability is Greenspan's hallmark," says David Jones, a veteran Fed watcher and vice chairman at the Wall Street firm Aubrey B. Lanston. "When he realized that the market crash had had little or no effect on the economy, he reversed policy quickly. For a Fed chairman, he has a rare ability to improvise. There's a parallel between that and his stint as a professional musician, I believe."

Greenspan's improvisational skill did not win plaudits from the Reagan administration. Tight monetary policy was exactly what they hoped to avoid during the 1988 election year. Such concerns had in fact helped precipitate the changeover from Volcker to Greenspan. But now tight monetary policy was what they were getting, and from a Republican no less.

Michael Darby, a Treasury official, sent a letter dated January 21, 1988, urging the Fed to speed up the economy. It wasn't received directly by Greenspan, but copies were sent to a number of the Fed's top brass. Darby accompanied his letter with charts showing that growth of the money supply was grinding to a halt. Within the Fed, this was considered an astounding breach of etiquette. The Fed is supposed to be independent, insulated from administration pressures.

During his February 24, 1988, Humphrey-Hawkins testimony, Greenspan complained about the Darby letter.

> When I heard about Dr. Darby's letter I objected quite strongly, and all I can say is, as best as I can judge, he was not aware of the implications of what he was doing. I myself am not particularly concerned that we will be unduly influenced by the administration . . . The only thing I hope does not happen is that concern of our responding to political pressure gets so

extraordinary that we will feel the necessity to do precisely the opposite, and we could very well be taking actions which would be counter to our best judgment.

In other words, Greenspan wasn't likely to allow himself to be influenced by Darby's letter. If anything, the Fed might lean toward actions that were the opposite of the letter's recommendations. Although delivered in code, and rather garbled code at that, Greenspan's statement was nothing short of a veiled threat.

Senator Proxmire immediately responded, "It is both deplorable and counterproductive for the Reagan administration to pressure you as much as they have in recent months."

This, too, was code—Greenspan's old adversary was hardly expressing sympathy. Rather, as a Democratic Senator, nothing could be more unsettling than a Republican Fed chairman in bed with a Republican president. He was simply checking Greenspan, reiterating that he shouldn't cave in to administration pressure.

Welcome to Washington. As Fed chairman, Greenspan was now party to political machinations far more Byzantine than anything he'd encountered during his time at the CEA.

Reagan, for his part, simply denied any knowledge of the offending letter. "I'm going to have to find out what this is all about," he told a reporter during the brouhaha, "because nothing of that kind had been directed to me."

It's possible that Reagan was in earnest, but even so, he had undoubtedly found ways to quietly exert pressure on the Fed. Presidents always do. They rarely snipe at the Fed chairman publicly, but there are other ways of getting the message across.

One way is through the traditional weekly breakfast meeting between the Fed chairman and Treasury secretary. During these sessions, the Treasury secretary has an opportunity to deliver the administration's perspective on economic policy. This is a time-honored way for presidents to make their views known, thereby exerting subtle pressure.

On the whole, Greenspan and Reagan got on fairly well, but their personal relationship was lukewarm at best. Prior to becoming Fed chief, Greenspan had been one of the president's outside advisers. Even as an adviser, the chemistry with Reagan was rather different than with Ford. Ford was extremely detail oriented, having spent years heading up the House Appropriations Committee. Greenspan, too, loves to get lost in an issue, to parse it out from various angles. Reagan tended not to ponder the details, focusing instead on matters of broad ideology. The former actor had a penchant for distilling big ideas—renewal, say—into inspirational catchphrases such as "It is morning in America."

When Reagan appointed Greenspan as Fed chairman, he was well into his second term, with only a year and a half in office remaining. During that time, the two had relatively little direct contact. Among other things, both men shared remoteness as a trait. Greenspan's reserve is far more manifest. But at heart, President Reagan was also surprisingly vague and abstracted. No one who worked with the man ever quite managed to unearth his core. He's so elusive, in fact, that the president's official biographer Edmund Morris resorted to creating a fictional character that interacted with Reagan in order to bring parts of his life, well, to life, in the 1999 national best-seller *Dutch*. Like two magnets with the same valence, Greenspan and Reagan were not inclined to connect.

"I don't think they were all that close," says Bill Seidman. "I spent a lot of time with Greenspan. I don't remember him dropping 'as I was saying to the president' into conversations very often. My impression is that Greenspan was far closer to Clinton than Reagan."

Obviously, Jim Baker, Reagan's Treasury secretary, is in an excellent position to assess their relationship. "He had a high regard for Greenspan," Baker says. "But it wasn't all that close a relationship."

Through the remainder of 1988, the tension intensified and even Vice President Bush got involved. Commenting during a May campaign stop in Maine, he offered "a word of caution" to Greenspan and the Fed: "I wouldn't want to see them step over some [line] that would ratchet down, tighten down on economic growth. So I think there is more room for the economy to grow without unacceptable increases in inflation."

Greenspan shut out the attacks and concentrated on managing a soft landing. On August 9, 1988, he raised rates yet again. This was considered an almost brazen act of independence, coming just days before the Republican National Convention in New Orleans. This latest hike brought the funds rate to 8 percent. In the months ahead, the Fed would keep tightening until the funds rate hit 9.75 percent, 3 percent above where it had been immediately following the crash.

But the administration needn't have worried. The Fed's actions didn't end up dampening Republican electoral prospects. The economy was still chugging along, and many voters fully expected that Bush would keep the Reagan juggernaut on course.

At the New Orleans confab, Bush chose Dan Quayle as his running mate. Andrea Mitchell was first to report the ticket, landing a scoop. Meanwhile, the Democratic nominee was Michael Dukakis, a former Massachusetts governor and onetime talk-show host who had actually interviewed Greenspan about the all-volunteer armed forces. Bush soundly defeated Dukakis in the general election. In fact, he picked up more votes than had Reagan during his decisive 1980 victory.

13

IT'S THE ECONOMY, STUPID

Bush's term in office would be different from Reagan's in almost every way. Where Reagan had presided over a boom, Bush got stuck nursing the inevitable morning-after hangover.

Businesses, banks, and individuals all began to stagger under the weight of massive debts taken on during earlier, more optimistic times. Bush also inherited a gigantic deficit, the legacy of a long line of profligate presidents. His immediate predecessor hadn't helped matters by pursuing a combination of low taxes and massive outlays for defense.

But that was Reagan: He dared to dream that America could have it all, and details be damned. He was a leader foremost, capable of grand gestures. By contrast, Bush—after eight years of apprenticeship—was in a position to do little more than keep the Reagan Revolution going. Bush's most memorable campaign sound bite is telling: "Read my lips. No new taxes." A show of resolve, perhaps, but hardly a statement that inspired devotion from the public.

During the course of Bush's term, the economy was destined to grow increasingly fragile. There were innumerable problems: a worsening trade deficit, factories moving overseas, and the real-estate market heading south.

Any Fed chairman, during any era, would have found it a challenge. Greenspan, for his part, wound up having immense difficulty formulating his monetary policy. It was not his finest hour on the public stage.

He attempted to carefully maneuver the economy, but a series of shocks to the system—a thrift crisis, widespread commercial banking failures, and hostilities in the Persian Gulf—combined to make this goal increasingly difficult. The economy gradually deteriorated, and Greenspan failed to read the signs at some critical junctures. Ultimately, the country slid into recession.

Over the course of the next four years, tensions between Greenspan and Bush would wind up like a watch spring. Immediately following the election, before Bush had even taken office, the two set to sparring.

Greenspan extended an invitation to the administration's transition team to meet and discuss the deficit. Bush declined to take him up on the offer. Shortly afterward, Greenspan stated in congressional testimony that he'd "err more on the side of restrictiveness than stimulus" in monetary policy. "I haven't talked to Alan lately," countered Bush in an interview, "but I don't want to see us move so strongly against the fear of inflation that we impede growth."

Back and forth they went, right from the start. Greenspan and Bush would end up having one of the worst president–Fed chairman relationships ever.

Shock number one was the thrift crisis.

Thrifts—also known as savings and loans—are a specialized type of bank that emerged back in the 1930s to help Americans finance their homes. At the outset, thrifts were extremely conservative institutions that followed what is commonly referred to as the "3-6-3 formula." Bankers who ran thrifts paid 3 percent interest on the deposits they took in, collected 6 percent on money lent out for mortgages, and left at 3:00 P.M. to play golf.

This was a great arrangement until the 1970s and 1980s. As inflation began to spiral, depositors were no longer content to receive a measly 3 percent in interest. In March 1980, Carter signed legislation that allowed thrifts to pay higher rates. Sometimes they offered as much as 18 percent in an effort to lure depositors away from money markets and other types of accounts offered by their competitors in the commercial banking industry.

But the 1980 legislation was a half measure. The thrifts now faced a problem known as maturity mismatch. While they were free to pay higher rates of interest to depositors, they were stuck with huge portfolios of long-term mortgages that paid a 6 percent return.

The obvious solution: Allow thrifts to engage in investments that promised a better return than mortgage lending. In 1982, Reagan signed a bill that essentially deregulated the industry.

Thrifts went wild, investing in junk bonds, bull-sperm banks, even Florida swampland. Such investments had the potential for higher returns but also carried vastly greater risk. The thrift industry—once a backwater for conservative bankers—started to attract all kinds of rogue speculators. Among the most notorious were Charles Keating, president of Lincoln Savings and Loan, and Don Dixon, president of the Vernon Savings and Loan Association.

Keating's thrift—headquartered in Irvine, California—loaded up on junk bonds and shaky real-estate schemes, such as a mall in the middle of the desert. A memo that circulated among his bond salesmen read, in part: "Remember the weak, meek and ignorant are always good targets."

Meanwhile, Dixon grew a sleepy thrift in a small Texas town into a behemoth with $1.7 billion in assets. Along the way, he awarded $40 million worth of bonuses to himself and others in top management. Dixon also used the thrift's own money to buy himself a Rolls Royce, a $2-million beach house, and $36,000 worth of fresh-cut flowers.

Of course, the fun could not last. Around the time Bush became president, thrifts were dropping like flies. The insurance fund that backed them up—the Federal Savings and Loan Insurance Corporation (FSLIC)—had been exhausted.

Congress created a new organization called the Resolution Trust Corporation, charged with cleaning up the mess. The job entailed selling off the assets of dead thrifts. This had to be done with great care. If a thrift had made a dicey investment in a half-built hotel, say, the RTC couldn't simply dump it at a fire-sale price. That might depress values in various local real-estate markets.

Instead, the RTC slowly worked its way through the portfolios of hundreds of insolvent thrifts, selling off speculative investments for the best prices they could fetch. The proceeds went to the depositors, every last one of whom had to be paid off. They were insured, after all. Maintaining confidence in the U.S. financial system was the paramount concern. In fact, Congress deemed that if the RTC couldn't raise enough to make depositors whole, the shortfall would have to be reconciled with taxpayer dollars. Eventually, that's exactly what happened, and it was a highly unpopular decision.

As Fed chairman, Greenspan sat on the advisory board of the RTC, along with Treasury Secretary Nicholas Brady and Jack Kemp, who was secretary of the Department of Housing and Urban Development at the time. The advisory board didn't really get involved in the day-to-day details of cleaning up the thrift industry. It was more a way of making sure that Greenspan and other economic-policy heavyweights stayed in the loop.

"Greenspan wanted to get our views," says Bill Seidman, who served as chairman of the RTC. "This was the most prominent problem of the day. He was very much in favor of getting insolvent institutions out of the system. He was not actively involved in doing it."

Mostly, Greenspan adopted a pose of watchful waiting. The Fed doesn't directly regulate thrifts as it does a portion of commercial banks. Still, there was talk of the Fed stepping in as lender of last resort if matters grew sufficiently dire. The financial crises never grew so ominous that the Fed felt obligated to lend a hand. Nevertheless, the thrift mess did manage to become a public scandal of epic proportions.

The crisis had remarkably long tentacles that stretched from the private sector to the public sector, touching every branch of government—local, state, and national—and stretching across party lines and beyond. Former presidents Carter and Reagan share blame for their deregulatory efforts. Neil Bush—son of George Bush and younger brother of George W. Bush—served as a director of Denver's Silverado S&L, which had to be bailed out at a cost of $1 billion. Drexel Burnham Lambert's Michael Milken sold junk bonds to thrifts such as Lincoln and Silverado. David Stockman, director of the Office of Management and Budget under Reagan, slashed funding for thrift regulation, making the high-risk-investment rampage all the easier. The list goes on and on and on.

Even William Proxmire was not above reproach. Back in 1974, Proxmire helped block an effort by the thrift industry to expand into the adjustable-rate mortgage market. As a populist, he felt that Americans had a right to mortgages fixed at low rates, per the "3-6-3 formula." Of course, adjustable-rate mortgages would have been a minor concession, compared to what came later—bull-sperm banks and the like. But they would have allowed the thrifts to eke out a bit more on their assets.

Greenspan also merits a place in the rogue's gallery. He, too, played a role in precipitating the thrift crisis. The actions in question took place while he was in private practice. Nevertheless, they came back to haunt him when he was Fed chairman, leading to his worst public moment since his notorious "percentage-wise" comment during the Ford administration.

Long a champion of deregulation, Greenspan, while working as a consultant in the mid-1980s, had accepted a consulting job from the white-shoe New York law firm Paul, Weiss, Rifkind, Wharton and Garrison. He was retained on behalf of Charles Keating's Lincoln Savings and Loan to assess whether the thrift was in adequate financial health to invest in real-estate development projects, known in the industry as direct investments.

In a four-page letter to thrift regulators, dated February 13, 1985, Greenspan presented his verdict: "Lincoln's new management, and that of its parent, American Continental Corporation, is seasoned and expert in selecting and making direct investments." He also stated: "[T]he new management effectively restored the association to a vibrant and healthy state, with a strong net worth position, largely through the expert selection of sound and profitable direct investments." His resounding conclusion was that the thrift should be allowed to continue to make such investments.

Of course, Lincoln didn't prove to be exactly "vibrant and healthy." Keating and the rest of his cronies were anything but "seasoned and expert." Greenspan was extremely embarrassed by this episode, in which he effectively gave his blessing to a den of thieves.

"When I first met the people from Lincoln, they struck me as reasonable, sensible people who knew what they were doing," he told the *New York Times:* "Of course, I'm embarrassed by my failure to foresee what eventually transpired. I was wrong about Lincoln. I was wrong about what they would ultimately do and the problems they would ultimately create."

Acting as a consultant, Greenspan offered some very bad advice—and collected a fee rumored at between $30,000 and $40,000. Unlike some others, however, he never faced any kind of criminal inquiry.

The Justice Department launched an investigation of five senators who had allegedly pulled strings to get regulators off Keating's back. The list included John Glenn, the once and future astronaut and Democratic senator from Ohio, who received a $234,000 contribution from Keating. In turn, he arranged a meeting between Keating and House Speaker Jim Wright.

Others in the so-called Keating Five included Senators Alan Cranston (Democrat, California), Donald Riegle (Democrat, Michigan), Dennis DeConcini (Democrat, Arizona), and John McCain (Republican, Arizona). McCain received a $112,000 contribution from Keating. In exchange, he regularly sang the praises of Lincoln S&L, often employing Greenspan's letter to regulators as an exhibit. As the S&L crisis heated up, a McCain spokesperson told the *New York Times:* "Senator McCain has cited the Greenspan study many times as a powerful force in his approach to Lincoln."

Remarkably, the Keating Five got off with little more than a rap on their collective knuckles. When asked whether his contributions had influenced the senators, Keating said, "I certainly hope so." But the special prosecutor Robert Bennett apparently failed to turn up anything substantive on this score. The senators were admonished for "poor judgment," and no further action was taken. By the time of his 2000 bid for the Republican presidential nomination, McCain had managed to repackage himself as a reformer with campaign-finance guidelines as one of his major policy concerns.

Keating was convicted in 1991 on charges of racketeering and fraud. But he spent only a few years in jail, largely because it was later determined that the judge assigned to his case—one Lance Ito—had bungled instructions to jurors. The cost to taxpayers of cleaning up Lincoln Savings and Loan: $3 billion.

Epic is the word for the thrift crisis—epic in its reach and epic in its cost. To this day, no one has a clue as to the actual price tag. Estimates range anywhere from $500 billion to $1 trillion. Basically, it cost a lot of money: Adjusted for inflation, more than Vietnam and at least twice as much as Korea. Although long gone from the headlines, the cost of the cleanup is still being borne. Assign the crisis a mid-range figure of $750 billion, and it means $25 a year for every household in this country until 2030.

Despite the eye-popping numbers, the U.S. economy proved robust enough to absorb the shock. If you picture the U.S. economy as a heavy-weight boxer, the thrift crisis was like a roundhouse right to the jaw. The economy was left woozy, but still standing.

"The S&L thing was nasty, and it had a huge political overlay to it," says Gerald Corrigan. "But I never considered the crisis truly life threatening in the way it would have been if two or three major globally active U.S. financial institutions hit the silk. That would have been a different ball game."

That would be the next challenge facing Greenspan.

Hot on the heels of the thrift crisis came problems in commercial banking—an industry that makes loans to individuals and businesses and one that dwarfs the S&Ls in its size and importance to the U.S. economy. Because the Fed regulates a portion of commercial banks, the fire was in the Fed's own house this time.

As with the thrift debacle, the banks' problems stemmed from overly speculative lending during earlier boom times. The crisis literally rolled from region to region. It started in the mid-1980s with small Midwestern agricultural banks, then hit the oil-producing Southeast, followed by New England, Florida, and then California.

During Bush's first year in office, 206 banks failed. Another 159 failed in 1990. None of these were on the scale of a Citibank or Bank of America, per Corrigan's fears, but some pretty big names went down: Bank of New England, with $21.9 billion in assets, and MCorp, headquartered in Dallas, with $15.7 billion worth of assets. All told, 882 banks went out of business between 1988 and 1992. More banks failed during the banking crisis than at any time since the Great Depression.

As the industry faltered, banks became extremely hesitant about lending. One way to avoid going out of business is to simply not make loans. Banks can instead plow depositors' money into very conservative investments, such as Treasury bills.

Greenspan and the Fed found themselves in a difficult position. Traditionally, the Fed is considered the toughest of the three regulators, far more of a hard case than either the Comptroller of Currency or FDIC.

What's more, strict new lending guidelines had recently been enacted for the banking industry. But now the Fed's examiners were forced to lighten up. They didn't want the banks to make risky loans. That was what got them in trouble in the first place. But they also didn't want the banks to make no loans at all.

In some ways, however, it was all a lost cause. Even when banks made loans available, businesses and consumers weren't exactly in a borrowing mood. They were too busy recovering from debt binges of their own. John LaWare, a former Fed governor, remembers this as an especially challenging time. "Greenspan is a great believer in a financial system based on confidence, what J. P. Morgan would have called 'character.' If you don't have confidence, you become more conservative. Both borrowers and lenders were being much more cautious."

The result was a so-called credit crunch.

In June 1989, as the economy began to show signs of weakness, Greenspan made another of his improvisations, switching from a tightening to easing mode. By June 1990, a series of moves had dropped the funds rate from 10 percent to 8.25 percent. As the economy struggled, Greenspan continued to bring down the funds rate.

But banks didn't respond in kind by lowering their prime rates. Instead, they continued buying T-bills and other conservative investments. A lower funds rate served to simply increase their spreads.

In the months ahead, the Fed would even resort to a rarely used tool, changing its reserve requirements. The amount that banks had to hold in reserve against certain types of deposits was cut by more than 20 percent. The 1990 move was the first change to reserve requirements in seven years. The hope was that new money—$12 billion worth by one estimate—would be freed up for lending. But it didn't work.

Nothing worked. Banks weren't lending and consumers weren't borrowing. Naturally, business activity began slowing down, and the economy started to contract. Soon the United States found itself mired in a recession.

The National Bureau of Economic Research—an organization once headed by Arthur Burns—is the official arbiter of recessions, declaring when they begin and when they end. A popular definition holds that a recession occurs when there are two consecutive quarters of negative GDP growth. Of course, the NBER can't weigh in until considerably after the fact. Retrospectively, it would pinpoint the month of July as the beginning of the 1990–1991 recession.

Greenspan's timing was way off on this one. At the very moment the economy headed south, he suddenly turned cautious about further rate cuts. This was another of his patented abrupt reversals. The Fed had been in an easing mode ever since it had identified the credit crunch. Now Greenspan began worrying that cutting rates too far might ignite inflation. The latest round of government economic statistics—most particularly one showing wages inching up—gave Greenspan and his Fed colleagues pause.

On August 2, 1990, Iraq invaded Kuwait. Over the next few months, oil prices nearly doubled to $40 a barrel. This served to add fuel to the Fed's inflationary fears. The summer of 1990 also featured a typical round of congressional budgetary bickering. Greenspan continued to hold out hope that something might be done about the bloated deficit—and he questioned the value of cutting rates further if headway wasn't made on the issue.

Meanwhile, the economy was sinking fast. Greenspan misread the clues. Or perhaps, as some have suggested, he was simply in denial. During an August 21, 1990, meeting of the FOMC, he stated: "I think there are several things we can stipulate with some degree of certainty, namely that those who argue that we are already in a recession . . . are reasonably certain to be wrong."

Of course, the economy was already in a recession, and had been for nearly a month. It was Greenspan who would be proved wrong.

Throughout the autumn of 1990, Greenspan refused to acknowledge that a recession had begun. At one point, he dubbed the economic situation "more of a rolling readjustment." At another, he referred to a "meaningful downturn in aggregate output." Greenspan was willing to admit that the economy was in bad shape. He just wouldn't use the "R" word.

But a recession, by any other name, still smells as foul. The public's faith in the economy was badly shaken. The Conference Board's consumer confidence index had dropped from 101 in July 1990 to 85 in August, right after Iraq's attack on Kuwait. By January 1991, it stood at 54, the lowest level in ten years. Meanwhile, the misery index—a measure that takes into account a mix of inflation and unemployment—spiked above 10.

There was plenty of misery to go around. Unemployment was pushing 7 percent in the winter of 1990–1991; it had been closer to 5 percent during 1989. Large companies such as AT&T, Digital Equipment, and General Motors started cutting employees loose in droves. All told, there would be nearly a quarter of a million layoffs announced during the recession.

Greenspan soon fell under renewed attack by the administration. In his January 1991 State of the Union speech, Bush was pretty baldfaced: "Interest rates should be lower—now."

The fact was, rates had come down in response to the worsening economic climate. The Fed had settled into a mode that might best be described as "cautious easing." But Bush felt that interest rates had been too high to begin with and needed to fall further and faster. As a president grappling with a recession, such sentiments aren't surprising. But a growing consensus, both inside and outside the government, shared Bush's view that Greenspan had failed to grasp the seriousness of the situation.

An article about Greenspan that ran in *Business Week* at around this time is a case in point. It carried the headline: "Attacking the Recession—with a Peashooter."

The tide was turning against Greenspan. These things occur with lightning speed and, as Fed chairman, managing perceptions is key. He hadn't helped himself by engaging in various semantic somersaults about "rolling readjustments."

Rumors began to circulate that Greenspan would not be renominated when his term ended in July 1991. When it wasn't Bush sniping at the Fed, it was Treasury Secretary Nicholas Brady. He kept up a furious campaign directed at Greenspan and his colleagues.

Congress, too, got in on the action. While testifying before the House Budget Committee on January 22, 1991, Greenspan received a dressing down from New York senator Alphonse D'Amato. D'Amato described the Fed's most recent rate cut as "too little, too late." He added: "No one wants to tell you because you're the big guru . . . People are going to starve out there and you're worried about inflation."

In January 1991, the United States invaded Iraq. Scuds flew, Patriot missiles intercepted them, Stormin' Norman Schwarzkopf talked tough, and Saddam Hussein backed down. It was all over within a matter of weeks, and Bush's approval ratings soared. Rapid resolution of the conflict gave the economy a needed boost.

By March, the recession had ended. It wound up being one of the shortest recessions on record, lasting just eight months. Of course, this wasn't immediately clear; the NBER would still have to study the data and render its official verdict.

But by the spring of 1991, it was clear that the economy was coming out of the doldrums, albeit very slowly. The recession of 1990–1991 had also been remarkably shallow. Inflation hadn't reached double-digits as it had during the mid-1970s recession; unemployment hadn't hit 10 percent as during the early 1980s downturn.

Bush renominated Greenspan in the summer of 1991.

With the Fed chief at his side, the president told reporters at a press conference: "I would not be standing here next to this man if I did not have full confidence in him."

Truth be told, Bush simply couldn't find a suitable alternative. Again, it's hard to change Fed chairmen. Treasury Secretary Brady championed Gerald Corrigan, but Corrigan was a Volcker protégé and a Democrat to boot. It's worth noting that Bush held off making his announcement until July 10, a month before Greenspan's first four-year term was to expire. He was renominated, but he received what was far from a ringing endorsement.

The economy limped along. Shallow recession slowly gave way to shallow recovery. During the fourth quarter of 1991, the economy grew at a rate of 2.5 percent. Better to have an expanding economy than a contracting one. At the same time, Bush faced the 1992 presidential race and worried that the growth rate left very little margin for error. Every time the economy has grown less than 2 percent in an election year, the incumbent party has been tossed out. It happened in 1960, and it happened in 1980.

The Bush camp kicked off 1992 in a state of alarm. Treasury Secretary Brady hammered on 3-percent GDP growth as the minimum acceptable target. Relations between Greenspan and Brady—strained even in the best of times—broke down entirely. The two discontinued their weekly breakfasts. "This was a low point between the Fed and Treasury during modern times," says Fed watcher David Jones. "Brady was very aggressive in his approach to the Fed. The people at the Fed didn't like him personally. He was viewed as a lightweight and an incompetent."

Meanwhile, the Fed was actually doing everything in its power to foster speedier growth. Greenspan may have been late to respond, but when he realized that the economy was flailing, he'd opened the spigots.

"The thing about Greenspan," observes Paul Samuelson, "is that he doesn't stay wrong."

Throughout 1992, the Fed pursued loose monetary policy. By September, the fed funds rate was at 3 percent, a thirty-year low. The Fed had enacted twenty-seven separate easings, going back to 1989 when the rate stood at 9.75 percent. But the economy remained unusually sluggish and seemed virtually immune to the Fed's medicine.

Of course, the administration kept up a steady drumbeat for even easier money—more, faster, looser, lower. It was an election year, and Bush was locked in a battle with Bill Clinton. Clinton wisely chose to make the stagnant economy his central campaign issue. The Cold War was winding down, after all, so foreign policy was no longer a pressing matter. Besides, when it came to the economy, Bush was vulnerable. He had presided over a recession, followed by a very tepid recovery, and then, to further damage his reelection chances, he'd reneged on his pledge to tow the line on taxes.

Reagan had declared, "It is morning in America." The Clinton campaign theme became the caveat: "It's the economy, stupid."

And Clinton was right. It was the economy. Exit George Bush.

Bush placed responsibility for his election loss squarely on Greenspan. And he would continue to blame him. Bush revisited the sore topic during an interview with David Frost that aired on the A&E network on August 25, 1998: "I think that if the interest rates had been lowered more dramatically that I would have been reelected president because the recovery that we were in would have been more visible. I reappointed him, and he disappointed me."

14

IRRATIONAL
EXUBERANCE

If his campaigning style was any indicator, Clinton was going to take a very different approach to economic issues than his predecessors. At one point during the race, he had actually criticized Jimmy Carter for failing to take inflation seriously. This was partly posturing to be sure, an effort to distinguish himself as a so-called New Democrat. But if there's ever a topic guaranteed to warm the cockles of a central banker's heart, it's inflation fighting. Carter had let the inflation genie out of the bottle; Volcker had to stuff it back in.

Then there were Clinton's comments during the campaign's first presidential debate, held on October 11, 1992. The candidate praised the Fed's approach to the economy, saying: "Their policies so far, it seems to me, are pretty sound." This, while Bush was harping away. Ever the charmer, Clinton was busy courting the Fed even before he'd won the election.

Shortly after his victory, Clinton extended an invitation to Greenspan to meet with him at the Governor's Mansion in Little Rock. New Treasury secretary Lloyd Bentsen—he of the celebrated you're-no-Jack-Kennedy quip aimed at Dan Quayle—suggested that the meeting was a first-rate idea. Clinton decided it should be a one-on-one affair and told Al Gore that he wanted to establish a chemistry with Greenspan.

For his part, Greenspan had no qualms about meeting in private with the president-elect. He felt that improved relations with the executive branch could only benefit the Fed. As for any concerns about being co-opted, he had shown himself to be a maddeningly independent chairman during two Republican administrations.

On December 3, 1992, Greenspan flew down to Arkansas, where the two were scheduled to meet for approximately an hour. They started the session off talking about economics and politics—the things you would expect a Fed chairman and president to discuss. But Greenspan was immediately struck by Clinton's grasp of the issues. The topic soon turned to one of Greenspan's gravest concerns, the budget deficit. It had soared in recent years, reaching nearly $300 billion in fiscal 1992. Greenspan explained to the president-elect—as reported by Bob Woodward in his book *The Agenda* and independently confirmed—that the Fed was relatively powerless as long as the deficit remained at record levels. The problem with deficits is that they crowd out other types of investments. The government is literally borrowing money from its citizens, money that they might otherwise choose to invest elsewhere—in the private sector, say.

If the deficit climbs high enough, Greenspan suggested, the Fed's monetary policy ceases to have its desired effect. The reason: Long-term interest rates stop falling in tandem with the short-term rates that the Fed controls. And it's long-term rates—paid by mortgage holders and corporate borrowers—that are most critical to the health of the economy.

In Greenspan's view, this was the key to the economy's current malaise. The funds rate was all the way down to 3 percent; the Fed couldn't go much lower or it would be giving money away. But thanks to towering deficits, long-term rates had a built-in inflation premium. They were hovering several percentage points above their historical levels. Bring down the deficit, urged Greenspan, and long-term rates will follow. Then and only then would the economy pick up momentum.

It was a splendid performance. Greenspan had been waiting a long time to deliver this spiel. He'd offered to meet with Bush's transition team to discuss deficit reduction and had been rebuffed, but Clinton was all ears.

One hour stretched into three.

Greenspan and Clinton really hit it off, in spite of differences between the two that bordered on the absurd. For starters, Greenspan was a Republican, Clinton a Democrat. Greenspan was a native New

Yorker, cautious, reserved, and a member of the Silent Generation; Clinton was an affable back-slapping Southern baby boomer. Greenspan liked Handel, Clinton liked Elvis.

When Greenspan abandoned his dreams of being a professional musician, he pretty much gave up the clarinet and saxophone, except for occasional recitals in the privacy of his own home. Clinton never played professionally, but as president, he'd ham it up every chance he got, wielding his sax at state functions, on MTV, and alongside Kenny G.

While in the White House, Clinton would even make a couple of discreet inquiries about borrowing a saxophone that once belonged to the late Stan Getz, jazz legend, and erstwhile Greenspan jamming partner. "There's no way that man will ever get his lips on my Dad's saxophone," says Beverly McGovern, Getz's daughter, and the executor of his estate.

Greenspan maintained a healthy diet; Clinton favored Big Macs. On and on and on.

But the two did connect in some significant ways. If there was one thing Greenspan valued, it was intelligence. That was the common denominator that connected him to everyone from Ayn Rand to Ted Kennedy. On that score, Greenspan and Clinton were particularly well matched. Both loved statistics, numbers, and minutia. They were policy wonks of the first magnitude. Both were also pragmatists.

Back in Washington, Greenspan briefed his Fed colleagues during a regularly scheduled Monday-morning policy meeting.

"He said he had a great time with Bill Clinton," recalls Susan Phillips, a former Fed governor and dean of George Washington University's School of Business and Public Management. "It turns out they really got on quite well intellectually. Alan likes to engage in banter, to debate."

Phillips adds: "As a general matter, he felt that the conversation showed a respect for the independence of the Fed. The Fed had gotten used to working with the Bush administration. When there's a change in administrations, you're not sure what you're going to get."

The favorable impression Greenspan formed in Little Rock continued to blossom when Clinton arrived in Washington. From the outset, the new president sent signals that he understood the deficit problem and intended to do something about it. Greenspan and Bentsen resumed the traditional weekly Fed-Treasury breakfast. The pair even started playing tennis together. And Bentsen regularly consulted Greenspan about deficit reduction. He would then relay Greenspan's views back to Clinton and to the other members of the new administration's economic team, which included OMB director Leon Panetta, CEA chair Laura D'Andrea Tyson, and Robert Rubin, who headed up the president's National Economic Council.

Rubin had left a job as co-chairman of investment bank Goldman Sachs to join the administration. He was a Democratic stalwart and tireless fund-raiser who had drummed up millions for Clinton, Walter Mondale, and others. He was also a savvy Wall Street insider who understood the interplay among monetary policy, the bond market, and the economy at large. "Rubin tended to be amenable to the Fed's perspective," says Fed watcher William Griggs. "He understood that the administration was more likely to get the kind of economic results it desired through a relationship with the Fed that was cooperative rather than antagonistic."

Greenspan even went as far as providing Clinton's economic team with a deficit-reduction formula. Every $100 billion in deficit reduction would pull down long-term rates by about 1 percent. This proved a useful guideline as Bentsen, Rubin, and the others on Clinton's economic team hammered out the details. They arrived at a target of reducing the deficit by $145 billion in fiscal 1997.

Greenspan, in turn, gave the plan his blessing during testimony before the Senate Budget Committee on January 28, 1993: "I don't find the number that President Clinton has indicated to be off base." He would continue to champion Clinton's plan in his public statements, calling it "credible" and "serious."

But Clinton was an odd hybrid. He thrilled at wading up to his neck in detail, like Greenspan. He was also given to Reaganesque bursts of cockeyed optimism. Clinton grew enamored of the idea of deficit reduction wedded to an oldfangled Keynesian stimulus package to jumpstart the economy. But a stimulus package, by necessity, would raise government spending, adding to the deficit.

This produced a tug-of-war within the administration. On one side was Clinton's economic team, urging fiscal restraint and deficit reduction. On the other was the stimulus set led by Hillary Clinton and Labor Secretary Robert Reich. Clinton stood in the middle, paying heed to both sides. This was quintessential Clinton and set the tone for the remainder of his administration.

Ultimately, Clinton would submit a hybrid plan to Congress, part deficit reduction, part economic stimulus. The 1992 elections had ushered in ninety-two new members of the House, many committed to doing something about the government's budgetary problems. They filibustered the stimulus part of the package to death, but what remained was a credible, serious budget bill.

The bill made little effort to reign in exorbitant government spending but instead tied deficit reduction to a record $241 billion worth of tax increases. The bill provided for $496 billion worth of deficit reduction over five years, or roughly $100 billion a year. The legislation passed, with Gore breaking a 50-50 tie. The first real blow against the deficit had been struck.

On February 15, 1993, Greenspan received another invitation from Clinton. This time, the occasion was the new president's very first State of the Union address, to be delivered two days later.

When Greenspan arrived at the capitol building for the big event, an usher showed him to his seat. He wound up in the balcony, in A6, directly between Hillary Clinton and Tipper Gore. Greenspan was shocked. He had assumed that he would be shunted off somewhere among the pocket-protector set. Instead, he found himself sitting between the nation's First and Second Ladies. Greenspan was literally in the hot seat. Throughout the evening, he was in the crosshairs of network television cameras. Whenever Clinton made a dramatic point—requiring an audience-reaction shot—the camera showed Hillary, Greenspan, and Tipper. In the course of the address, Greenspan was forced to stand roughly two dozen times to applaud various Clinton plans and proposals.

The following day, Greenspan faced an avalanche of criticism. There was a widespread feeling that he had sent an unsettling message about the independence of the Fed, or lack thereof. Many felt that Greenspan had revealed an unseemly thirst for publicity; others thought the Fed chairman was merely naive.

Supreme Court justices often avoid State of the Unions for exactly this reason; Fed chairmen usually skip them, too. On one occasion,

Volcker actually refused to meet Reagan at the White House for fear that there would be cameras present.

"Alan was personally embarrassed," recalls former Fed governor John LaWare. "I think he got blindsided. He was thinking, 'Gee, I'd love to be present for a historic moment.' When he arrived, and was shown where his seat was, he was really dismayed. . . . From Clinton's point of view, it was like saying 'Here's my pal, Alan.' Clinton was communicating, 'Greenspan's my man.'"

The public perception that he was in Clinton's thrall was troubling to Greenspan. As a consequence, the honeymoon between the two was short-lived. One year into the new administration, on January 21, 1994, during a closed-door meeting with Clinton and his top economic advisers, Greenspan indicated that the Fed intended to raise interest rates. Clinton was furious and viewed the move as a betrayal. It seemed as though Greenspan was going back on his word.

At their initial meeting in Little Rock, Greenspan had suggested that deficit reduction would result in lower interest rates. Clinton had known at the time that this didn't constitute any kind of explicit deal. No Fed chairman would ever paint himself into a corner policywise.

Nevertheless, Clinton felt that he'd done his part. A budget bill had passed that promised to hack away at the deficit, knocking down long-term rates per Greenspan's formula. Now the Fed was preparing to raise short-term rates. What's more, it was doing this while inflation was pretty much under control. During 1993, the consumer price index had grown at a rate of just 3.3 percent.

But Greenspan and his colleagues had their reasons. By January 1994, the Fed had left rates unchanged at 3 percent for eighteen months, the longest time in its history. Because the recovery from the recession had been slow and shallow, the Fed kept the rate low. But a 3-percent funds rate provided banks with unusually cheap money by historical standards.

Greenspan was starting to worry that such easy monetary policy might spark a fresh round of inflation. Certain early-warning indicators favored by the Fed were already becoming evident: People were working additional overtime hours, delays in the delivery of industrial parts were increasing, the trucking industry was reporting capacity shortages. All of this hinted that the economy might be revving up faster than was generally realized. To the vast majority, the economy appeared to be in a sluggish recovery mode, but Greenspan worried that it was actually showing the first faint signs of overheating.

Monetary policy works with a time lag, anywhere from three months to two years. Greenspan knew that if he was going to stifle inflation, he'd do well to get a head start. "If you wait to see the eyes of inflation, then it's too late," he once commented.

Thus began Greenspan's preemptive strike on inflation, one of the most controversial of the chairman's many policy prescriptions. Between February 1994 and February 1995, the Fed initiated seven separate tightenings, ratcheting the funds rate from 3 percent up to 6 percent.

There's an impression—widely held and mistaken—that Clinton simply stood by and accepted this change in direction by Greenspan and the Fed. Hardly. The president was livid. He wanted nothing so much as to attack the Fed in public statements, just as Bush had done. But his economic team urged him to hold off. "We had to restrain him," says Alice Rivlin, former director of OMB, and a senior fellow at the Brookings Institution. "It was his economists that said, 'Don't say that, Mr. President.' We certainly suggested that any public discussion of interest rates or Fed policy was not appropriate."

This proved to be wise counsel. Clinton didn't really have to make any statement—he had the benefit of the tide of public opinion. Greenspan had always been seen as an inflation hawk, but now people began to question whether he was an inflation cuckoo. Trying to stave off something that did not even exist yet did not make for popular policy. Radio talk show host Rush Limbaugh—then at the zenith of his popularity and influence—referred to Greenspan's "paranoia with inflation." Meanwhile, countless newspaper and magazine articles criticized him for tilting at imaginary windmills. A *Time* magazine article entitled "Fighting the Right Foe?" questioned whether Greenspan's preoccupation with inflation was stifling the recovery. The article concluded by quoting a famous remark by General Omar Bradley, to the effect that if the Korean War were expanded into China, the United States would be fighting "the wrong war, at the wrong place, at the wrong time, and with the wrong enemy."

That was the general perception about the Fed's preemptive strike against inflation. It was the wrong war, the wrong time, and so on.

Clinton also had the benefit of the hue and cry that went up among congressional Democrats. Here, too, the president was able to sit back and let others do the Fed-baiting. And Congress was also only too happy to fight this battle for him.

When the Fed was originally created in 1913, it was by an act of Congress, a fact that Congress has always been loath to let the Fed forget. Senator Paul Douglas once handed Fed chairman William McChesney Martin a note that read: "The Federal Reserve Board is an agency of Congress." Then he handed Martin a piece of tape, the better to hang the note on his bathroom mirror as a reminder.

Probably the Fed's greatest congressional critic was Wright Patman. Born in a log cabin in 1894, the Texas populist was elected to the House in 1928 and served continuously until his death in 1976, at age eighty-two. Throughout his long career, he complained loudly, harshly, and frequently that the Fed was locked in a conspiracy to choke small businesses and farmers. At every opportunity, he presented new legislative schemes—most of them unsuccessful—designed to reorganize the institution.

The time-honored conflict between Congress and the Fed centers around the issue of accountability. Setting monetary policy is an excruciatingly complex business. Traditionally, the Fed has adhered to the notion that the less that is known about its inner workings the better. That way it's possible to surprise the markets. When Volcker launched his all-out assault on inflation, for example, he announced the decision in an impromptu Saturday press conference.

The Fed has long made a fine art of furtiveness. Until 1994, the interest-rate decisions made at FOMC meetings did not get announced until six weeks afterward, sometimes more. Trained Fed specialists on Wall Street—known as Fed watchers—had to study various measures of the money supply to see if an easing or tightening had occurred.

Fed watchers also developed all kinds of tricks for trying to anticipate interest-rate moves. One of the most common: parsing statements made by Fed officials in search of clues, like a baseball coach trying to steal a rival team's signals. For example, the word "would" was considered a strong declaration; "might" was a weak one. Over the years, Fed watching developed into an extremely specialized discipline.

Even the Eccles Building in Washington—the physical building itself—has a tradition of secrecy. During World War II, the joint chiefs of U.S. and British military convened in the boardroom where the FOMC conducts its discussions. They held thirteen meetings there between December 24, 1941, and January 14, 1942. The reason the venue was chosen: If there was one place in America perceived as secure from wiretaps, intruders, and spies, it was the place where monetary policy was hashed out.

When William Greider, a former assistant managing editor for the *Washington Post*, published a history of the Fed in 1987, it was entitled *Secrets of the Temple*.

But Congress created the Fed, and Congress vested the Fed with its power over monetary policy. Thus, Congress has always tried to keep tabs.

Fed officials are regularly summoned to appear before various commissions and committees. Humphrey-Hawkins testimony—a semiannual rite for Fed chairmen—is actually the result of a 1978 law seeking to foist greater openness on the various government agencies responsible for setting economic policy, especially the Fed. But Fed chairmen have ways of keeping the secrets safely in the temple. The preferred method, of course, is obfuscation. Arthur Burns would literally throw up a smokescreen, meandering with great abandon and puffing on his pipe all the while, until his head was surrounded by a halo of smoke. Volcker favored a similar technique but preferred short stubby cigars.

While serving on the CEA, Greenspan had ample opportunity to practice. But Fed chairman was the big leagues. As a lifelong nonsmoker, he was forced to work doubly hard on verbal pyrotechnics.

Greenspan has proved to be the most bedazzling obfuscator of them all. As he once told Congress: "I know you believe you understand what you think I said, but I am not sure you realize that what you heard is not what I meant."

As Fed chairman, Greenspan was guaranteed some scrapes with Congress. It was built into the job. But the preemptive strike on inflation stepped up the volume to a whole other level. *Highly secretive government agency risks shaky recovery to fight inflation that hasn't even shown up in the statistics*—it was a recipe for conflict. Congress was all over Greenspan and the Fed.

Foremost among the Fed bashers was Henry Gonzalez. As a Democrat and as a populist, Gonzalez picked up where fellow Texan Wright Patman left off. Gonzalez, who served as chairman of the House Banking Committee, would quickly eclipse Proxmire—who retired in

1988—to become the most formidable and vocal congressional critic Greenspan had faced yet.

Gonzalez was born in San Antonio in 1916, a descendant of Basques who had settled in Mexico during the sixteenth century. Growing up, he recited Greek classics with rocks in his mouth in order to improve his elocution. He did stints on the San Antonio City Council and in the Texas state government before being elected to the House of Representatives in 1961.

Gonzalez had large drooping features that lent his face a permanent hangdog expression. As a congressman, he became legendary for his "special orders"—after-hours rants on the floor of the House, broadcast on C-Span, and delivered for the benefit of constituents back home. He also had a fiery temper. Once, in a San Antonio restaurant, he decked a man who suggested that his voting record showed Communist leanings.

On various occasions, Gonzalez called for the impeachment of both Reagan and Bush. Upon Clinton's election, with a Democrat in the White House, Gonzalez turned his attention to Greenspan and the Fed.

He quickly developed a whole list of measures designed to increase Fed accountability, some contained in bills, others simply tossed off as recommendations. He called on the FOMC to release detailed transcripts one week after meetings rather than vague summaries six weeks later, and he suggested that FOMC meetings be videotaped.

While introducing a bill meant to foster greater diversity at the Fed, Gonzalez derided the institution as an "old-boy network." He added: ". . . women and minorities have little or no say in the conduct of our nation's monetary policy and bank regulation." He also complained about the size of the Fed staff's pay increases in 1992. While the inflation rate was 2.9 percent, certain officers received raises in excess of 4 percent. "There is a certain irony about the nation's chief inflation fighters giving themselves raises greater than the rate of inflation," he wrote in an April 1993 letter to President Clinton.

While the Fed pursued its preemptive strike on inflation, Gonzalez maintained maximum pressure. He was joined in his efforts by a number of others, including fellow Democrats Paul Sarbanes of Maryland and Lee Hamilton of Indiana. At every opportunity, Greenspan and the various governors were hauled before Congress to testify.

"Seemed like every time we turned around someone was asking these probing questions," recalls Robert Parry, president of the San Francisco Fed. "This was something that was quite irritating and quite time-consuming."

Parry adds that Greenspan remained surprisingly unruffled. "He's a very consistent person," he says, "not given to swings of emotion. He doesn't seem to be flustered by things. My recollection is that he approached this in a dispassionate way, figuring answering the questions raised by Congress was the most effective way to go."

But Clinton wasn't entirely silent. As president, he had one particularly effective source of leverage over the Fed—the power to make appointments. Presidents nominate and renominate Fed chairmen, and they also fill vacancies on the Fed's Board of Governors. In 1994, Clinton got the chance to name the Fed's vice chairman, the second in command behind Greenspan. This was the first appointment by a Democratic president in fourteen years. Clinton relished the opportunity to appoint someone more ideologically in sync with the administration.

He selected Alan Blinder, a brilliant, outspoken, and unabashedly liberal economics professor from Princeton. Blinder had once written a book entitled *Hard Heads, Soft Hearts: Tough-Minded Economics for a Just Society*. More recently, Blinder had done a stint as a member of the Clinton administration's CEA. He had also been called upon periodically to help Chelsea Clinton with her algebra homework.

Stepping into the Fed's hidebound culture, Blinder found himself embattled from the outset. His first misstep occurred at Jackson Hole, Wyoming, during a retreat that's hosted every August by the Kansas City Fed. Various sessions are held on the state of the economy and potential policy responses. In off-hours, the nation's central bankers ride horseback and eat barbecue.

During 1994's Jackson Hole retreat, Blinder appeared on a panel alongside such prominent international bankers as Hans Tietmeyer, president of Germany's Bundesbank. Blinder indicated that he felt the Fed should make unemployment a priority, alongside inflation. At one point, he stated: "In my view, central banks—or, more generally, macroeconomic policies—do indeed have a role in reducing unemployment as well as reducing inflation."

Blinder's comments were met with gasps of horror from fellow Fed deputies. Never mind that the theme of the session was actually titled "Reducing Unemployment." Never mind that the 1978 Humphrey-Hawkins Bill spells out the Fed's mandate as: "To promote effectively the goals of maximum employment, stable prices and moderate long-term interest rates." Concern about Blinder's comments came down to nuances, points fine enough to stack neatly on the head of a pin. The Fed's old guard perceived something soft in him. As a liberal, an academic, and a Clinton appointee, he was a quintessential outsider. He simply didn't fit into the Greenspan Fed.

It's worth noting that throughout Greenspan's career, he has fostered a collegial environment—provided, of course, there's no argument that he is the one in charge. During his stint on the CEA, two of his colleagues quit in frustration when Greenspan hogged all the glamorous assignments and monopolized access to President Ford. And at the outset of his Fed tenure, Greenspan had considerable tension with Vice Chairman Manuel Johnson. So it was with Blinder. He was talented, ambitious, and a threat to replace Greenspan when his term ended in 1996.

If Clinton showed uncanny instincts in getting elected, Greenspan was no less savvy in managing his own unelected realm. Because of his calm demeanor, people have often mistakenly assumed Greenspan is apolitical. But there's no way to sit atop an organization as fractious as the Fed without engaging in some clashes. In his own quiet, careful way Greenspan has always known how to get what he wants. "Greenspan is an absolutely superb politician," says Bill Seidman.

Greenspan knew exactly how to handle Blinder. He gave him just enough rope. The irrepressible Blinder was happy to oblige. He continued to make comments and continued to irk his colleagues. He even jumped on the Fed-openness bandwagon, stating at one point: "When we take actions, they are not reversible by any other body of government, and I think that gives us a tremendous obligation to explain what we're up to, why we're up to doing it, and why we think it is the right thing." On another occasion, he told the *New York Times:* "My biggest disagreement with my colleagues at the Fed is over openness. I believe we should talk to society more and say what we are doing and why we think it is right. But the position of this institution has always been to be extremely tight-lipped."

Blinder wound up very isolated at the Fed. His office was right next to Greenspan's, yet the two men often went weeks at a time without even speaking.

By the end of 1995, Blinder was back at Princeton.

"Blinder came in a bit naively as vice chairman," says Mickey Levy, the chief economist of Bank of America, who was present at the controversial Jackson Hole session. "The Fed is a pretty conservative body. I'm not sure that Blinder was aware of the structure."

Others think Blinder simply realized that his outspoken reformist instincts made him better suited for academia.

"I can see that a good chair at Princeton bulks up large compared to the best chair at the Federal Reserve," says Paul Samuelson.

Despite a deteriorating relationship with Clinton, Greenspan still wound up getting renominated in early 1996. Clinton became another president in a long line who simply didn't have a choice. Blinder hadn't worked out, and Clinton knew he'd have a tough time bringing another candidate in from outside the Fed. Republicans made up the majority in Congress now. An election loomed in 1996, and they weren't about to let the president select a new Fed chairman without a fight.

"If they send us any name other than Greenspan," said Senator Robert Bennett of Utah, "we just might not act on it."

Clinton's response was to propose a package deal. He decided to tie Greenspan's reappointment to the nomination of a new vice chairman. That way, Clinton could at least replace Blinder with someone to his liking. Clinton's choice was Felix Rohatyn, a senior partner at Lazard Frères and a major force in helping bail out New York City during its 1970s fiscal crisis. Rohatyn's perspective—long-held and widely known—was that government should take an activist approach to economic problems.

Clinton felt a dual nomination could create a balanced ticket. Greenspan was an inflation hawk of the first order. As vice chairman, Rohatyn could pursue policy aimed at growth and job creation. In an election year, Clinton wanted to exert at least some influence over the Fed.

From the start, Clinton's balanced ticket faced insurmountable hurdles. Within the administration, Rubin privately expressed doubts about the ticket; from without, Connie Mack, a Florida Republican and member of the Banking Committee, mounted a vigorous campaign against Rohatyn. Faced with an uphill battle, Rohatyn asked that his name be withdrawn as a nominee. Presently, Clinton had to settle for a less controversial dual ticket. Alice Rivlin, director of OMB, became Clinton's choice.

Now it was the Democrats' turn to gripe. The Senate grants its individual members generous rights of delay. Tom Harkin decided to hold up Greenspan's and Rivlin's nominations until he got what he wanted. His demand: three days of debate over monetary policy.

Harkin hailed from Iowa, a state with widespread agricultural interests. Going back to the first Bank of the United States, farmers have been suspicious of central banks. Harkin framed the Fed's preemptive strike squarely in terms of this centuries-old conflict.

"The Fed today is not concerned about the threat of inflation," he stated, "nor even about the shadow of a threat, but about the reflection of the shadow of the threat. To keep our economy in harness when there is all this potential for growth does us all a disservice."

Harkin managed to delay the two nominations for several months. Finally, the Senate acceded to his demand for three days of monetary debate, but in the end, nothing of consequence was agreed to in the sessions.

On June 20, 1996, Greenspan was confirmed in the Senate for a third term as chairman of the Federal Reserve. The vote was 91 to 7 in favor. Clinton won the presidential election in November, defeating Bob Dole. Thus concluded another contentious chapter in the saga of Fed chiefs versus commanders in chief.

Lost in all the bickering and posturing and hoopla was one key fact: The preemptive strike against inflation actually worked. As an initiative, it was much despised and woefully unpopular, but Greenspan's tough policy prescription did the trick.

Inflation dropped to 2.7 percent in 1996. For the remainder of the decade, the rate would never rise above 3 percent. That compares to an average annual rate of 3.8 percent for the period 1990–1995. Meanwhile, the economy grew at a robust pace. The result was the Fed's dream combination: low inflation and steady, sustainable growth. Viewed through the lens of history, the preemptive strike helped set the stage for the most explosive boom the United States has ever seen.

Greenspan and his colleagues at the Fed would eventually feel vindicated. "My own feeling is that the preemptive strike was one of the most successful pieces of monetary policy in recent Fed history," said J. Alfred Broaddus Jr., president of the Richmond Fed. "It broke inflationary expectations and laid the foundation for great economic performance."

The clashes of the mid-1990s also had another consequence. The Fed, under pressure from Gonzalez and others, made the most significant moves toward openness in its long, dodgy history. In 1993, Greenspan agreed to release detailed transcripts of FOMC meetings with a five-year time lag. In 1994, the Fed agreed to disclose FOMC meeting results on the day they take place, at 2:15 P.M. That meant Fed watchers would never again have to spend six weeks guessing whether the Fed had changed interest rates or not. Between 1993 and 1994, the Fed also doubled the number of women and minorities in its senior ranks.

During the mid-1990s, Greenspan had to contend with a sad event in his personal life. His mother, Rose, died during the summer of 1995, at age ninety-four.

Even well into her eighties, Rose had remained a vibrant woman. She played tennis every morning and did yoga every day. She continued to delight in the piano and would regularly drop by the DeWitt nursing home on 79th Street and Third Avenue in Manhattan to entertain the residents. Her showstoppers were "Getting to Know You" from *The King and I* and "Try to Remember" from the musical *The Fantasticks*. But in 1987, Rose's sister Mary Halpert, Wesley's mother, died. The two sisters had always been very close. After Mary's death, Rose just kind of gave up on life.

By this time, Greenspan was down in Washington, though he called his mother every morning at 7 A.M. On Saturdays, he would often take an early shuttle up to New York to visit her at her apartment at 68th Street and Broadway, near Lincoln Center. Later, he'd swing by the apartment he still maintained at 860 UN Plaza to water his plants. Then he'd catch a return shuttle to Washington, to be back in time for whatever gala event was on his calendar for Saturday evening.

Greenspan—second most powerful man in America—always remained devoted to his mother. "He loved her and I think it was very easy for him to show that," says Joan Mitchell Blumenthal. "It was probably easier for him to show her than anybody else. He would often hug her. I think he was at his most expressive with her. He was deeply grateful for the way she had raised him."

Rose had been the last of seven siblings. Her passing marked the end of an era. A small graveside service was held in northern New Jersey, with mostly family present, along with a few of Greenspan's intimates such as Blumenthal and Andrea Mitchell. Greenspan delivered a eulogy, visibly shaken.

Greenspan's father had also died, but years earlier. The two men never managed any kind of rapprochement. In fact, late in his life the elder Greenspan showed up at Townsend-Greenspan to ask his son for money.

"Alan's dad was smart enough to write a book once," says Wesley Halpert. "So he had something there. But I got the impression that he was always sort of a dreamer, a guy who could never really make it. And the facts seemed to bear that out."

By the mid-1990s, the U.S. economy was truly on an even keel. If the Fed is forever trying to navigate between dangerous shoals, per the ship analogy, then by 1996, the economy had broken into open water and had started to really cruise. Real GDP grew at a heartening 3.7-percent clip. Inflation was low, as was unemployment, and the Dow had climbed into record territory, above 6,000. All was right in the world.

But vigilance is Greenspan's middle name. Strip away the tête-à-têtes with presidents and dates with media divas, and Greenspan remained at his core measured and cautious, a born central banker. He wasn't about to rest easy. Someone once joked that Greenspan's tombstone should read: "I am guardedly optimistic about the next world, but remain cognizant of the downside risk."

So it was during these high times that Greenspan made what will surely go down as his most famous utterance ever. It was a mere two words, buried in an avalanche of highly technical and otherwise befuddling words. But it served to capture people's imagination. For better or worse, those two words were to become for a time Greenspan's catchphrase, his tag line, and his slogan. On the evening of Thursday,

December 5, 1996, Greenspan suggested that investors might be suffering from "irrational exuberance."

The occasion was a reception in Greenspan's honor, held by the American Enterprise Institute for Public Policy Research (AEI), a think tank located in Washington. He was on hand to receive the Francis Boyer Award, an annual honor bestowed on someone who has made notable contributions to American society. Past recipients included Arthur Burns, Gerald Ford, Henry Kissinger, Ronald Reagan, and Paul Volcker. Greenspan's speech, entitled "The Challenge of Central Banking in a Democratic Society," was eighteen pages long and nearly 4,500 words.

His audience was soon nodding from cocktail-hour martinis, growing hungry for dinner, and otherwise fidgeting. "Frankly, it was a long and boring speech about the history of the Fed," recalls James Glassman, a fellow at the AEI and coauthor of the book *Dow 36,000*.

But about halfway through, Greenspan delved into territory that perked people up. He discussed Japan's so-called bubble economy, characterized by an inflated stock market, sky-high real estate, and overextended banks. The bubble burst in 1989, pitching Japan into a deep and intractable recession. Greenspan asked: "But how do we know when irrational exuberance has unduly escalated asset values, which then become subject to unexpected and prolonged contractions as they have in Japan over the past decade?"

Directly addressing the stock market was a highly unusual move for a Fed chairman. The Fed has no direct control over stock prices, or "asset values," as Greenspan termed them. The Fed's bottom-line concern has always been GDP growth—is the economy growing too slow or too fast? Obviously, there's a relationship between the stock market and the economy in general. But the stock market is merely a reflection of the health of the overall economy. It's a fine distinction, but an important one. Historically, the Fed has tended to view the relative levels of the Dow, Nasdaq, and other indexes as components in its bevy of inflation indicators.

Prior to Greenspan's 1996 speech, in fact, Fed chairmen have publicly commented on the stock market per se on only two occasions. In March 1929, Fed chairman Roy Young made some relatively mild statements about the rise in stock speculation. On June 1, 1965,

William McChesney Martin referred to "disquieting similarities between our present prosperity and the fabulous Twenties." At the time, the Dow was flirting with 1,000.

Greenspan's comments were virtually without precedent. They grabbed the attention of his sophisticated and economics-savvy audience. Glassman snapped to and actually jotted the "irrational exuberance" passage in a notebook. "I wrote down the quote, thinking it was pretty interesting," he says.

Herb Stein also took notice. Stein was Glassman's AEI colleague and Greenspan's predecessor as CEA chairman. Stein said, "Good thing the markets are closed."

Soon the buzz was spreading among the 1,000-plus guests in attendance at the Washington Hilton. Greenspan, it seemed, was suggesting that the stock market was overvalued. He appeared to have drawn an analogy between the Japanese bubble economy and the high-flying U.S. stock market. People zeroed in on that single phrase, "irrational exuberance." It was picked up by some of the press in attendance, who rushed to file stories, which then traveled out over the wires.

The impact was instantaneous. The U.S. markets may have been closed, but Greenspan's note of caution reached exchanges on the other side of the world like a bolt out of the blue. Markets in Australia and New Zealand—open for Friday trading—immediately fell. The Nikkei 225—Japan's corollary to the Dow—suffered its biggest loss of the year, falling 3 percent. As happened during the Crash of '87, the sell-off rolled westward, causing exchanges in Germany, France, and England to fall. Presently, it hit the United States. Not long after the opening bell on Friday, the Dow was down 145 points. It bounced back, to finish the day off 55 points, at 6,382.

All in all, Greenspan's words did not have a profound effect on global fortunes. No market anywhere in the world was thrown into a lasting tailspin. But for one man to cause even so much as a small worldwide shudder indicates awesome power. The effect on Greenspan—and how he was viewed by the world—would be lasting. Greenspan the mortal was fast becoming Greenspan the myth—a man who could literally move markets.

Never mind that his "irrational exuberance" comment was actually framed as a question. It was not altogether clear that Greenspan even felt that the stock market was overvalued. As his onetime colleague Susan Phillips said: "Alan likes to engage in banter, to debate." As a master obfuscator, Greenspan had long made a point of avoiding decisive statements. But the simple two-word elegance of "irrational exuberance" was irresistible to the press and public.

Ever afterward, Greenspan would have to be even more vigilant about his comments. Once upon a time, Fed watchers were content to sort decisive "woulds" from tentative "mights." Going forward, every nuance of every sentence Greenspan uttered would be endlessly dissected. The media would build a hall of mirrors to rival Versailles. "If Greenspan said what we think he said, does he mean what we think he means?"

A footnote on the famous "irrational exuberance" comment: If Greenspan did in fact mean what people thought he meant—namely, that the market was overvalued—then that's another black mark on his spotty record as a prognosticator.

Greenspan used remarkably similar language in a March 1959 article in *Fortune*, when he warned of "overexuberance" in the S&P 500. The following year, the S&P returned 43 percent. History also would not vindicate his 1996 statement. The Dow stood around 6,000, and it had a long way yet to climb.

Greenspan may have feared irrational exuberance in the markets, but he wasn't averse to letting a little creep into his personal life.

On April 6, 1997, Greenspan and Andrea Mitchell got married. They had been living together for several years and dating for more than a decade.

Greenspan proposed on Christmas Day in 1996, shortly after a visit with Al Hunt, an editor at the *Wall Street Journal*, Hunt's wife, Judy Woodruff, and their kids. The visit was an annual rite for Greenspan and Mitchell.

"After being with that wonderful family we came back to our place to open some presents," says Mitchell. "He asked me whether I would like a large wedding or a small wedding."

Greenspan had phrased his marriage proposal in a way that left Mitchell with no out—the only choice was the size of the wedding. The very first time he'd asked out wife number one, Joan Mitchell, he hadn't given her the option of saying yes or no but rather made her choose: a movie, a sporting event, or a concert. Nearly half a century had passed, and he was still employing the same tricks.

The wedding was held at the Inn at Little Washington in the heart of Virginia horse country. It was a garden ceremony with ninety-seven guests—a mix of family and the famous. The guest list included: Henry and Nancy Kissinger, Colin and Alma Powell, Senator Daniel Patrick Moynihan, NBC's Tim Russert, and ABC's David Brinkley. Barbara Walters was there, accompanied by Senator John Warner.

Wesley Halpert and Mitchell's sister, Susan Greenstein, were the attendants. Supreme Court Justice Ruth Bader Ginsburg conducted the ceremony. "It was very meaningful for both of us to have her preside," says Mitchell. "She's someone we both admired tremendously. We weren't having a religious service and wanted someone who could bless our wedding and consecrate it in our own fashion."

Mitchell wore a silk dress designed by Oscar de la Renta, while Greenspan wore an old blue suit of indeterminate make. The couple's honeymoon was essentially an addendum to a business trip Greenspan already had planned. He had to be in Basel, Switzerland, for a meeting of central bankers from various nations and tacked on a side trip to Venice, where a Vivaldi concert was a high point for the newlyweds.

Afterward, they settled into domestic life in a Victorian house in the Palisades section of northwest Washington. Mitchell had purchased it in 1976, when she first moved to the city. They had the house renovated, putting special emphasis on building custom shelving for their many books.

As a wedding gift, Mitchell's parents gave the couple a Steinway piano. "Sometimes he'd play it and amuse himself or me," says Mitchell.

But mostly Greenspan worked, morning to midnight, seven days a week. During Greenspan's first year of marriage, he was far busier than most new husbands. He was called upon to stave off a global financial crisis—the Asian Contagion.

On July 2, 1997, the Thai baht collapsed, the trigger point for an international crisis. Within weeks, the contagion had spread through Asia, rocking Malaysia, Indonesia, and the Philippines. Soon major U.S. trading partners—Japan and South Korea—were under siege. Then, with chilling insidiousness, the crisis crept into Russia. On August 17, 1998, Russia unexpectedly defaulted on a portion of its sovereign debt. Global markets worldwide were in a free fall.

Meanwhile, back in Connecticut, the former head of Salomon's bond department and a couple of Nobel laureates made a series of wrong-way bets on international currency movements. In the blink of an eye, their hedge fund was $4 billion under water. Just like that, the crisis had washed up on U.S. shores.

The Fed helped put together a consortium of investors who bought stakes to keep the ailing hedge fund afloat. The Fed also lowered interest rates several times in rapid succession, helping keep the Asian Contagion at bay. There were some uneasy moments, when it seemed as if the crisis would throw the markets into lasting turmoil. It was a tense period, but no other cracks appeared in the U.S. financial system and confidence was soon restored. The crisis was successfully averted.

Greenspan's savvy handling of the Asian Contagion brought together skills accumulated during a half a century as an economist and thirty years on the public stage. During those dire days in 1998, it often appeared inevitable that the crisis would overtake the United States. But it never did. The boom just kept on booming, and for that Greenspan was about to receive considerable acclaim.

15

THE CULT OF GREENSPAN

Question: How many central bankers does it take to screw in a light-bulb?

Answer: One. Greenspan holds the bulb and the world revolves around him.

Greenspan's deft handling of the Asian Contagion turned him into a bona fide celebrity. Years in the future, social historians will look back on the heady days of economic prosperity that immediately followed the crisis as Greenspan's defining moment. The Fed chairman was promoted to iconic status and joined the ranks of Harry Houdini, General Douglas MacArthur, and Madonna.

This was all somehow strangely fitting, given the number of famous people he'd rubbed shoulders with in the course of a lifetime. Ayn Rand had showed an uncanny knack for mining the zeitgeist, always managing to find a huge popular audience for her work. Kissinger was a star during the 1970s, when complicated geopolitical issues occupied the national consciousness.

But it was economic issues that took center stage during the turn of the twentieth century. As a technology revolution swept the nation, millions of Americans jumped into the stock market to get a piece of the action, and Greenspan became a touchstone. Even if it was unclear exactly what the Fed did—or perhaps precisely because of that—he captured the popular imagination. Here was this enigmatic man who seemed to hold the fate of the nation's economy in his hands. As a consequence, Greenspan managed to achieve a level of acclaim never before bestowed on a Fed chairman and probably never to be bestowed again.

Call it the cult of Greenspan.

In the wake of the famous "irrational exuberance" comment, his power to move markets became legendary. Regardless of his intent, the reality was that stocks bobbed and wove on his every word.

Perceived positive comments on February 11, 1999, helped send the Nasdaq soaring to 2,406, up 96 points, at the time its largest single-day gain ever. But what Greenspan giveth, he also taketh away. Two weeks later, he suggested that the economy was "stretched in a number of directions" and that "something will give at one point or another." The Dow dropped 145 to 9,400. The Nasdaq fell 37 to 2,339.

Sometimes, the mere fact that Greenspan said nothing of substance was heartening. His congressional testimony of July 27, 1999, was blessedly free of pithy observations, warnings, or surprises. On the news—or lack of news—the Nasdaq jumped 1 percent.

On at least one occasion, Greenspan actually assigned an aide to follow the markets in real time during his testimony. That way, if a particular speaking point seemed to be having a deleterious effect on stocks, he could change course in midstream.

Greenspan's powers of equivocation continue to inspire awe. "He is a genius for being able to blur the issues," says Milton Friedman. "I listen to his testimony before Congress and I am rapt with admiration for his ability to take all that crap and turn back around and deliver sentences that sound like he's saying something when he's really not."

Mentor Burns had been an exceptional obfuscator, but student Greenspan turned out to be the finest ever. Burns tended to drone on in a tone that was dripping with high seriousness. By contrast, the winking, ironic quality of Greenspan's style has proved winning with Congress and the public. He shows that he is in on the joke. As he said at one point, "I spend a substantial amount of my time endeavoring to fend off questions and worry terribly that I might end up being too clear." On another occasion, he answered a congressman's query by saying, "I'm trying to think of a way to answer that question by putting more words into fewer ideas than I usually do."

Greenspan got a big laugh. People ate it up.

CNBC turned into GNBC—all Greenspan, all the time. The cable network took to providing live coverage even of some of the Fed chairman's minor testimony, with the tag line: "Greenspan Speaks." It also introduced a wildly popular and widely imitated feature called the Briefcase Indicator.

The idea behind the Briefcase Indicator: On days when the FOMC meets, the thickness of Greenspan's briefcase offers a clue as to the direction of interest rates. A thick briefcase means he's been reading voluminously and doing plenty of pondering. A change in rates is probable. A thin briefcase denotes an unclouded mind on the part of the chairman—no rate change likely. According to CNBC, the indicator called interest-rate decisions correctly on nineteen of its first twenty tries. Of course, most of the time the "decision" was simply to leave interest rates untouched.

On days when FOMC meetings are held, CNBC cameramen even took to staking out the path that Greenspan walks to the Eccles Building. Appropriate theme music would accompany his stroll. If he was looking cagey, the producers might cue up the theme from *Mission Impossible*. If he appeared confident, they'd play "Mr. Big Stuff." Back in the studio, CNBC anchors such as Maria Bartiromo made the official call: thick or thin briefcase, rates changed or left alone.

Though obviously tongue-in-cheek, the indicator managed to carve out its own little niche in the monetary-policy guessing game. Was Greenspan aware of the indicator? Was he actually using CNBC to send signals to the markets? "He often walks down the street in full view of the cameras," says CNBC producer Matt Quayle. "This is one of the most powerful men in the world. Why doesn't he just get dropped off at the front door?"

The Internet also began to offer a trove of Greenspanalia. Web sites started to crop up, such as GetExuberant.com: home of the Official Alan Greenspan Fan Club. Visitors can post messages, read a brief tutorial on monetary policy, or follow links to recent news stories on Greenspan.

During 1999, a reporter for TheStreet.com put up a site called the Greenspan Game. It featured a "Fedspeak generator" that created statements even more inscrutable than those uttered by the man himself. Using Greenspan's actual July 1999 Humphrey-Hawkins testimony as a framework, the program randomly inserted choice nonsense phrases. It sliced and diced Greenspan's speech to produce forty different madcap iterations. Here, for example, is the program's mutant version of Greenspan's opening statement: "Thank you for this opportunity to answer my critics, who claim I am making up every word of the Federal Reserve's semiannual report on how I used to beat the living snot out of Bob Rubin at tetherball."

Meanwhile, an artist named Phillip A. Boyd II tried selling limited-edition Greenspan portraits over the web for $75 a pop. The portrait bore the inscription "Rational Exuberance." Boyd—who has done portraits of Abraham Lincoln, Malcolm X, and Babe Ruth—decided it was simply the Fed chairman's time.

Internet chat rooms also started to buzz with talk of Greenspan. On any given day, a search on Deja News was likely to turn up hundreds of thousands of hits, particularly at financial chat rooms.

Here's a message posted August 25, 1999:

I "talked" to mama this morning. Of course, it was a "one sided" conversation, but I talked to her, nevertheless. I don't know why.

Maybe it's because August 4th was the 1 year anniversary of her death. Maybe it's because the 26th is my 13th anniversary, or because September 4th is my 42nd birthday. I don't know why.

Maybe just because.

All I know is I got up early on my day off, stood outside on the porch, looked at mama's (and father's) memorial garden (where their cremains were buried), looked to the sky, and talked.

I didn't say anything special. Not by my standards. I discussed the economy (Alan Greenspan, rising interest rates) versus having purchased my home before the recent trends, work, my sister, and things in general.

The phenomenon soon grew truly global—it is the World Wide Web, after all.

Here's a message posted August 10, 1999: "DIMENTICAVO. . . . Greenspan farà di sicuro la COSA GIUSTA. . . . onde ragion x cui . . . mettiamoci il cuore in pace!!! p.s.: domani esce il Q. report di CISCO SYSTEM (se a qualcuno può interessare. . . .)."

That's Italian. Rough translation: "FORGET ABOUT IT. . . . Greenspan will perform the PROPER ACTION. . . . We must have peace in our hearts!!! P.S.: Tomorrow CISCO SYSTEMS issues its quarterly report (if anyone is interested. . . .)."

Greenspan fever quickly moved from the sublime to the ridiculous.

For more than two decades, Lenny Gilleo had run a barber shop concession in the basement of the Eccles Building. Over the years, he trimmed Burns's abundant tresses and snipped away at Volcker's spare locks. He got a charge out of handing out his custom business cards, which read: "Hairman of the Board. My monetary policy is greatly affected by your growth rate."

But otherwise, nothing doing. He was barber to Fed chairmen—big deal. But when Greenspan followed in the tradition of Burns and Volcker by employing Gilleo as his barber, Gilleo became the subject of a profile in the *Washington Post*.

Then there's the table flap. Since 1977, the FOMC has conducted its business around a twenty-seven-foot-long table fashioned out of Honduran mahogany, with a center section made of black granite. It weighs two tons. Since becoming Fed chairman, Greenspan had always sat at the head of this table. But in November 1998, attendees at one of the Fed's periodic public meetings noticed that he had moved to a spot in the middle.

The hubbub began immediately. What did it mean? Was Greenspan sending a message about increased "collegiality" at the Fed? Turns out the move was for the sake of acoustics. "Given the speed of sound, the advice arrived too late and inadvertently we got behind the curve," joked Greenspan, during a meeting of the Fed's Board of Governors.

A&E Biography selected Greenspan as the "most fascinating person of 1999." Filling in the top ten beneath him were, among others, Cher, Tiger Woods, Ricky Martin, and Yugoslav strongman Slobodan Milosevic.

Greenspan also made a cameo on *The Simpsons*, or at least a suitably dour animated likeness of the Fed chairman appeared on the show. The plot line: Lisa has become president. Bart tries to high-five the Fed chairman, but Greenspan ignores him.

Greenspan, Greenspan, Greenspan—on TV, on the web, on everybody's mind.

Late in 1999, Americans were treated to the spectacle of the leading presidential candidates for the 2000 election falling all over one another to see who could heap the highest praise on Greenspan.

"I am his biggest fan," said Al Gore in a CNBC interview. "I think he's doing a great job. I can't think of anybody who can do a better job."

"He has done a great job managing the monetary side of our economy," said George W. Bush. "The best way to keep inflation in check is to appoint somebody who's got a track record of doing that."

But the prize went to John McCain. During a primary debate, he gushed: "And by the way, I would not only reappoint Alan Greenspan; if he would happen to die, God forbid, I would do like they did in the movie *Weekend at Bernie's*. I would prop him up and put a pair of dark glasses on him."

Clinton beat McCain to the punch. On January 4, 2000, Clinton nominated Greenspan to a fourth term as Fed chairman. Although the two had never managed to recapture the spark of that initial meeting in Little Rock, they were again on comfortable terms, at least. Granted, their conversations had grown less and less frequent over the years, but what was there to talk about? The economy was soaring.

Greenspan's Senate confirmation hearing—a tense scene on previous occasions—was more like a coronation this time around. Phil Gramm, Republican senator from Texas, sent the following valentine Greenspan's way: "If you were forced to narrow down the credit for the golden age that we find ourselves living in, I think there are many people who would be due credit, and there are more who would claim credit. But of those who are in a position of authority, I think your name would have to be at the top of the list."

Long a Greenspan fan, Gramm had attached a rider to a bill a few years back that raised the Fed chairman's salary to $133,800. When Greenspan started in 1987, he was paid $89,500. His salary stood at $141,300 at the beginning of his fourth term.

By the dawn of the new millennium, it was nearly impossible to find anyone in America who wasn't gaga over Greenspan. Democrats and Republicans, Wall Street and Main Street, dogs and cats—all were high on the Fed chairman.

In fact, a survey of the cultural landscape revealed exactly two dissenting parties capable of summoning any real vinegar.

One was Steve Forbes. During a primary-race debate, he made the following pronouncement:

We have a Federal Reserve that is starting to tighten up [and] raise interest rates because of a bogus economic theory that says that prosperity causes inflation. So unlike George [W.] Bush, I'm not sure I'm going to reappoint Alan Greenspan, if he's addicted to that theory. It's a destructive one. It has already done immense harm to agriculture in America. And if he continues in that course of action, it's going to do real harm to the economy.

Forbes would continue to flog this theme while stumping in Iowa—a clear echo of William Jennings Bryan's populist rhetoric of more than a century before.

The other source of anti-Greenspan invective, though diffuse and deep underground, was unreconstructed Objectivists. Ayn Rand's most fervent followers never forgave Greenspan for the heresy of heading up a central bank. Central banks are, after all, agents of big government that meddle in the economy.

Of course, Rand never lived to see Greenspan become a central banker. But she seemed pleased enough with his first foray into government, during the Ford administration. He was one of the few people whom she had not "excommunicated" from her movement by the time she died.

Leonard Peikoff took care of that. The man who had vied with Greenspan for Rand's attention during the 1950s strongly denounced Greenspan on his talk show, heard on ten stations across the country, including KIEV in Los Angeles.

Fellow Objectivists were equally harsh.

"Ayn Rand must be turning in her grave at what Greenspan has become," says Bert Ely, a prominent banking consultant and Rand follower. "To me, the guy is a hypocrite. Central banking is central planning. Here's the great Objectivist, running this organization. Alan Greenspan is a real political prostitute."

Ely even printed up a set of buttons with slogans such as "Who Needs the Fed?" and the sarcastic "Happy Humphrey-Hawkins Day." Like WIN buttons, they're printed in noninflationary duo-tones, yellow and black.

"The story of Greenspan is the story of a gradual surrendering of principles," says Richard Salsman, an economic consultant and Objectivist. "The general view is the guy has sold out. Some people say he's doing the best he can within a fairly ridiculous regime, buying time for us. I think he's become a very political animal. At some point along the line he must have decided he'd rather be known than be right. He must have decided he preferred to be influential."

But so long as Greenspan steered clear of Steve Forbes and stray Objectivists, he could do no wrong. Within Washington social circles, Greenspan was invincible. The man who had made a splash with Barbara Walters during the Ford administration reached the pinnacle of popularity.

"Greenspan is at the top of the ziggurat socially," says Lloyd Grove, a gossip columnist for the *Washington Post*. "If you're talking dinner circuit, he's somebody that everybody in Washington would love to have at their table."

"He's definitely A-list," concurs Kevin Chaffee, social editor for the rival *Washington Times*. "Clearly, the president is always number one. But Greenspan's social rank is elevated up into the stratosphere, more than any previous Fed chairman."

Greenspan had the requisites: powerful friends and invitations to all the right parties.

Over the years, he and Andrea Mitchell had become close to such players as PBS news host Jim Lehrer and his wife, Kate; World Bank president Jim Wolfensohn and his wife, Elaine; and Katherine Graham, retired chairman of the Washington Post Company and one of the doyennes of Washington society. Graham's father, Eugene Meyer, was chairman of the Fed from 1930 to 1933.

Greenspan made an annual tradition of holding a March 6 birthday luncheon with three other people born on the same date—former CIA director William Webster, former House speaker Tom Foley, and Missouri senator Kit Bond.

Another annual tradition: the White House Correspondents' Dinner. Held each spring, it's the event of the Washington social season. Various news agencies invite celebrities such as Barbra Streisand, Warren Beatty, and Sharon Stone. Typically, the attendees are treated to an appearance by the president.

Also on the Greenspan-Mitchell social circuit: Ben Bradlee and Sally Quinn's New Year's Eve party. Bradlee is former editor of the *Post;* Quinn is his wife and a D.C. social fixture. The party is held at the couple's elegant Georgetown home. The guest list is relatively small—only about 100—and it's been the hottest ticket in town on December 31 going back many years.

The Fed also throws its own party, a Fourth of July bash. It's a tradition started by Volcker. Greenspan and other Fed officials rub shoulders with various muckety-mucks in government and the media. The Eccles Building affords a great view of fireworks exploding over the Washington Mall.

The U.S. economy achieved a landmark in February 2000. The expansion reached its 107th month, making it the longest one on record. Real GDP had been growing steadily—at an average annual rate of 3.6 percent—since March 1991. The old record of 106 months spanned the period February 1961 to December 1969.

The expansion was extraordinary by any measure. The Dow grew from 3,000 in March of 1991 to above 10,000 in February 2000. The Nasdaq climbed from 500 to right beneath 5,000 over the same period.

During those 107 months, 5,000 companies had initial public offerings, raising a total of $300 billion dollars. More than 100,000 Americans joined a select group—people with annual salaries in excess of $1 million.

In January 2000, the Conference Board's consumer confidence index hit a record high of 144.7. The previous record of 142.3 had been set in October 1968. The misery index was down around 6, versus 11 during the recession in 1991.

In perhaps the most stunning turn of all, the U.S. budget moved into surplus territory in September 1999 for the first time in thirty years. The deficit had reached a record $290 billion in fiscal 1992. Deficit-cutting initiatives during the Clinton years played a role, but the real credit goes to all those thriving new companies and all those freshly minted millionaires. Their tax dollars swelled the government's coffers, putting a real dent in the deficit.

A good many factors contributed to the record expansion. The end of the Cold War allowed the United States to shift focus from national security to economic growth. Deregulation—initiated by Carter and adopted wholesale by Reagan—helped create a more competitive business environment. The North American Free Trade Agreement—

hatched on Bush's watch and stewarded through by Clinton—increased free trade.

Deregulation, NAFTA, the end of the Cold War—each played a part in creating a positive economic climate. The right conditions were in place so that when the Internet and a host of related technological innovations came onto the scene, they had room to run wild. Top it all off with wise monetary policy on the part of Greenspan and the Fed and the result was a boom to end all booms. Everything just came together.

Greenspan addressed this period of economic grace during a speech cosponsored by the Gerald Ford Museum in Grand Rapids, Michigan, on September 8, 1999: "It is safe to say that we are witnessing this decade, in the United States, history's most compelling demonstration of free peoples operating in free markets."

The comment carried an echo of Burns, an echo of Rand, and is about as close as Alan Greenspan has ever come to declaring victory.

Soon the Fed chairman was back in his typical watchful mode.

Presiding over a long boom is a challenge unto itself. In some ways, it's even more difficult than dealing with a crisis. People come to expect prosperity. They start to take it for granted. It becomes the backdrop of their lives, just part of the scenery. Woe be to the Fed chairman who screws that up.

The winter of 2000 found Greenspan beginning his fourth term as Fed chairman. But he was hardly complacent. "I don't think people realize how hard Alan works," said Mitchell during a March 2000 interview. "He is up and working by 5:30 or 6:00 every single morning, including weekends. People in government are always judged by their last decision. And an amazing amount of data goes into those decisions. With so much at stake, Alan has to really do his homework."

Going forward, Greenspan and the Fed face some major challenges.

The most significant is what priority to assign to the stock market in setting monetary policy. Ever since his famous "irrational exuberance" statement, Greenspan has puzzled over this question. His concerns have centered around the stock market's potential to cause inflation.

The expansion that began in 1991 was different from those that came before. The Roaring Twenties, for example, was a so-called rich man's boom. By the year 2000, however, more than half of all American households owned stocks either directly or in corporate retirement or pension plans.

Many Americans saw their investments climb to dizzying heights. Even if their gains were mostly on paper—a bloated IRA account, say, or galloping Microsoft options—it gave people a feeling of confidence and security. Feeling flush, people naturally began to spend more. Greenspan began to worry that this was increasing the strain on the economy's productive capacity. It's a phenomenon known as the "wealth effect."

Here's how it works: A thirty-five-year-old computer programmer wakes up one morning, checks his 401(k), and realizes that he has $86,000. Technically, that money is earmarked as retirement savings, and he faces tax penalties if he withdraws it early. He decides not to touch it, but just knowing that he has that much money makes him feel wealthier in general. It puts an extra spring in his step, and he decides to buy a new car.

All along the automobile production chain, a little extra work has to be done to accommodate his purchase—by lug-nut manufacturers, seat-belt makers, and showroom service help.

Multiply the computer programmer's decision by several million and you get the wealth effect. According to one study, consumers are likely to spend 3 to 5 percent of newfound wealth. As a result, companies are flooded with extra orders and must hire new people. In a tight labor market, that can be a problem. Now the ingredients for inflation are in place.

How, then, to stop that process? One way is to cool down the stock market, thereby dampening the wealth effect.

During the year 2000, the Nasdaq went through some gut-wrenching gyrations. Greenspan faced some harsh criticism, the first he's received in a while.

On Wall Street, there was a feeling that repeated Fed tightenings, along with a number of Greenspan's recent comments, had been aimed squarely at the stock market. Greenspan countered that he was targeting the effects the booming markets were having on the underlying economy. This struck many as a rather too-fine distinction.

Ultimately, the Fed's control over the stock market is limited, anyway. Interest-rate increases certainly dampen the market, but not with any precision. Hiking rates a quarter point can't be counted on to cause a 5-percent drop in the Nasdaq. About the only other tool the Fed has is talk. Many of Greenspan's public statements were seen as jawboning, an effort to talk the stock market down into more comfortable territory.

But investors can choose to ignore the Fed chairman entirely. As Greenspan's fourth term got underway, they often appeared to be doing exactly that. Of course, if the boom turns into a bubble, the blame lies squarely in the Fed's corner. It's quite a predicament.

Another challenge for the Fed is developing new ways to measure a new economy. The Fed tracks more than 20,000 different indicators. Various measures are constantly coming in and out of vogue. During the credit crunch that preceded the 1990–1991 recession, the Fed looked at an array of data on lending activity. In the mid-1990s, a measurement called P* (pronounced "P star") was all the rage. It was a measure designed to assess whether the money supply was growing in sync with GNP potential.

But some of the most time-honored gauges have broken down. It used to be an article of faith that if unemployment fell beneath 6 percent, the labor market would grow too tight, spurring inflation. This was known among economists as NAIRU, the "nonaccelerating inflation rate of unemployment." But by the late 1990s, unemployment had plummeted through that threshold and had fallen down into the 4-percent range.

Another rule of thumb: GDP growth above 3 percent is too fast, hence inflationary. But during three straight years in the late 1990s, real GDP growth broke the 4-percent barrier.

Despite GDP growth that's too fast and unemployment that's too low—by historical standards—inflation stayed tamed, at between 2 and 2.5 percent throughout the late 1990s. The explanation: Increases in worker productivity—thanks to the computer revolution—have made it possible to pay higher wages without raising prices.

During Greenspan's tenure, the Fed has been unusually flexible about ignoring the old benchmarks and letting the economy roam. But Greenspan has also been fond of pointing out that the old rules still apply. "The laws of supply and demand have not been repealed," he has said on a number of occasions.

Although February 2000 ushered in the longest expansion ever, it was still part of a business cycle. Meaning: The boom will eventually be followed by a bust. What goes up, must come down, unless that inviolable law has somehow been altered.

It won't be until after the cycle has run its course that it will be better understood. "When we look back at the 1990s, from the perspective of say 2010, the nature of the forces currently in train will have presumably become clear," said Greenspan during an address at the Economic Club of New York on January 13, 2000.

At some point, after this business cycle ends, it will be possible to do a postmortem. Then the Fed will have some fresh ways of gauging a new economy. It will be possible to assign a GDP speed limit appropriate to a postindustrial information age. Or perhaps the Fed will identify a new minimum unemployment threshold appropriate to a fluid and dynamic tech-driven economy.

In the meantime, Greenspan has plenty to contend with. He may be the architect of the longest economic expansion in U.S. history, but if it all comes crashing down, that's what people will remember come 2010.

Greenspan's legacy is still a work in progress. Economic conditions can change in an instant: The only constant is constant change.

Bibliography

Anderson, Martin. Revolution. *Harcourt Brace Jovanovich (San Diego), 1988*

Beckner, Steven. Back From the Brink: the Greenspan Years. *John Wiley & Sons (New York), 1996*

Binswanger, Harry. The Ayn Rand Lexicon. *Penguin (New York), 1986*

Branden, Barbara. The Passion of Ayn Rand. *Doubleday (New York), 1986*

Branden, Nathaniel. My Years with Ayn Rand. *Jossey-Bass Publishers (San Francisco), 1999*

Elsner, Harry. The Technocrats. *Syracuse University Press (Syracuse, New York), 1967*

Fredland, J. Eric, Curtis Gilroy, Roger Little and W.S. Sellman. Professionals on the Front Line: Two Decades of the All-Volunteer Force. *Brassey's (Washington, D.C.), 1996*

Friedman, Milton and Rose. Two Lucky People. *University of Chicago Press (Chicago), 1998*

Garment, Leonard. Crazy Rhythm. *Times Books (New York), 1997*

George Washington High School Yearbook, *1943*

Gitler, Ira. Swing to Bop. *Oxford University Press (New York), 1985*

Glassman, James & Kevin Hassett . Dow 36,000. *Times Business (New York), 1999*

Greenspan, Herbert. Recovery Ahead! *H.R. Regan & Co. (New York), 1935*

Greider, William. Secrets of the Temple. *Touchstone (New York), 1987*

Hargrove, Erwin & Samuel Morley. The President and the Council of Economic Advisers: Interviews with CEA Chairmen. *Westview Press, 1984*

Jackson, Kenneth. The Encyclopedia of New York. *Yale University Press (New Haven, Connecticut), 1995*

Jones, David. The Politics of Money: the Fed Under Alan Greenspan. *New York Institute of Finance (New York), 1991*

Kalb, Marvin and Bernard. Kissinger. *Little Brown and Company (Boston), 1974*

Katznelson, Ira. City Trenches. *The University of Chicago Press (Chicago), 1982*

Levy, Peter. Encyclopedia of the Reagan-Bush Years. *Greenwood Press (West-port, Connecticut), 1996*

Lewis, Michael. Liar's Poker. *Penguin Books (New York), 1989*

Lowenstein, Steven. Frankfurt on the Hudson. *Wayne State University Press (Detroit), 1989*

Matusow, Allen. Nixon's Economy. *University Press of Kansas (Lawrence, Kansas), 1998*

Nominations of Philip A. Loomis, Jr. and Alan Greenspan, Hearing Before the Committee on Banking, Housing and Urban Affairs, United States Senate. *U.S. Government Printing Office (Washington), 1974*

Nomination of Alan Greenspan: Hearing Before the Committee on Banking, Housing and Urban Affairs, United States Senate. *U.S. Government Printing Office (Washington), 1987*

Porter, Roger. Presidential Decision Making. *Cambridge University Press (New York), 1980*

Rand, Ayn. The Fountainhead. *Bobbs-Merrill (Indianapolis), 1943*

Rand, Ayn. Atlas Shrugged. *Random House (New York), 1957*

Rand, Ayn. Capitalism: the Unknown Ideal. *Signet (New York), 1967*

Schieber, Sylvester & John Shoven. The Real Deal: the History and Future of Social Security. *Yale University Press (New Haven, Connecticut), 1999*

Sciabarra, Chris Matthew. Ayn Rand: Her Life and Thought. *The Atlas Society*

Schoenebaum, Eleanora. Political Profiles: The Nixon/Ford Years. *Facts on File (New York), 1979*

Sicilia, David & Jeffrey Cruikshank. The Greenspan Effect. *McGraw-Hill (New York), 2000*

Simon, George. The Big Bands. *Macmillan (New York), 1967*

Wells, Wyatt. Economist in an Uncertain World: Arthur F. Burns and the Federal Reserve, 1970–1978. *Columbia University Press (New York), 1994*

Woodward, Bob. The Agenda. *Simon & Schuster (New York), 1994*

Notes

PREFACE

xi   "On July 2, 1997 . . ." WashingtonPost.com (Time Line, Asia's Financial Crisis 1997–1999)

xi   "As the value . . ." Ibid.

xi   "Each had achieved . . . " *Time*, February 15, 1999

xii   "On July 24, 1997 . . ." UKEC.com (Chronology of the Asian Currency Crisis)

xii   "He even went . . . " *Wall Street Journal*, April 26, 1999

xii   "The Philippine peso . . ." WashingtonPost.com (Time Line, Asia's Financial Crisis 1997–1999)

xii   "Indonesia was the . . ." Ibid.

xii   "1,200 people were killed . . . " *Wall Street Journal*, April 26, 1999

xii   "Then bang, bang . . . " *Newsweek*, December 29, 1997

xiii   "At the close . . . " *Time*, November 10, 1997

xiii   "The next morning . . ." Ibid.

xiii   "In November 1997 . . ." WashingtonPost.com (Time Line, Asia's Financial Crisis 1997–1999)

xiii   "When the number . . . " *Newsweek*, December 1, 1997

xiii   "The Fed quietly . . ." Susan Phillips to JM, interview on February 10, 2000

xiv   "Throughout the winter . . ." Edward Boehne to JM, interview on February 25, 2000

xiv   "Fully 40 percent . . . " *Time*, February 15, 1999

xiv   "During testimony before . . . " *Wall Street Journal*, February 25, 1998

xiv   "Greenspan decided to . . . " *Washington Post*, December 22, 1998

xiv   "In May 1998 . . ." Wsws.org "A Warning from Dr. Greenspan"

xiv   "It had also finalized . . . " *New York Times Magazine*, May 31, 1998

xv   "Then, on August 17, 1998 . . . " *The New Yorker*, July 5, 1999

xv   "Russia, as it turned . . ." Alice Rivlin to JM, interview on February 28, 2000

xv   "He remained outwardly . . ." J. Alfred Broaddus to JM, interview on February 25, 2000

xv   "The most conspicuous . . ." Edward Boehne to JM, interview on February 25, 2000

xv   "Such spreads had . . . " *Business Week*, October 12, 1998

xv   "In September 1998 . . . " *USA Today*, October 2, 1998

xvi   "His antics . . ." Michael Lewis, *Liar's Poker*, p. 17

xvi   "In the blink . . ." *Los Angeles Time*s, December 17, 1998

xvi   "Meriwether and Mullins . . ." Peter Bakstansky, New York Fed, to JM, April 21, 2000

xvi   "On September 23, 1998 . . ." Ibid.

xvii   "The Fed initiated . . . " *Washington Post*, December 22, 1998

xvii   "The Fed announced . . . " *New York Times*, October 16, 1998

xvii   "The Fed issued . . . " *Washington Post*, November 18, 1998

xvii   "Meanwhile, Congress pushed . . . " *Wall Street Journal*, April 26, 1999

xvii   "Greenspan saved the . . ." William Griggs to JM, interview on February 23, 2000

CHAPTER 1

1   "The area is so. . . " *Metropolis*, April 1991

1   "The colonization of . . ." Ira Katznelson, *City Trenches*, p. 76

1   "The section came . . ." Steven Lowenstein, *Frankfurt on the Hudson*

1   "Into this thriving . . . " *Who's Who 1999*, p. 1737

1   "His father, Herbert Greenspan . . ." Wesley Halpert to JM, interview on May 10, 2000

2   "Alan's mother, Rose . . ." Wesley Halpert to JM, interview on December 14, 1999

2   "Rose, née Rose . . ." Wesley Halpert to JM, interview on February 16, 2000

2   "When Alan was . . . " *New York Times Magazine*, April 25, 1976

2   "Rose took Alan . . ." Wesley Halpert to JM, interview on December 14, 1999

3   "As a young . . . " *New York Times Magazine*, April 25, 1976

3   "His intellect served . . ." Bill Callejo to JM, interview on November 12, 1999

3   "'Alan was good . . ." Stanford Sanoff to JM, interview on November 10, 1999

3   "At P.S. 169 . . ." Bill Callejo to JM, interview on May 4, 2000

3   "During summers . . ." Stanford Sanoff to JM, interview on November 10, 1999

4   "He even developed . . . " *Business Week*, July 31, 1989

4   "In the summertime . . . " Wesley Halpert to JM, interview on December 14, 1999

4   "When Alan was 9 . . ." Herbert Greenspan, *Recovery Ahead!*

4   "'May this my . . . " *New York Times Magazine*, January 15, 1989

4   "Both the Goldsmiths . . ." Wesley Halpert to JM, interview on December 14, 1999

5   "'Rose was such . . ." Claire Rosen to JM, interview on February 14, 2000

5   "And then there was . . ." Wesley Halpert to JM, interview on February 16, 2000

5   "During the mid–1930s . . ." Bill Callejo to JM, interview on November 12, 1999

6   "He was placed . . ." Leila Kollmar to JM, interview on May 1, 2000

6   "Classroom seating was . . ." Bill Callejo to JM, interview on November 12, 1999

6   "It was during . . ." Leila Kollmar to JM, interview on May 1, 2000

6   "'He had a . . ." Bill Callejo to JM, interview on November 12, 1999

6   ". . . he was a thinker . . ." Stanford Sanoff to JM, interview on November 10, 1999

6   "One way Greenspan . . ." Wesley Halpert to JM, interview on December 14, 1999

7   "In the autumn . . ." Nomination of Alan Greenspan: Hearing Before the Committee on Banking, Housing, and Urban Affairs, United States Senate, July 21, 1987, p.69

7   "It was occupied . . ." Bill Gononsky, GWHS science teacher, to JM, interview on February 22, 2000

7   "Between 1933 and . . . " *Northern California Jewish Bulletin*, January 13, 1988

7   "In 1938, among . . ." Marvin and Bernard Kalb, *Kissinger*, p. 35

7   "By day he . . . " *New York Times*, October 19, 1999

7   "Despite a backbreaking . . ." Marvin and Bernard Kalb, *Kissinger*, p. 37

7   "Among his favorite . . ." Lee Hilton to JM, interview on May 1, 2000

7   "He was president . . ." George Washington High School Yearbook, 1943

7   "George Washington High . . ." Warner Soelling, GW H.S. class of '43, to JM, interview on February 22, 2000

8   "Greenspan played clarinet . . ." Lee Hilton to JM, interview on May 1, 2000

8   "As one might . . ." Stanford Sanoff to JM, interview on April 28, 2000

9   "During his teens . . ." Wesley Halpert to JM, interview on December 14, 1999

9   "Sheiner was a . . ." Ron Naroff to JM, interview on March 27, 2000

10   "Through Sheiner's lessons . . ." Bob Getz to JM, interview on April 18, 2000

10   "He graduated . . ." Walter Scally, GW H.S. class of '43, to JM, interview on May 1, 2000

CHAPTER 2

11   "He was asked . . . " *Institute of Musical Art*, 1942–43 catalog, courtesy Juilliard archives

11   "Greenspan managed to . . ." publicly available portion of school records, courtesy of Juilliard archives

12   "Piano, chorus, music theory . . ." Ibid.

12   "Christmann, a finicky . . ." Christmann's c.v., courtesy Juilliard achives

12   "The school paper . . ." *IMA News* issues covering Greenspan's 1943–44 tenure, courtesy of Juilliard archives

12   "Years later, Christmann . . ." Courtesy of Juilliard archives

12   "According to the . . . " *Institute of Musical Art*, 1942–43 catalog, courtesy Juilliard archives

13   "When Greenspan auditioned . . ." Leonard Garment to JM, interview on September 25, 1999

13   "Jerome offered him. . . " *A&E Biography* "Alan Greenspan," broadcast December 13, 1999

13   "Greenspan accepted, and . . ." publicly available portion of school records, courtesy of Juilliard archives

13   "'Alan was good . . ." Henry Jerome to JM, interview on September 29, 1999

13   "'He was a . . ." Leonard Garment to JM, interview on September 25, 1999

13   "Jerome had begun . . ." Ira Gitler, *Swing to Bop*, p.202

13   "He, too, had . . ." Henry Jerome to JM, interview on September 29, 1999

13   "A New York City . . ." Leonard Garment, *Crazy Rhythm*, p.4

14   "Both Greenspan and . . ." Ibid, p.10

14   "Upon coming to . . ." Ibid, p.20

14   "Henry Jerome's peripatetic . . ." Leonard Garment to JM, interview on September 25, 1999

14   "His orchestra, though . . ." George Simon, *The Big Bands*, p.471

14   "He enjoyed the . . ." Henry Jerome to JM, interview on April 28, 2000

14   "Within the swing . . ." George Simon to JM, interview on September 21, 1999

14   "Middle-aged couples . . ." Leonard Garment to JM, interview on September 25, 1999

14   "In fact, Henry . . ." Ira Gitler, *Swing to Bop*, p. 204

15   "Nice people, hello . . ." Lyrics from album "Hello Nice People," Henry Jerome & His Orchestra, Roulette label, catalog number 25056

15   "Greenspan toured all . . ." Henry Jerome to JM, interview on September 29, 1999

15   ". . . more often, they'd . . ." Henry Jerome interview and Leonard Garment, *Crazy Rhythm*, p.27

15   "They thoroughly enjoyed . . ." Leonard Garment to JM, interview on April 28, 2000

15   "A highlight for . . ." Henry Jerome to JM, interview on April 28, 2000

15   "'It's the old . . ." Henry Jerome to JM, interview on September 29, 1999

16   "Bop, like swing . . ." Ira Gitler, *Swing to Bop*, p. 3

16   "Bop basically upped . . ." Martin Johnson, music critic, to JM, interview on September 21, 1999

16   "For Greenspan, it . . ." Leonard Garment to JM, interview on April 28, 2000

16   "Garment was actually . . ." Leonard Garment to JM, interview on September 25, 1999

16   "'Look what's happening . . ." Henry Jerome to JM, interview on September 29, 1999

17   "Greenspan had joined . . ." Leonard Garment to JM, interview on September 25, 1999

17   "Jerome deep-sixed . . ." Ira Gitler, *Swing to Bop*, p.204

17   "The new band . . ." Leonard Garment, *Crazy Rhythm*, p.37

17   "Another ringer was . . ." Johnny Mandel to JM, interview on October 1, 1999

17   "Circa 1944, bookings . . ." Henry Jerome to JM, interview on September 29, 1999

17   "About the only . . ." Leonard Garment, *Crazy Rhythm*, p.36

17   "The Child's Restaurant . . ." Henry Jerome to JM, interview on September 29, 1999

18   "'Everybody came to . . ." Johnny Mandel to JM, interview on October 1, 1999

18   "Mandel remembers that . . ." Ibid.

18   "'We had to . . ." Leonard Garment to JM, interview on September 25, 1999

18   "During set breaks . . ." Leonard Garment, *Crazy Rhythm*, p.37

18   "'Alan was in . . ." Johnny Mandel to JM, interview on October 1, 1999

18   "Aside from Garment . . ." Leonard Garment to JM, interview on September 25, 1999

19   "The answer, according . . ." Harry Elsner, *The Technocrats* and *American History Illustrated*, March 1983

19   "'He and Greenspan . . ." Jackie Eagle to JM, interview on April 28, 2000

19   "One day in . . ." Bill Callejo to JM, interview on November 12, 1999

20   "The strike had . . ." Don Kennedy, swing music expert and syndicated radio show host, to JM, interview on September 24, 1999

20   "Henry Jerome and His . . ." E.P. DiGiannantonio, expert on V-disks, to JM, interview on September 24, 1999

20   "Greenspan appears, too . . ." Henry Jerome to JM, interview on September 29, 1999

20   "Years later, when . . ." courtesy of Institute of Jazz Studies at Rutgers University

21   "In 1945, Jerome . . ." Henry Jerome to JM, interview on September 29, 1999

21   "Nevertheless, the band . . ." Loren Schoenberg to JM, interview on September 21, 1999

21   "Sax player Larry . . . " *New York Times*, September 25, 1984
21   "Jackie Eagle became . . ." Jackie Eagle to JM, interview on April 28, 2000
21   "As for Jerome . . . " . . . " Henry Jerome to JM, interview on September 29, 1999
22   "Greenspan didn't actually . . ." Jackie Eagle to JM, interview on April 28, 2000
22   "Playing in a . . ." Leonard Garment to JM, interview on September 25, 1999
22   "As Greenspan would . . ." Steven Beckner, *Back from the Brink*, page 11

CHAPTER 3

23   "By contrast, NYU . . ." NYU.edu
23   "But when Greenspan . . ." Kenneth Cohen, NYU class of '48, to JM, interview on September 22, 1999
23   ". . . churned out graduates . . . "Commerce Violet yearbook, 1948
23   "Classes for the School . . ." Robert Kavesh to JM, interview on September 30, 1999
24   "There was Walter . . ." Ibid.
24   "As a consequence . . ." Ibid.
24   "Keynes was cutting-edge . . ." Bizednet.com, biography of Keynes
25   "'I remember Greenspan . . ." Robert Kavesh to JM, interview on September 30, 1999
25   "'Greenspan really wasn't . . ." Betty Schwimmer to JM, interview on September 24, 1999
26   "Another of Greenspan's . . ." Ernest Kurnow to JM, interview on October 11, 1999
26   ". . . notoriously poor lecturer . . ." source to JM, on background
26   "Moore's future inflation . . ." Geoffrey Moore to JM, in response to written query, courtesy of his colleague Anirvan Banerji
26   "One of the textbooks . . ." Ibid.
26   "Mitchell was one . . ." Wyatt Wells, *Economist in an Uncertain World*, p.2
26   "He had an . . ." Ernest Kurnow to JM, interview on October 11, 1999
26   "'Greenspan was a . . ." Commerce Violet yearbook, 1948
27   "Greenspan was also . . ." Commerce Violet yearbook, 1947
27   ". . . got a mention . . ." *The International Economy,* January/February 2000
27   ". . . managed straight A's . . . " *New York Times Magazine*, January 15, 1989
27   "Wesley Mitchell and . . ." Milton Friedman to JM, interview on October 11, 1999
27   "His book, *Business* . . ." Milton and Rose Friedman, *Two Lucky People*, p.68
27   "In 1920, Mitchell . . ." Wyatt Wells, *Economist in an Uncertain World*, p.2

27   "The simple fact . . ." Ibid. p.4

28   "After earning his . . ." Ibid. p.6

28   "Later, Burns returned . . ." Ibid. p.5

28   "Burns and his mentor . . ." Ibid. p. 7

28   "Burns was one . . ." Wyatt Wells to JM, interview on October 20, 1999

28   "The way in . . ." Milton and Rose Friedman, *Two Lucky People*, p.233

28   "That Burns and Keynes . . ." Wyatt Wells to JM, interview on October 20, 1999

29   "At Columbia, Greenspan . . ." Judith Mackey to JM, interview on January 28, 2000

29   "Accuracy and precision . . ." Milton Friedman to JM, interview on October 11, 1999

29   "The rap on Burns . . ." Robert Lipsey, National Bureau of Economic Research, to JM, interview on October 25, 1999

30   "He could be . . ." Milton Friedman to JM, interview on October 11, 1999

30   "'Burns clearly had . . ." Judith Mackey to JM, interview on January 28, 2000

30   "In 1952, he . . ." Joan Mitchell Blumenthal to JM, interview on November 8, 1999

31   "Mitchell agreed to . . ." Joan Mitchell Blumental to JM, interview on May 15, 2000

31   "'He was an interesting . . ." Joan Mitchell Blumenthal to JM, interview on November 8, 1999

31   "There had been . . ." Wesley Halpert to JM, interview on December 14, 1999

31   "He finally wound . . ." Joan Mitchell Blumental to JM, interview on May 15, 2000

31   "The young couple . . ." Joan Mitchell Blumenthal to JM, interview on November 8, 1999

31   "So Greenspan went . . ." Nominations of Philip A. Loomis, Jr. and Alan Greenspan, Hearing Before the Committee on Banking, Housing and Urban Affairs, United States Senate, August 8, 1974, p.54

32   "Greenspan earned a . . ." *Worth*, May 1995

32   "The Conference Board . . ." Conference Board publication entitled, *In the Beginning. . .*

32   "Greenspan thoroughly enjoyed . . ." Joan Mitchell Blumenthal to JM, interview on November 8, 1999

32   "His job involved . . ." M. Kathryn Eickhoff to JM, interview on December 28, 1999

32   "He borrowed countless . . ." Randy Poe, the Conference Board's communications director, to JM, interview on September 29, 1999

32   ". . . close to Al Sommers . . ." Lucie Blau, the Conference Board, interview on September 29, 1999

32   "Sommers was liberal-leaning . . . " *Across the Board*, April 1994

33   "... legendary Sandy Parker ..." M. Kathryn Eickhoff to JM, interview on December 28, 1999

33   "He introduced a... " *Fortune*, April 7, 1980

33   "Parker took to ... " *Fortune*, February 9, 1981

33   "'Parker had a ..." M. Kathryn Eickhoff to JM, interview on December 28, 1999

33   "While Greenspan was immersed ..." Joan Mitchell Blumenthal to JM, interview on November 8, 1999

33   "During this time. . . " Ibid.

CHAPTER 4

36   "... Alisa Zinovievna Rosenbaum ..." courtesy of Jeff Britting, archivist, Ayn Rand Institute

36   "As a young child ..." Barbara Branden, *The Passion of Ayn Rand*, p.6

36   "Upon entering school ..." Chris Matthew Sciabarra, *Ayn Rand: Her Life and Thought*, p.6

36   "Her mother introduced ..." Ibid. p.7

36   "One entry read ..." Barbara Branden, *The Passion of Ayn Rand*, p.35

36   "Zinovy Rosenbaum's pharmacy ..." Chris Matthew Sciabarra, *Ayn Rand: Her Life and Thought*, p.8

36   "One time, Alisa ..." Barbara Branden, *The Passion of Ayn Rand*, p.44

36   "Whenever she planned ..." Ibid. p.50

37   "In 1921, Alisa ..." courtesy of Jeff Britting, archivist, Ayn Rand Institute

37   "Two years later ..." Barbara Branden, *The Passion of Ayn Rand*, p.50

37   "'I knew it ... " *Saturday Evening Post*, November 11, 1961

37   "In 1925, she ..." Barbara Branden, *The Passion of Ayn Rand*, p.59

37   "... Alisa changed her first ..." courtesy of Jeff Britting, archivist, Ayn Rand Institute

37   "The 'Rand' was ..." Nathaniel Branden to JM, interview on May 19, 2000

37   "She drove her ..." Barbara Branden, *The Passion of Ayn Rand*, p. 70

37   "Rand's cousin, Sarah ..." courtesy of Jeff Britting, archivist, Ayn Rand Institute

37   "She lived in ..." Barbara Branden, *The Passion of Ayn Rand*, p. 74

37   "Rand found work ..." courtesy of Jeff Britting, archivist, Ayn Rand Institute

37   "She proceded to ..." Barbara Branden, *The Passion of Ayn Rand*, p. 105

38   "Universal expressed interest ..." Ibid. p.107

38   "During the same ..." Chris Matthew Sciabarra, *Ayn Rand: Her Life and Thought*, p.9

38   "But Al Woods ..." Barbara Branden, *The Passion of Ayn Rand*, p. 121

38   "It became a ..." Ibid. p.124

38   "Rand made just ..." Ibid. p.127

38	"At the height . . ." Ibid. p.125
38	"Rand submitted the . . ." AynRand.com
38	"Ultimately, she found . . ." Barbara Branden, *The Passion of Ayn Rand*, p. 170–71
38	"Among the book's . . . " *Life*, April 7, 1967
38	"Blumenthal had been . . . " *Saturday Evening Post*, November 11, 1961
39	"'Nathan was the . . ." Ibid.
39	"Soon Blumenthal and . . ." Barbara Branden to JM, interview on October 12, 1999
39	"Another name change . . ." Nathaniel Branden to JM, interview on May 19, 2000
39	"It now numbered . . ." Barbara Branden, *The Passion of Ayn Rand*, p. 254
39	"He had enjoyed . . ." Joan Mitchell Blumenthal to JM, interview on November 8, 1999
39	". . . very somber young . . ." Nathaniel Branden, *My Years with Ayn Rand*, p.113
39	"It was through . . ." Joan Mitchell Blumenthal to JM, interview on November 8, 1999
39	"Over several months . . ." Nathaniel Branden to JM, interview on October 18, 1999
40	"He'd already been . . ." Ibid.
40	"'I think that . . ." Ibid.
40	"Rand would periodically . . ." Nathaniel Branden, *My Years with Ayn Rand*, p.113
40	"'I thought Greenspan . . ." Nathaniel Branden to JM, interview on October 18, 1999
41	"A few years hence . . ." Barbara Branden, *The Passion of Ayn Rand*, p. 255
41	"The Collective met . . ." Fred Cookinham, Ayn Rand walking tour guide, to JM, October 22, 1999
41	"It was a . . ." Robert Hessen to JM, interview on October 29, 1999
41	". . . a self-professed . . ." Ayn Rand, *Capitalism: the Unknown Ideal*, p. vii
42	"A frequent topic . . ." Nathaniel Branden, *My Years with Ayn Rand*, p.160
42	"They forswear logic . . ." Harry Binwanger, *The Ayn Rand Lexicon*, p.531
42	"Or she might . . . " *Saturday Evening Post*, November 11, 1961
43	"'Alan became wildly . . ." Nathaniel Branden to JM, interview on October 18, 1999
43	"What sticks with . . ." Barbara Branden to JM, interview on October 12, 1999
43	"Near the end . . ." courtesy of Jeff Britting, archivist, Ayn Rand Institute
43	"Rand had extremely . . ." Ibid.
43	"'Alan loves Mozart . . ." Barbara Branden to JM, interview on October 12, 1999
43	"She also appreciated . . ." Jeff Walker, *The Ayn Rand Cult*, p.204
44	"In fact, she . . ." Kathryn Eickhoff to JM, interview on December 29, 1999

44	"Ultimately, Greenspan was . . ." Nathaniel Branden, *My Years with Ayn Rand*, p.159
44	"As for Rand's . . . " *The Passion of Ayn Rand*, Showtime movie
44	"One thing is . . ." Robert Hessen to JM, interview on October 29, 1999
45	"Being party to . . ." Robert Kavesh to JM, interview on September 30, 1999
45	"Published in 1957 . . ." Barbara Branden, *The Passion of Ayn Rand*, p. 218
45	"'Alan was just . . ." Barbara Branden to JM, interview on October 12, 1999
46	"Her editor at . . ." Barbara Branden, *The Passion of Ayn Rand*, p. 292
46	"So *Atlas Shrugged* . . . " *Saturday Evening Post*, November 11, 1961
46	"The reviews were . . ." Ibid.
46	"Not in any . . . " *New York Times*, October 13, 1957
46	"The Collective rallied . . ." Barbara Branden to JM, interview on October 12, 1999
47	"To the Editor . . . " *New York Times*, November 3, 1957
47	"In 1958, he . . ." Nathaniel Branden, *My Years with Ayn Rand*, p.205
47	"Branden kicked off . . ." Barbara Branden, *The Passion of Ayn Rand*, p. 306
47	"The series was . . ." Jerome Tuccille, *It Usually Begins with Ayn Rand*, p.10–11
47	". . . The Destructiveness of . . . " *Saturday Evening Post*, November 11, 1961
47	". . . Why Human Beings . . ." Nathaniel Branden, *My Years with Ayn Rand*, p.253
47	"He worked up . . ." R.W. Bradford, editor of *Liberty* magazine, to JM, interview on October 20, 1999
48	"'I remember he . . ." Barbara Branden to JM, interview on October 12, 1999
48	"John Hospers was . . . "John Hospers to JM, interview on October 12, 1999
48	". . . NBI created audiotaped . . ." Chris Matthew Sciabarra, *Ayn Rand: Her Life and Thought*, p.18
48	"By 1965, audiotaped . . ." Barbara Branden, *The Passion of Ayn Rand*, p. 313
48	"In 1967, the NBI . . ." *Lingua Franca*, September 1999
48	"Rand and Branden next . . ." Nathaniel Branden, *My Years with Ayn Rand*, p.255
48	"In one essay . . ." Ayn Rand, *Capitalism: the Unknown Ideal*, p.63
48	". . . in another he . . ." Ibid. p.118
49	"Probably his most . . ." Ibid. p.96–101
49	"*Playboy* made her . . ." Barbara Branden, *The Passion of Ayn Rand*, p. 319
49	"Of all things . . ." Ibid. p.325
49	"Her standard outfit . . . " *Time*, February 29, 1960
49	"These were favorite . . ." Kathryn Eickhoff to JM, interview on December 29, 1999
49	"The Collective also . . ." Ibid.

50   "Eugene Schwartz, a fellow . . ." quote taken from Eugene Schwartz letter to JM, dated May 3, 2000

50   "Rand was becoming . . ." Barbara Branden to JM, interview on October 12, 1999

50   "A couple of new . . ." Barbara Branden, *The Passion of Ayn Rand*, p. 269, p.275

50   "Greenspan managed to . . ." Nathaniel Branden to JM, interview on October 18, 1999

50   "'Alan distanced himself . . ." Barbara Branden to JM, interview on October 12, 1999

50   "She did so . . . " *The Objectivist*, May 1968

51   "We the undersigned . . . " Ibid.

51   "In later years . . ." Barbara Branden to JM, interview on October 12, 1999

51   "Hundreds of calls . . ." Barbara Branden, *The Passion of Ayn Rand*, p. 350

51   "'And almost no one . . ." Barbara Branden to JM, interview on October 12, 1999

51   "'Peikoff sided with . . ." Barbara Branden, *The Passion of Ayn Rand*, p. 352

51   "'Nathaniel Branden and . . ." Joan Mitchell Blumental to JM, interview on May 15, 2000

52   "Rand's vituperative attacks . . ." Barbara Branden, *The Passion of Ayn Rand*, p. 385

52   "Frank O'Connor, Rand's . . . " *The Passion of Ayn Rand*, Showtime movie

52   "Leonard Peikoff hung . . ." R.W. Bradford to JM, interview on October 20, 1999

52   "Greenspan also never . . ." Barbara Branden to JM, interview on October 12, 1999

CHAPTER 5

53   "He got started . . ." Judith Mackey to JM, interview on January 28, 2000

53   "There, Greenspan specialized . . ." Bess Kaplan to JM, interview on February 15, 2000

53   "He provided them . . ." Judith Mackey to JM, interview on January 28, 2000

53   "Greenspan wanted very . . ." Nathaniel Branden to JM, interview on October 18, 1999

54   "Within the small . . ." Kathryn Eickhoff to JM, interview on December 29, 1999

54   "But their ranks . . . " *New York Times Magazine*, January 15, 1989

54   "Greenspan chided himself . . ." Nathaniel Branden to JM, interview on October 18, 1999

54   "Furthermore, Herbert Greenspan . . . " *New York Times Magazine*, January 15, 1989

54   "By a stroke . . ." Judith Mackey to JM, interview on January 28, 2000

54 "When the two . . ." Ibid.

54 "Townsend was sixty-five . . . " *New York Times*, March 25, 1958

54 "Townsend-Skinner had . . ." Lowell Wiltbank to JM, interview on November 8, 1999

54 "The firm's primary . . ." Judith Mackey to JM, interview on January 28, 2000

55 "Skinner died in . . ." Kathryn Eickhoff to JM, interview on December 29, 1999

55 "His daughter – also . . ." Judith Mackey to JM, interview on January 28, 2000

55 "Townsend took an . . ." Bess Kaplan to JM, interview on February 15, 2000

56 "He'd get behind . . ." Kathryn Eickhoff to JM, interview on December 29, 1999

56 "Bob Kavesh, Greenspan's . . ." Robert Kavesh to JM, interview on September 30, 1999

56 "From Conference Board . . ." Kathryn Eickhoff to JM, interview on December 29, 1999

57 "He recalls Rand's . . ." Lowell Wiltbank to JM, interview on November 8, 1999

57 "'I get the same . . . " *New York Times Magazine*, April 25, 1976

57 ". . . paperboard sales . . ." David Rowe to JM, interview on October 20, 1999

57 "This would help . . ." Judith Mackey to JM, interview on January 28, 2000

57 "One of Townsend-Greenspan's . . ." Kathryn Eickhoff to JM, interview on December 29, 1999

58 "By the late 1950s . . ." Client names culled from interviews with various Townsend-Greenspan employees

58 "Despite having done . . ." Robert Kavesh to JM, interview on September 30, 1999

58 "In 1958, at . . . " *New York Times*, March 25, 1958

58 "Left alone and . . ." Judith Mackey to JM, interview on January 28, 2000

58 "Presently, Greenspan set . . ." Kathryn Eickhoff to JM, interview on December 29, 1999

59 "Larry Klein at . . ." Larry Klein to JM, interview on April 21, 2000

59 "Greenspan – the economic . . ." Kathryn Eickhoff to JM, interview on December 29, 1999

59 "To stay on trend . . ." Lowell Wiltbank to JM, interview on November 8, 1999

59 "'Alan didn't think . . ." Kathryn Eickhoff to JM, interview on December 29, 1999

60 "When Eickhoff got . . ." Jim Smith to JM, interview on December 29, 1999

61 "Greenspan remained close . . ." Joan Mitchell Blumenthal to JM, interview on November 8, 1999

61 "Blumenthal had briefly . . ." Barbara Branden, *The Passion of Ayn Rand*, p. 254

61   "'We became friends . . ." Allan Blumenthal to JM, interview on November 8, 1999

61   "'Any economist who . . ." quote taken from Eugene Schwartz letter to JM, dated May 3, 2000

61   "But Greenspan confided . . ." Joan Mitchell Blumenthal to JM, interview on November 8, 1999

62   "The other woman . . ." Robert Hessen to JM, interview on October 29, 1999

62   "'Alan projected a . . ." Barbara Branden to JM, interview on October 12, 1999

62   "Judith Mackey, a . . ." Judith Mackey to JM, interview on January 28, 2000

63   "As he once . . . " *New York Times*, June 5, 1983

63   "Greenspan also proved . . ." Judith Mackey to JM, interview on January 28, 2000

63   "One story – perhaps . . ." David Rowe to JM, interview on October 20, 1999

63   "Edgar Fiedler, an . . ." Edgar Fiedler to JM, interview on August 24, 1999

63   "Meanwhile, Frank Ikard. . . " *New York Times Magazine*, April 25, 1976

63   "In 1966, he . . . " *Fortune*, April 1966

64   ". . . first to 39 Broadway . . . " *New York Times* , March 25, 1958

64   ". . . later to 80 Pine . . ." Recollection of consensus of Townsend-Greenspan employees during interviews with JM

64   "The spaces were. . . " *New York Times*, June 5, 1983

64   "As an aesthetic . . ." Kathryn Eickhoff to JM, interview on December 29, 1999

64   "In the mid–1960s . . ." Ibid.

64   "As she didn't . . ." Bess Kaplan to JM, interview on February 15, 2000

64   "Typically, Herbert Greenspan . . ." Kathryn Eickhoff to JM, interview on December 29, 1999

64   "In 1967, Greenspan . . ." Gary Seevers to JM, interview on September 17, 1999

65   "Even Joan Mitchell . . ." Joan Mitchell Blumenthal to JM, interview on November 8, 1999

Chapter 6

67   ". . . Garment had graduated . . ." Leonard Garment, *Crazy Rhythm*, p.44–45, 51, and 54

67   "Due to numerous . . ." Ibid. p.62

67   "He'd lost the . . . " *US News & World Report*, September 20, 1999

67   "Thereupon, he'd delivered . . . " *New York Times Magazine*, January 21, 1968

68   "Nixon was in . . . " *US News & World Report*, September 20, 1999

68   "The price tag . . . " *New York Times Magazine*, January 21, 1968

68   "Partner John Mitchell . . ." Leonard Garment, *Crazy Rhythm*, p.117–120

68   "Garment also served . . ." Eleanora Schoenebaum, *Political Profiles: The Nixon/Ford Years*, p.223

68   "Now, Nixon had . . ." Leonard Garment to JM, interview on October 6, 1999

68   "He sat by . . ." *Worth*, May 1995

69   "'Nixon was favorably . . ." Leonard Garment to JM, interview on October 6, 1999

69   ". . . another political intimate . . ." Wyatt Wells, *Economist in an Uncertain World*, p.18

69   "Because this was . . . " *New York Times Magazine*, January 21, 1968

70   "As a young . . . " *US News & World Report*, November 18, 1968

70   "He ran as . . ." Allen Matusow, *Nixon's Economy*, p.1

70   "The thirty-year-old . . ." composite portrait drawn from multiple sources including Current Biography, 1985 Yearbook

71   "Nixon's media team . . ." Leonard Garment, *Crazy Rhythm*, p.132

71   "It was with . . ." Martin Anderson to JM, interview on February 17, 2000

71   "Greenspan's role was . . ." Martin Anderson to JM, interview on September 30, 1999

71   "An economic advisory . . . " *New York Times*, July 3, 1968

72   "'Nixon was very . . ." Dwight Chapin to JM, interview on September 15, 1999

72   "When he saw . . ." Martin Anderson to JM, interview on September 30, 1999

72   "He had a mind . . ." Ray Price to JM, interview on September 28, 1999

72   "'Nixon was extremely . . ." Martin Anderson to JM, interview on February 17, 2000

73   "This time Nixon . . ." gi.grolier.com, "The American Presidency"

73   "Nixon asked Greenspan. . . " *Wall Street Journal*, December 6, 1968

73   "Johnson's fiscal 1970 . . . " *New York Times*, December 11, 1968

74   "In the end, Johnson chose . . ." Allen Matusow, *Nixon's Economy*, p.40

74   "*Newsweek* described this . . . " *Newsweek*, January 27, 1969

74   "It wasn't until . . ." Allen Matusow, *Nixon's Economy*, p.39–51

74   "He'd been offered . . . " *Business Week*, April 28, 1975

74   "He'd also been . . ." Fred Malek, chairman of Thayer Capital Partners to JM, interview on September 30, 1999

74   "[Nixon] and I . . ." Erwin Hargrove, *The President and the Council of Economic Advisers*, p.414–415

75   "He found Nixon's . . ." Courtesy of Gerald Ford Library, A. James Reichley interview transcripts, 1977–81, "Economic Policy, Alan Greenspan"

75   "'I'm disturbed,' he . . . " *Business Week*, April 28, 1975

75   "Burns and Garment . . ." Eleanora Schoenebaum, *Political Profiles: The Nixon/Ford Years*, p.223 and Leonard Garment, *Crazy Rhythm*, p.161

75   "Even though Greenspan . . ." *Who's Who*, 1976–77, p.1238

75   "Opponents could count . . ." J. Eric Fredland et al., *Professionals on the Front Line*, p. 45

75   "During a campaign . . ." Milton & Rose Friedman, *Two Lucky People*, p.377

75   "Anderson's instincts told . . ." Martin Anderson to JM, interview on September 30, 1999

76   "Thomas Gates Jr., a . . . " *New York Times*, March 28, 1969

76   "Also squarely in . . ." Milton & Rose Friedman, *Two Lucky People*, p.630

76   "While at Chicago . . ." Eleanora Schoenebaum, *Political Profiles: The Nixon/Ford Years*, p.218

78   "According to Walter . . ." Walter Oi to JM, interview on September 28, 1999

78   ". . . Pentagon had concluded . . . " *Time,* January 10, 1969

78   "'Conceivably, Negroes could . . ." Ibid.

78   "The result was . . ." Milton & Rose Friedman, *Two Lucky People*, p.380

79   "While Friedman played . . ." Stephen Herbits to JM, interview on February 22, 2000

79   "On February 20, 1970 . . ." Milton & Rose Friedman, *Two Lucky People*, p.379

80   "'I still have . . ." Milton Friedman to JM, interview on October 11, 1999

CHAPTER 7

81   "By the summer . . ." Kathryn Eickhoff to JM, interview on December 29, 1999

81   "The building had . . . " *New York Daily News*, August 6, 1970

81   "About a half . . ." Kathryn Eickhoff to JM, interview on December 29, 1999

82   "By now, the building . . . " *New York Daily News*, August 6, 1970

82   "Greenspan and Eickhoff . . ." Kathryn Eickhoff to JM, interview on December 29, 1999

82   "Two people wound . . . " *New York Daily News*, August 6, 1970

82   "As for Townsend-Greenspan's . . ." Kathryn Eickhoff to JM, interview on December 29, 1999

83   "His consulting position . . ." Bill Franklin to JM, interview on October 27, 1999

83   ". . . administration's official forecast . . . " *New York Times*, February 24, 1971

83   "He went before . . . " *New York Times*, February 3, 1971

83   ". . . Greenspan and Ralph Nader . . . " *New York Times*, June 22, 1971

84   "An op-ed he . . . " *New York Times*, July 25, 1971

84   "He worried that . . ." Allen Matusow, *Nixon's Economy*, p.5

84   "On the evening . . ." Ibid. p.154–55

84   "In Nixon's view . . ." Ibid. p. 112, 157

85   "As a twenty-eight-year-old . . . " *Newsweek*, September 13, 1971

85   "During the 1968 . . . " *US News & World Report*, November 25, 1968

85   "After ninety days . . . " *US News & World Report*, December 6, 1971

86   "The IRS printed . . . " *US News & World Report*, January 31, 1972

86   "Railroad signalmen managed . . . " *US News & World Report*, December 13, 1971

86   "But only a . . . " *US News & World Report*, January 17, 1972

86   "Meat processors shipped . . ." Edgar Fiedler to JM, interview on August 24, 1999

86   "Milton Friedman concluded . . ." Allen Matusow, *Nixon's Economy*, p.231

86   "Ayn Rand weighed . . . " *Ayn Rand Letter*, October 25, 1971 & November 8, 1971

86   "In a *New* . . . " *New York Times*, July 31, 1973

86   "He was part . . ." C. Jackson Grayson to JM, interview on September 24, 1999

87   "Greenspan also met . . ." Donald Rumsfeld to JM, interview on August 27, 1999

87   "In June 1973 . . ." Allen Matusow, *Nixon's Economy*, p.231

87   "By April 1974 . . ." Allen Matusow to JM, interview on May 8, 2000

87   "Early in 1974 . . ." Eleanora Schoenebaum, *Political Profiles: The Nixon/Ford Years*, p.252

88   "The CEA was . . ." Whitehouse.gov/WH/EOP/CEA

88   "Edwin Nourse, the . . ." David Munro to JM, interview on September 16, 1999

89   "It retaliated by . . ." Wyatt Wells, *Economist in an Uncertain World*, p.14

89   "Burns set himself . . ." Murray Weidenbaum to JM, interview on August 13, 1999

89   "Stein was a . . . " *New York Times*, September 9, 1999

89   "Among the media . . . " *New York Times*, July 28, 1974

89   "Congressional Democrats thought . . . " *Time*, July 29, 1974

89   "By the spring . . . " *New York Times*, July 28, 1974

89   ". . . more than $300,000 . . . " *Newsweek*, February 24, 1975

89   "He'd have to . . ." NYU Alumni News, October 1974

90   ". . . the prospect of . . ." Robert Kavesh to JM, interview on September 30, 1999

90   "Overtures were also . . . " *New York Times*, July 24, 1974

90   "Nixon chief-of-staff . . ." Erwin Hargrove, *The President and the Council of Economic Advisers*, p.414

90   "It took Arthur . . ." Ibid. p.414

90   "I changed my . . ." *New York Times*, July 24, 1974

90   "What is at . . . " *Time*, August 4, 1974

91   "A couple of . . ." Joan Mitchell Blumenthal to JM, interview on November 8, 1999

91   "On August 8 . . ." Nominations of Philip A. Loomis, Jr. and Alan Greenspan, Hearing Before the Committee on Banking, Housing and Urban Affairs, United States Senate, August 8, 1974

91   "Even if we . . ." Howard Shuman to JM, interview on September 9, 1999

92   "On this day..." Nominations of Philip A. Loomis, Jr. and Alan Greenspan, Hearing Before the Committee on Banking, Housing and Urban Affairs, United States Senate, August 8, 1974, p.11

92   "At this point..." Ibid. p.12

92   "He also suggested..." Ibid. p.15

93   "'Well, I want..." Ibid. p.52

CHAPTER 8

95   "Ford, thirteen years..." Biographical sketch of Ford, courtesy of Gerald Ford Library

96   "Ford's distinguished congressional..." Eleanora Schoenebaum, *Political Profiles: The Nixon/Ford Years*, p.207

96   "One of Ford's..." Biographical sketch of Ford, courtesy of Gerald Ford Library

96   "Eight months later..." Eleanora Schoenebaum, *Political Profiles: The Nixon/Ford Years*, p.208

96   "At his swearing..." grolier.com/presidents/nbk/bios/

97   "The Dow Jones... " *US News & World Report*, August 26, 1974

97   "So, too, did... " *Newsweek*, September 30, 1974

98   "'Watergate still had..." Donald Rumsfeld to JM, interview on August 27, 1999

98   "Leonard Garment would..." Eleanora Schoenebaum, *Political Profiles: The Nixon/Ford Years*, p.224

99   "On August 13, 1974..." *New Republic*, September 14, 1974

99   "'I think it..." Courtesy of Gerald Ford Library, Alan Greenspan files, Box 29, General Correspondence, 1974 (S)(2)

99   "Greenspan left his..." Courtesy of Gerald Ford Library, Alan Greenspan files, Box 19, "AG–1976"

99   "He placed his..." Current Biography, 1974, p.155

99   "He chose to..." Harry Winston, general manager of Watergate complex circa 1974, to JM, interview on October 27, 1999

100   "He rented it... " *New York Times*, August 22, 1976

100   "A brief swearing-in..." Courtesy of Gerald Ford Library, Robert Orben files, Box 2, "9/4/74, Swearing in Greenspan"

100   "'I'm very proud... " *Time*, September 30, 1974

101   "This comment to... " *Newsweek*, February 24, 1975

101   "'I am a... " *Time*, September 30, 1974

101   "Greenspan moved into... " *New York Times Magazine*, April 25, 1976

101   "For instance, wages..." Steven Landsburg, University of Rochester, to JM, interview on September 14, 1999

102   "'If inflation continues..." Eleanora Schoenebaum, *Political Profiles: The Nixon/Ford Years*, p.252

102   "Always deeply conservative..." Ibid. p.209

102   "They covered a . . . " *New York Times Magazine*, September 22, 1974

102   "At the Health . . ." Courtesy of Gerald Ford Library, L. William Seidman files, Box 6,"Health, Education, Income Security and Social Services" 9/19/74 bound transcript

103   "'Mr. Wurf,' Greenspan . . ." Ibid.

103   "The AFL-CIO. . . " *Wall Street Journal*, October 8, 1974

103   "Meanwhile, some home. . . " *Wall Street Journal*, October 4, 1974

103   "'This may be . . ." Murray Weidenbaum to JM, interview on August 13, 1999

103   "Greenspan was quick . . . " *New York Times*, September 27, 1974

104   "Held at the . . ." Ibid.

104   "It kicked off . . ." Courtesy of Gerald Ford Library, Alan Greenspan files, Box 54, "Summit Conference on Inflation – Washington September 27–28, 1974"

104   "'No new ideas,. . . " Edgar Fiedler to JM, interview on August 24, 1999

104   "Paul McCracken, Nixon's . . ." Paul McCracken to JM, interview on September 9, 1999

104   "He was pushed . . ." Courtesy of Gerald Ford Library, Alan Greenspan files, Box 7, "Economic Policy Board (2)"

104   "Greenspan, fresh from . . ." Erwin Hargrove, *The President and the Council of Economic Advisers*, p.425

105   "He confirmed that . . . " *New York Times*, October 13, 1974

105   "'Shop wisely, look . . ." Public Papers of the Presidents, Gerald Ford, August 9 to December 31, 1974

105   "'It was Republican . . ." William Niskanen to JM, interview on August 16, 1999

105   "But the most . . . " *The New Yorker*, October 21, 1974

105   "Lester Kinsolving, a . . . " *New York Times*, November 15, 1974

105   "'I plan to . . ." Courtesy of Gerald Ford Library, Alan Greenspan files, Box 49, "Presidential Speeches, Addresses and Interviews on the Economy, 1974"

106   "Greenspan and my . . ." Edgar Fiedler to JM, interview on August 24, 1999

106   "Greenspan would later . . ." Erwin Hargrove, *The President and the Council of Economic Advisers*, p.425

106   "'We went dutifully . . ." Paul Samuelson to JM, interview on August 17, 1999

106   "Industrial production fell. . . " *Newsweek*, February 24, 1975

106   "General Motors laid . . . " *New York Times*, January 16, 1975

106   "As the New . . ." courtesy of the Conference Board

106   "Between 1960 and . . . " *New York Times*, February 5, 1975

107   "Although it averaged . . ." Ibid.

107   "'A recession is. . . " *New York Times*, March 7, 1975

107   "Upon taking the . . . " *Current Biography*, 1974, p.155

107   "During the first . . ." Eleanora Schoenebaum, *Political Profiles: The Nixon/Ford Years*, p.209

107   "'Everyone knows Greenspan . . ." David Munro to JM, interview on September 16, 1999

107   "Thus, Greenspan urged . . ." Erwin Hargrove, *The President and the Council of Economic Advisers*, p.411

107   "During his 1975 . . . " *New York Times*, January 16, 1975

107   "But the Democratic . . . " *New York Times*, March 30, 1975

108   "Ford asked his. . . " *New York Times Magazine*, April 25, 1976

108   "In a memo . . ." Courtesy of Gerald Ford Library, Alan Greenspan files, Box 19, "AG 1975 (2)"

108   "But the real . . . " *New York Times*, March 30, 1975

108   ". . . Dick Cheney. . . " *Fortune*, July 6, 1987

108   ". . . only non-Ph.D. . . ." *Current Biography*, 1974, p.155

109   "It's usually a . . ." Murray Weidenbaum to JM, interview on August 13, 1999

109   "An unwritten CEA . . ." Paul MacAvoy to JM, interview on October 1, 1999

109   "'When you take . . ." Murray Weidenbaum to JM, interview on August 13, 1999

109   "An unnamed CEA. . . " *New York Times*, March 12, 1975

109   "Gary Seevers, a . . ." Gary Seevers to JM, interview on September 17, 1999

109   "Eventually, they were . . . " *New York Times*, July 22, 1975

110   "MacAvoy recalls that . . ." Paul MacAvoy to JM, interview on October 1, 1999

110   "The trough of . . ." Courtesy of the Conference Board

110   "There had been . . . " *New York Times*, January 5, 1975

110   "'One thing that . . . " *US News & World Report*, June 28, 1976

110   "At a later . . ." Erwin Hargrove, *The President and the Council of Economic Advisers*, p.451

111   "Trade Minister Nikolai . . ." Allen Matusow to JM, interview on August 13, 1999

111   "Before anyone quite . . . " *New York Times*, August 1, 1975

111   ". . . roughly one-fourth . . ." Allen Matusow to JM, interview on August 13, 1999

111   "One day in . . ." Paul MacAvoy to JM, interview on October 1, 1999

111   "Estimates put the . . . " *Time*, August 25, 1975

111   ". . . yet the country's . . . " *Reader's Digest*, December 1976

112   "The Canadian Wheat . . ." Courtesy of Gerald Ford Library, Alan Greenspan files, Box 24, "Edward G. Schuh, Sept. 74-Sept. 75 (1)"

112   "An alarm bell . . ." G. Edward Schuh to JM, interview on October 21, 1999

112   "At this point. . . " *Reader's Digest*, December 1976

112   "Secretary of Agriculture . . ." G. Edward Schuh to JM, interview on October 21, 1999

112   "At the same . . . " *Time*, September 8, 1975

113   "In their corner . . ." G. Edward Schuh to JM, interview on October 21, 1999

113   "'Greenspan's view was . . ." Ibid.

113   "Rather than the . . ." Paul MacAvoy to JM, interview on October 1, 1999

113   "The Soviets were . . . " *US News & World Report*, November 3, 1975

113   "The worst-case estimate . . . " *Reader's Digest*, December 1976

114   "The imperious Kissinger . . ." Courtesy of Gerald Ford Library, Alan Greenspan files, Box 7, "Economic Policy Board (1)"

114   "Relying on a . . ." Composite portrait drawn from multiple sources

114   "Kissinger saw a . . . " *US News & World Report*, October 20, 1975

115   "'I had very . . ." Henry Kissinger to JM, interview on May 16, 2000

115   "By 1975, New . . . " *Reader's Digest*, November 1975

115   "By 1974, the . . . " *Newsweek*, December 15, 1975

115   "As a consequence . . . " *Reader's Digest*, November 1975

115   "It became common . . ." Ibid.

116   "But in March . . ." Kathleen Hulser, New-York Historical Society, to JM, interview on September 15, 1999

116   "The city's next . . ." Kenneth Jackson, editor, *The Encyclopedia of New York*, p. 781

116   "Felix Rohatyn, a . . ." Ibid. p. 1017

116   "Instead of being . . ." Ibid. p. 781

116   "The bonds were . . ." Kathleen Hulser to JM, interview on September 15, 1999

116   "A giant sales . . . " *Reader's Digest*, November 1975

117   "As a first . . ." Kathleen Hulser to JM, interview on September 15, 1999

117   "Then came the . . ." Robert Bailey, Rutgers University, to JM, interview on September 20, 1999

117   "Angry sanitation workers . . ." Eleanora Schoenebaum, *Political Profiles: The Nixon/Ford Years*, p. 716

117   ". . . 20,000 tons of . . . " *Reader's Digest*, November 1975

117   "Laid-off policemen . . ." Kathleen Hulser to JM, interview on September 15, 1999

117   ". . . Ross Perot, who . . ." Ibid.

117   "On October 9 . . . " *New York Times*, October 10, 1975

118   "Ron Nessen, Ford's . . . " *Newsweek*, October 27, 1975

118   "Toughest among the . . ." Gerald Ford to JM, interview on December 2, 1999

118   "Before joining the . . ." Eleanora Schoenebaum, *Political Profiles: The Nixon/Ford Years*, p. 597

118   "'I would say . . ." L. William Seidman to JM, interview on September 16, 1999

118   ". . . Ford delivered a . . . " *New York Daily News*, October 30, 1975

118   "Frightening studies began . . ." David Munro to JM, interview on September 16, 1999

118   "In a memo . . ." Courtesy of Gerald Ford Library, Alan Greenspan files, Box 19, "AG 1975"

119   "'If Paris is . . ." David Munro to JM, interview on September 16, 1999

119   "In November, Governor . . ." Robert Bailey to JM, interview on September 20, 1999

119   "The city would . . ." Eleanora Schoenebaum, *Political Profiles: The Nixon/Ford Years*, p. 717

119   "The loan would . . . " *Time*, December 8, 1975

119   "'Alan Greenspan to . . ." Gerald Ford to JM, interview on December 2, 1999

119   "But the lingering . . ." Robert Bailey to JM, interview on September 20, 1999

119   "Even at the . . ." Kathleen Hulser to JM, interview on September 15, 1999

119   "But perhaps most of . . ." Raymond Horton, Columbia University business school, to JM, interview on September 20, 1999

CHAPTER 9

121   "Members of Congress . . ." Courtesy of Gerald Ford Library, Alan Greenspan files, Box 28, "General Correspondence, 1974 (H)(3)"

121   "Greenspan grew so . . . " *New York Times Magazine*, April 25, 1976

121   "Lenny Garment has . . ." Leonard Garment to JM, interview on October 6, 1999

122   "'There was a . . ." Donald Rumsfeld to JM, interview on August 27, 1999

122   "As chairman of . . ." David Munro to JM, interview on September 16, 1999

122   "By contrast, Arthur . . ." Hendrik Houthakker, former CEA member, Harvard University, to JM, interview on September 28, 1999

122   ". . . Warren Harding apparently . . . " *Newsweek*, February 24, 1975

123   "'I don't give . . ." Allen Matusow to JM, interview on August 13, 1999

123   "'He had all . . ." Paul McCracken to JM, interview on September 9, 1999

123   "Ford had become . . . " *New York Times Magazine*, April 25, 1976

123   "He voted against . . ." Eleanora Schoenebaum, *Political Profiles: The Nixon/Ford Years*, p. 207

123   "In fact, Ford . . ." Courtesy of Gerald Ford Library, Alan Greenspan files, Box 6, "Miscellaneous"

123   "They met in . . . " *New York Times Magazine*, April 25, 1976

123   "Others such as . . ." Roger Porter, *Presidential Decision Making*, p.127

124   "That left Greenspan . . . " *New York Times Magazine*, April 25, 1976

124   "While Greenspan struck . . ." L. William Seidman to JM, interview on September 16, 1999

124   "'Greenspan treated the . . ." Paul MacAvoy to JM, interview on October 1, 1999

124   "'He is unquestionably . . ." Erwin Hargrove, *The President and the Council of Economic Advisers*, p.422

125   "Ford, in turn . . ." Gerald Ford to JM, interview on December 2, 1999

125   ". . . Eagle Scout and . . ." Biographical sketch of Ford, courtesy of Gerald Ford Library

125   ". . . beer excise taxes . . ." Courtesy of Gerald Ford Library, Alan Greenspan files, box 2, "James Cannon (3)"

125   ". . . U.S. postal system . . ." Courtesy of Gerald Ford Library, Alan Greenspan files, box 21, "Paul MacAvoy, June 1975 – October 1976"

125   "He regularly shot . . ." Courtesy of Gerald Ford Library, Alan Greenspan files, box 1 "April '75"

125   "'Observe that the . . ." Courtesy of Gerald Ford Library, Alan Greenspan files, box 19, "AG—1975 (2)"

125   "Indeed, the consensus . . ." Burton Malkiel to JM, detailed answering machine message left on September 20, 1999. Supported by interviews with numerous other sources.

125   "The pair even . . . " *Washingtonian*, April 1995

125   "The two attended . . . " *Business Week*, June 15, 1987

125   "In the wake . . ." Courtesy of Gerald Ford Library, Alan Greenspan files, box 1, "December 74"

126   "Joan Mitchell Blumenthal . . ." Joan Mitchell Blumenthal to JM, interview on November 8, 1999

127   "'To prepare for . . ." Paul MacAvoy to JM, interview on October 1, 1999

127   "As Schuh recalls . . ." G. Edward Schuh to JM, interview on October 21, 1999

127   ". . . cover of *Newsweek* . . . " *Newsweek*, February 25, 1975

127   "*Penthouse* asked if . . ." Courtesy of Gerald Ford Library, Alan Greenspan files, Box 3, "General Correspondence, 1975, C (2)"

127   "'I appreciate your . . ." Courtesy of Gerald Ford Library, Alan Greenspan files, Box 36, "General Correspondence, 1976 (XYZ)"

128   "'What has happened . . ." Courtesy of Gerald Ford Library, Alan Greenspan files, Box 32, "General Correspondence, 1975 (W)(1)"

128   "'Dear Mr. Greenspan . . ." Courtesy of Gerald Ford Library, Alan Greenspan files, Box 30, "General Correspondence, 1975 (B)(2)"

128   "Former Nixon counselor . . ." Courtesy of Gerald Ford Library, Alan Greenspan files, Box 34, "General Correspondence, 1975 (T)"

128   "Tom Brokaw attended . . ." Courtesy of Gerald Ford Library, Alan Greenspan files, Box 33, "General Correspondence, 1976 (M)(1)"

128   "Many a night . . ." David Munro to JM, interview on September 16, 1999

128   "Henry Mitchell of . . . " *New York Times Magazine*, April 25, 1976

128   ". . . David Munro describes . . ." David Munro to JM, interview on September 16, 1999

129   "Suspect health had . . ." Bill Callejo to JM, interview on November 12, 1999
129   "During late-night . . ." Donald Rumsfeld to JM, interview on August 27, 1999
129   "It was during . . ." geocities.com
129   "'It was apparently . . ." L. William Seidman to JM, interview on September 16, 1999
129   "The pair were . . . " *New York Times* , April 16, 1976
129   "A story about . . ." *Pittsburgh Post Gazette*, May 19, 1976
130   "'He's a lovely . . ." geocities.com
130   "It was 'almost . . . " *New York Times Magazine*, January 15, 1989
131   "The Dow began . . . " *New York Times*, February 27, 1976
131   "Meanwhile, corporate profits . . . " *New York Times*, July 7, 1976
131   "'Freeing individuals is . . ." Courtesy of Gerald Ford Library, Alan Greenspan files, Box 52, "State of the Union 1976 (5)"
131   "The evening before . . ." Courtesy of Gerald Ford Library, A. James Reichley interview transcripts, 1977–81, "Economic Policy, Alan Greenspan"
131   "It went through nine . . ." Courtesy of Gerald Ford Library, Robert Hartmann files, Box 180, "1/19/76, A Greenspan's comments"
131   "Ford referred to . . ." Courtesy of Gerald Ford Library, Alan Greenspan files, Box 51, "State of the Union, 1976 (1)"
132   "'It is often . . ." Courtesy of Gerald Ford Library, "Ron Nessen files, Box 68, "Issues & Answers, June 29, 1976" transcript
132   "Unemployment stood at . . ." Courtesy of the Conference Board
132   "Unemployment among blacks . . . " *New York Times*, September 4, 1976
132   "'We are now. . . " *New York Times Magazine*, April 25, 1976
132   "If elected president . . . " *Time*, April 26, 1976
132   "He suggested that . . . " *US News & World Report*, October 1, 1976
132   "By contrast, Ford. . . " *New York Times*, November 4, 1976
132   "Carter's advisers included . . . " *Time*, April 26, 1976
133   "A relief bill . . . " *Time* , March 1, 1976
133   "Serving as Hawkins's . . . " *New York Times*, May 22, 1976
133   "Humphrey-Hawkins offered. . . " *Time*, March 1, 1976
133   "The legislation would . . . " *New York Times*, July 23, 1976
133   "The unemployment rate . . . " *New York Times*, September 4, 1976
133   "Greenspan described the . . . " *New York Times*, August 31, 1976
134   "By the CEA's . . ." Courtesy of Gerald Ford Library, A. James Reichley interview transcripts, 1977–81, "Economic Policy, Alan Greenspan"
134   "Kissinger was present . . ." Ibid.
134   "Despite being the . . ." Eleanora Schoenebaum, *Political Profiles: The Nixon/Ford Years*, p. 212
134   "Ford selected Kansas . . ." Ibid. p.213
134   "More bad news . . . " *New York Times*, October 30, 1976
134   "On October 31 . . ." Courtesy of Gerald Ford Library, Ron Nessen files, Box 65, "Face the Nation, October 31, 1976" transcript

135   "On November 2 . . ." Eleanora Schoenebaum, *Political Profiles: The Nixon/Ford Years*, p. xxiii

135   ". . . to pardon Nixon . . ." Ibid. p.218

136   "It read in . . ." Courtesy of Gerald Ford Library, Arthur Burns files, Box K13, "Alan Greenspan"

Chapter 10

137   "Ford had promised . . ." Judith Mackey to JM, interview on January 28, 2000

137   "'I think there . . ." Ibid.

138   "'You had to . . ." David Rowe to JM, interview on October 20, 1999

138   "The firm even . . ." Lowell Wiltbank to JM, interview on November 8, 1999

138   "While CEA chair . . ." Kathryn Eickhoff to JM, interview on December 29, 1999

138   "Instead, the degree . . ." Robert Kavesh to JM, interview on September 30, 1999

138   "The collection totaled . . ." Courtesy of NYU's Stern School, viewing of Greenspan's Ph.D. papers by JM on October 11, 1999

139   "Barbara Walters threw . . ." Robert Kavesh to JM, interview on September 30, 1999

139   "In typical fashion . . ." Kathryn Eickhoff to JM, interview on December 29, 1999

139   "Greenspan managed to . . ." Detail courtesy of Harry Walker Agency

139   "Reportedly, Greenspan commanded . . ." multiple sources

139   "Immediately following his. . ." Kathryn Eickhoff to JM, interview on December 29, 1999

139   "'You never had . . ." Bill Franklin to JM, interview on October 27, 1999

140   "'Alan was always . . ." Murray Weidenbaum to JM, interview on August 13, 1999

140   "During the late . . ." Nomination of Alan Greenspan: Hearing Before the Committee on Banking, Housing, and Urban Affairs, United States Senate, July 21, 1987, p.75

140   "He was even tapped . . . " *Fortune*, April 8, 1991

140   "The South Dakota . . . " *New York Times*, July 3, 1972

140   "Greenspan organized a . . ." David Rowe to JM, interview on October 20, 1999

141   "Greenspan had met . . ." Martin Anderson to JM, interview on February 17, 2000

141   "'Reagan basically asked . . ." Ibid.

141   "On June 5, 1980 . . . " *Time*, July 28, 1980

141   "Ford took a . . . " *Newsweek*, July 28, 1980

142   "... hopefully defeat Carter." Ibid.

142   "Within hours, a ..." Ibid.

142   "Late that night ... " *Time*, July 28, 1980

143   "The two sides. . . " *Newsweek*, July 28, 1980

143   "At one point . . ." Ibid.

143   "He felt that Kissinger . . . " *Time*, July 28, 1980

143   "That evening, Ford . . ." Ibid.

143   "... breach of confidence . . ." Ibid.

144   "At 11:00 PM . . ." Ibid.

144   "... at 11:37 PM . . ." Ibid.

144   "'Neither Greenspan nor . . ." Henry Kissinger to JM, interview on May 16, 2000

144   "Donald Rumsfeld, who . . ." Donald Rumsfeld to JM, interview on August 27, 1999

144   "... zealous disciple of . . ." Martin Anderson, *Revolution*, p.147

145   "Wanniski served as . . ." Ibid. p.157

145   "Reagan immediately dropped . . ." Ibid. p.160

145   "... the belief persisted . . ." Ibid. p.160

145   "The fact is, Greenspan . . ." Annelise Anderson to JM, interview on February 25, 2000

146   "Between 1977 and . . ." Sylvester Schieber & John Shoven, *The Real Deal*, p.184

146   "In May 1981 . . ." Ibid. p. 186

146   "Organized labor and . . ." Ibid. p.187

146   "Members of Congress . . ." Ibid. p.188

146   "On September 24 . . ." Ibid. p.189

146   "'He was chosen . . ." James Baker to JM, interview on January 26, 2000

147   "The commission worked . . ." Sylvester Schieber & John Shoven, *The Real Deal*, p.190

147   "... slid $20,000 deeper . . ." Sylvester Schieber to JM, interview on February 22, 2000

147   "The Greenspan Commission's . . ." Sylvester Schieber & John Shoven, *The Real Deal,* p.195

147   "... year 2000, the . . ." Sylvester Schieber to JM, interview on February 22, 2000

148   "'Alan this is . . ." Barbara Branden to JM, interview on October 12, 1999

148   "Being good Objectivists . . ." Barbara Branden, *The Passion of Ayn Rand*, p. 259

148   "Along the way . . ." Ibid. p.345

148   "For New Year's Eve . . ." Nathaniel Branden, *My Years with Ayn Rand*, p.324

148   "She was also angry . . ." Barbara Branden, *The Passion of Ayn Rand*, p. 345

148   "'He was dumfounded . . ." Barbara Branden to JM, interview on October
        12, 1999
148   "Thoughout her adult . . ." Barbara Branden, *The Passion of Ayn Rand*, p.
        383
148   ". . . publishing party for . . ." Barbara Branden, *The Passion of Ayn Rand*,
        p. 295
149   "In November 1981 . . ." Barbara Branden, *The Passion of Ayn Rand*, p.
        400–402
149   " . . . on March 6, 1982. . . " *New York Times*, March 7, 1982
149   "Two days later . . . " *New York Times*, March 10, 1982
150   "She left her . . . " *New York Times*, March 28, 1982
150   "The truth is . . ." Barbara Branden, *The Passion of Ayn Rand*, p.318
150   "For example, he . . . " *Newsweek*, June 15, 1987
150   "For the new . . ." David Rowe to JM, interview on October 20, 1999
150   "Thus, the firm . . ." Nomination of Alan Greenspan: Hearing Before the
        Committee on Banking, Housing, and Urban Affairs, United States Senate,
        July 21, 1987, p.75
150   "Kissinger had launched . . ." Henry Kissinger to JM, interview on May 16,
        2000

CHAPTER 11

154   "As a Reagan . . . " *Time*, June 15, 1987
154   "'There's no telling . . ." Ibid.
154   "The value of . . . " *Wall Street Journal*, June 3, 1987
155   "Were it to . . ." Nomination of Alan Greenspan: Hearing Before the Com-
        mittee on Banking, Housing, and Urban Affairs, United States Senate, July
        21, 1987, p.4
155   "'If some person . . ." Ibid. p.21
155   "'Dr. Greenspan,' said . . ." Ibid. p.3
155   "Proxmire chided Greenspan . . ." Ibid. p.41
156   ". . . philosophical objections to . . ." Ibid. p.55
156   "Townsend-Greenspan had . . . " *New York Times*, July 24, 1987
156   "On antitrust, Greenspan . . ." Ibid. p.55–6
156   "Ultimately, Greenspan was . . . " *New York Times*, July 22, 1987
156   "He was required . . . " *New York Times*, June 30, 1987
156   "'It was a . . ." Bess Kaplan to JM, interview on February 15, 2000
156   "Kathryn Eickhoff – Greenspan's . . ." Kathryn Eickhoff to JM, interview on
        May 16, 2000
156   "Filings show that . . . " *New York Times*, August 4, 1987
157   "Greenspan was confirmed . . ." Ibid.
157   "'Prox often voted . . ." Howard Shuman to JM, interview on September 9,
        1999
157   "That day, Greenspan . . ." Carolyn Halpert to JM, interview on February
        25, 2000

157   "The ceremony was . . ." *Current Biography Yearbook*, 1989

157   "A number of . . ." Carolyn Halpert to JM, interview on February 25, 2000

157   "Greenspan's mother, Rose . . ." Wesley Halpert to JM, interview on December 14, 1999

158   "Reagan said a . . ." Steven Beckner, *Back From the Brink*, p.28

158   "'Perhaps I should . . ." *Federal Reserve Bulletin*, September 1987

158   "No one laughed . . ." Carolyn Halpert to JM, interview on February 25, 2000

158   "I am particularly . . ." *Federal Reserve Bulletin*, September 1987

158   "Burns had died . . . " *New York Times*, June 27, 1987

159   "The Federal Reserve . . ." Description of Fed's duties a composite of multiple sources.

162   "The issue precipitated . . ." Richard Sylla to JM, interview on February 14, 2000

162   "He submitted a . . ." *Encyclopedia Americana*, 1999 edition, p.738

162   "Hamilton mounted a . . ." Richard Sylla to JM, interview on February 14, 2000

162   "Washington was won . . ." *Encyclopedia Americana*, 1999 edition, p.738

162   "The First Bank . . ." Richard Sylla to JM, interview on February 14, 2000

162   "The First Bank . . ." Anjan Thakor, University of Michigan business school, to JM, interview on February 2, 2000

162   ". . . it competed very . . . "George Bentson, Emory University, to JM, interview on February 4, 2000

162   "The bank lost . . ." Richard Sylla to JM, interview on February 14, 2000

162   "A tie in . . ." *American Eras: 1783–1815*, p.82

163   "Following the War . . ." Donald Kettl to JM, interview on January 25, 2000

163   "To finance the . . ." Richard Sylla to JM, interview on February 14, 2000

163   "A second Bank . . ." *Encyclopedia Americana*, 1999 edition, p.164

163   "In an opinion . . ." Richard Sylla to JM, interview on February 14, 2000

163   "He trounced his . . ." *Encyclopedia Americana*, 1999 edition, p.642

163   "The country entered . . ." Alan Greenspan, speech before Conference of State Bank Supervisors in Nashville on May 2, 1998

163   "During this period . . ." George Bentson to JM, interview on February 4, 2000

164   "Merchants got into . . ." Alan Greenspan, speech before Conference of State Bank Supervisors in Nashville on May 2, 1998

164   "A merchant in . . ." Richard Sylla to JM, interview on February 14, 2000

164   "In 1863, the . . ." Roger Johnson, *Historical Beginnings . . . the Federal Reserve*, booklet courtesy of Federal Reserve Bank of Boston

164   ". . . the checking account . . ." George Bentson to JM, interview on February 4, 2000

164   "For example, banks . . ." Donald Kettl to JM, interview on January 25, 2000

164   "Frequently credit was . . ." Richard Sylla to JM, interview on February 14, 2000

164   "A currency backed . . ." Donald Kettl, to JM, interview on January 25, 2000

165   "The government's decision . . ." Richard Sylla to JM, interview on February 14, 2000

165   ". . . William Jennings Bryan . . ." *Encyclopedia Americana*, 1999 edition, p.662

165   "There were panics . . ." Richard Sylla to JM, interview on February 14, 2000

165   "The last straw . . . "

165   "Massive insurance payouts . . ." American Decades: 1900–1909, p.93

165   "Following the Panic . . ." Richard Sylla to JM, interview on February 14, 2000

165   "Charles Lindbergh, a . . ." *The Region*, August 1988, publication courtesy of Federal Reserve Bank of Minneapolis

165   "So it was . . ." Roger Johnson, *Historical Beginnings . . . the Federal Reserve*, booklet courtesy of Federal Reserve Bank of Boston

166   "Wilson signed the . . ." *The Region*, August 1988, publication courtesy of Federal Reserve Bank of Minneapolis

166   "Next came the . . ." Roger Johnson, *Historical Beginnings . . . the Federal Reserve*, booklet courtesy of Federal Reserve Bank of Boston

166   "The board and . . . " *A Historical and Architectural Retrospective of the Board of Governors of the Federal Reserve System* monograph courtesy of the Federal Reserve

166   "Otherwise, it was . . ." Ibid.

167   "'The Fed flunked . . ." Richard Sylla to JM, interview on February 14, 2000

167   "Eccles was a . . ." Eccles portrait a composite drawn from numerous sources.

167   "For example, the . . ." *A Historical and Architectural Retrospective of the Board of Governors of the Federal Reserve System* monograph courtesy of the Federal Reserve

167   "Even before Keynes . . ." *The International Economy*, January/February 2000

167   "During Eccles's tenure . . ." *A Historical and Architectural Retrospective of the Board of Governors of the Federal Reserve System* monograph courtesy of the Federal Reserve

168   "Another formidable Fed . . ." Martin portrait a composite drawn from numerous sources.

168   "One time, LBJ . . ." David Jones, *The Politics of Money*, p. 92

168   "He died in . . . " *New York Times*, July 29, 1998

168   "Appointed by Carter . . . " *Time*, June 15, 1987

168   "Miller seriously botched . . . " *US News & World Report*, June 15, 1987

168   "The prime rate . . ." *The International Economy*, January/February 2000
169   "The consumer price . . . " *US News & World Report*, June 15, 1987
169   "According to one . . ." David Jones, *The Politics of Money*, p. 89
169   "Even at this . . ." Wayne Angell to JM, interview on January 18, 2000
169   "He pointed to . . . " *Business Week*, June 15, 1987
169   "When Volcker and . . . " *Newsweek*, June 15 1987
169   "Instead, he accepted . . . " *Time*, June 15, 1987
170   "One possible candidate . . . " *Wall Street Journal*, June 3, 1987
170   "'It's not easy . . ." James Baker to JM, interview on January 26, 2000
170   "Here was a . . ." Wayne Angell to JM, interview on January 18, 2000

CHAPTER 12

171   "Greenspan – a mere . . ." *Current Biography Yearbook*, 1989
171   "A few days . . . " *New York Times*, September 16, 1987
171   "On his first . . ." Preston Martin, former vice chairman of Fed, to JM, interview on January 18, 2000
171   "He wore off-the-rack. . . " *Washingtonian*, April 1995
172   "He once reportedly . . . " *Manhattan Inc.*, November 1988
172   "The Dow had . . . " *US News & World Report*, November 2, 1987
172   "On September 4 –" *New York Times*, September 16, 1987
172   "A Commerce Department . . . " *Time*, November 2, 1987
172   "Treasury Secretary Baker . . ." David Jones to JM, interview on January 19, 2000
172   "The colossal federal . . ." Wayne Angell to JM, interview on January 18, 2000
172   "The yield had . . . " *Business Week*, December 14, 1987
172   "The market dropped . . . " *Business Week*, November 2, 1987
172   "Friday featured a . . . " *Wall Street Journal*, October 19, 1987
173   "Even before the . . . " *Newsweek*, November 2, 1987
173   "He was scheduled . . . " *New York Times*, September 16, 1987
173   "When the Panic . . ." Vincent Tompkins, *American Decades: 1900–1909*, p.93
173   "When Greenspan left . . . " *Wall Street Journal*, November 25, 1987
173   "'How did the . . ." Fed spokesperson to JM, interview on February 15, 2000
173   "'Crashes always come . . ." Robert Heller to JM, interview on February 15, 2000
174   "As grim testimony . . . " *Fortune*, October 19, 1987
174   "The Dow had . . ." Steven Beckner, *Back from the Brink*, p.50
174   "The Crash of '87 . . . " *Business Week*, November 2, 1987
174   "Ashen-faced traders . . . " *The New Yorker*, November 2, 1987
174   "A voice came . . ." Ibid.

174   "At the close . . . " *Time*, November 2, 1987

174   "Warren Buffett lost . . . " *Fortune*, November 23, 1987

174   "Reportedly, the value . . . " *Wall Street Journal*, October 30, 1987

175   "But the lasting . . ." Roger Johnson, *Historical Beginnings . . . the Federal Reserve*, booklet courtesy of Federal Reserve Bank of Boston

175   "The discussion centered . . ." Gerald Corrigan to JM, interview on January 21, 2000

175   "Back in Washington . . ." Wayne Angell to JM, interview on January 18, 2000

175   "The Paris bourse . . . " *Time*, November 2, 1987

175   "Tokyo was down . . . " *Fortune*, November 23, 1987

175   "Greenspan went to . . . " *Reader's Digest*, December 1987

175   "A senior Fed . . ." Fed spokesperson to JM, interview on February 15, 2000

176   "Former Treasury secretary . . ." James Baker to JM, interview on January 26, 2000

176   "He flew back . . . " *Wall Street Journal*, August 25, 1997

176   "Also on Tuesday . . ." Courtesy of the Federal Reserve

176   "That task fell . . ." Robert Hetzel, research director, Federal Reserve Bank of Richmond to JM, interview on February 8, 2000

176   "Corrigan gathered several . . ." Gerald Corrigan to JM, interview on January 21, 2000

177   "'There's a real . . ." Ibid.

177   "He huddled with . . . " *Time*, November 2, 1987

177   "Savvy observers couldn't . . ." Ibid.

178   "He stated that . . . " *US News & World Report*, November 2, 1987

178   "On Wednesday, the . . . " *Newsweek*, November 2, 1987

178   "The Fed repeatedly. . . " *Fortune*, November 23, 1987

178   "Following the crash . . . " *US News & World Report*, November 2, 1987

178   "By week's end . . . " *Time*, November 2, 1987

178   "Roughly fifty small . . . " *Time*, November 9, 1987

179   "Some cited his . . ." William Griggs to JM, interview on February 23, 2000

179   "'The crisis established . . ." Edward Boehne to JM, interview on February 25, 2000

179   "When the two . . . " *New York Times Magazine*, January 15, 1989

179   "Mitchell was a . . ." Portrait of Mitchell a composite drawn from multiple sources including *Who's Who in America 2000* and NBC's website.

180   "Greenspan and Mitchell . . ." Andrea Mitchell to JM, interview on March 9, 2000

180   "One of her . . . " *Washingtonian*, April 1995

180   "'Why don't you . . ." Andrea Mitchell to JM, interview on March 9, 2000

180   "'My impression of . . ." Ibid.

180   "From the beginning . . ." Joan Mitchell Blumenthal to JM, interview on November 8, 1999

180   "The two became . . . " *New York Times Magazine*, January 15, 1989

181   "'He didn't think . . ." Andrea Mitchell to JM, interview on March 9, 2000

181   "'Greenspan could have . . ." Paul Samuelson to JM, interview on August 17, 1999

182   "Not long after . . ." David Jones to JM, interview on January 19, 2000

182   "Real gross domestic . . ." Courtesy of the Conference Board

182   "By year's end . . ." Steven Beckner, *Back from the Brink*, p. 71

183   "By early 1988 . . ." Ibid. p. 75

183   "'Adaptability is Greenspan's . . ." David Jones to JM, interview on January 19, 2000

183   "Michael Darby, a . . . " *New York Times*, February 25, 1988

183   "'When I heard . . ." Ibid.

184   "Senator Proxmire immediately . . ." Steven Beckner, *Back from the Brink*, p. 79

184   "Reagan, for his . . . " *New York Times*, February 25, 1988

185   "'I don't think . . ." L. William Seidman to JM, interview on January 20, 2000

185   "Obviously, Jim Baker . . ." James Baker to JM, interview on January 26, 2000

185   "I wouldn't want . . ." Steven Beckner, *Back from the Brink,* p. 91

185   "On August 9 . . . " *Business Week*, July 31, 1989

185   "This latest hike . . . " *New York Times*, February 25, 1989

186   "Andrea Mitchell was . . ." Andrea Mitchell to JM, interview on March 9, 2000

186   "Meanwhile, the Democratic . . ." Walter Oi to JM, interview on September 28, 1999

186   "In fact, he . . ." Peter Levy, *Encyclopedia of the Reagan-Bush Years*, p. 64

CHAPTER 13

188   "In March 1980 . . . " *US News & World Report*, October 1, 1990

189   "In 1982, Reagan . . ." Ibid.

189   "'Remember the weak . . . " *Time*, October 1, 1990

189   "Dixon also used . . . " *Reader's Digest*, April 1990

189   "The insurance fund . . ." James Barth, Auburn University, to JM, interview on January 19, 2000

190   "In fact, Congress . . ." Ibid.

190   "As Fed chairman . . . " *New York Times*, August 28, 1989

190   "'Greenspan wanted to . . ." L. William Seidman to JM, interview on January 20, 2000

190   "Still, there was . . . " *New York Times*, February 24, 1989

190   "Neil Bush – son . . . " *Time*, October 8, 1990

190   "David Stockman, director . . . " *US News & World Report*, October 1, 1990

190 "Even William Proxmire . . ." Ibid.
191 "Long a champion . . . " *New York Times*, November 20, 1989
191 "In a four-page . . ." Letter from Alan Greenspan to Thomas Sharkey, Federal Home Loan Bank, dated February 13, 1985
191 "'When I first . . . " *New York Times*, November 20, 1989
192 ". . . collected a fee . . ." Bert Ely to JM, interview on January 19, 2000
192 "The Justice Department . . . " *New York Times*, November 20, 1989
192 "The list included . . . " *Time*, March 11, 1991
192 "Others in the . . ." Ibid.
192 "As the S&L. . . " *New York Times*, November 20, 1989
192 "Basically, it cost . . . " *Time*, October 1, 1990
193 "The S&L thing . . ." Gerald Corrigan to JM, interview on January 21, 2000
193 "The crisis literally . . ." David Barr, FDIC, to JM, interview on January 19, 2000
193 "During Bush's first . . ." Ibid.
193 "More banks failed . . ." John LaWare to JM, interview on February 4, 2000
193 "Traditionally, the Fed . . ." Bernard Shull, Hunter College, to JM, interview on February 9, 2000
194 "'Greenspan is a . . ." John LaWare to JM, interview on February 4, 2000
194 "The amount that . . . " *Business Week*, December 17, 1990
194 "The 1990 move . . . " *US News & World Report*, December 17, 1990
195 "Retrospectively, it would . . ." Courtesy of National Bureau of Economic Research
195 "Over the next . . ." Steven Beckner, *Back from the Brink*, p. 192
195 "During an August 21 . . . " *Wall Street Journal*, January 24, 1996
195 "At another, he . . . " *Business Week*, December 17, 1990
195 "By January 1991 . . . " *New York Times*, February 22, 1991
195 "Meanwhile, the misery . . ." Courtesy of the Conference Board
196 "All told, there . . ." Courtesy of Challenger, Gray & Christmas
196 "In his January 1991 . . . " *New York Times*, January 31, 1991
196 "An article about . . . " *Business Week*, December 17, 1990
196 "Rumors began to . . ." Steven Beckner, *Back from the Brink*, p. 174
196 "D'Amato described the . . ." Ibid. p. 219
197 "It wound up . . ." Courtesy of National Bureau of Economic Research
197 "Bush renominated Greenspan . . . " *New York Times*, July 11, 1991
197 "With the Fed . . . " *Business Week*, July 22, 1991
197 "Treasury Secretary Brady . . ." Ibid.
197 "It's worth noting . . . " *New York Times*, February 28, 1992
197 "During the fourth . . ." Courtesy of the Conference Board
197 "Every time the . . . " *New York Times*, January 30, 1992
197 "Treasury Secretary Brady . . . " *New York Times*, September 24, 1992
197 "The two discontinued . . . " *Washingtonian*, April 1995
197 "'This was a . . ." David Jones to JM, interview on January 19, 2000

198   "'The thing about . . ." Paul Samuelson to JM, interview on August 17, 1999

198   "By September, the . . . " *New York Times*, October 11, 1992

198   "The Fed had . . ." Steven Beckner, *Back from the Brink*, p.285

198   "'I think that . . . " *Wall Street Journal*, August 25, 1998

CHAPTER 14

199   "At one point . . . " *Business Week*, March 8, 1993

199   "The candidate praised . . . " *New York Times*, November 2, 1992

199   "New Treasury secretary . . ." Bob Woodward, *The Agenda*, p. 61

199   "Clinton decided it. . . " *Washington Post*, June 6, 1994

199   "He felt that . . ." Susan Phillips to JM, interview on February 22, 2000

200   "On December 3 . . ." Bob Woodward, *The Agenda*, p. 68

200   "They started off . . ." John LaWare to JM, interview on February 4, 2000

200   "Greenspan explained to . . ." Bob Woodward, *The Agenda*, p.69

200   "One hour stretched . . ." Susan Phillips to JM, interview on February 22, 2000

201   "'There's no way . . ." Beverly McGovern to JM, interview on March 27, 2000

201   "'He said he . . ." Susan Phillips to JM, interview on February 22, 2000

201   "Greenspan and Bentsen . . ." Steven Beckner, *Back from the Brink*. p. 292

202   "He would then . . ." Bob Woodward, *The Agenda*, p.98, confirmed with multiple sources

202   "'Rubin tended to . . ." William Griggs to JM, interview on February 23, 2000

202   "Greenspan even went . . ." Steven Beckner, *Back from the Brink*. p. 299–300

202   "Greenspan, in turn . . . " *New York Times*, February 20, 1993

202   "This produced a . . ." Bob Woodward, *The Agenda*, p.110

203   "They filibustered the . . ." Gov.Exec.com

203   "On February 15 . . ." Bob Woodward, *The Agenda*, p. 134–5

203   "Greenspan was shocked . . ." John LaWare to JM, interview on February 4, 2000

203   "In the course . . ." *The Economist*, March 13, 1993

203   ". . . Fed chairman usually . . ." John LaWare to JM, interview on February 4, 2000

204   "'Alan was personally . . ." Ibid.

204   ". . . on January 21 . . . " *Time*, April 18, 1994

204   "By January 1994 . . . " *Business Week*, February 7, 1994

204   "Certain early-warning . . . " *New York Times*, June 7, 1996

205   "Monetary policy works . . ." John LaWare to JM, interview on February 4, 2000

205   "'If you wait . . ." Steven Beckner, *Back from the Brink*. p. 68

205   "Between February 1994 . . ." Robert Parry to JM, interview on February 28, 2000

205   "There's an impression . . ." Alice Rivlin to JM, interview on February 28, 2000

205   "Radio talk show . . ." *Liberty*, November 1999

205   "A *Time* magazine . . . " *Time*, May 23, 1994

205   "Here, too, the . . ." Steven Beckner to JM, interview on January 27, 2000

206   "Senator Paul Douglas . . . " *Manhattan Inc.*, November 1988

206   "Probably the Fed's . . ." composite portrait drawn from multiple sources

206   "Until 1994, the . . ." *Barron's*, April 19, 1999

206   "One of the most . . . " *Manhattan Inc.*, November 1988

206   "They held thirteen . . ." Courtesy of the Federal Reserve

207   "'I know you . . . " *Reader's Digest*, December 1997

207   "As a Democrat . . ." composite portrait drawn from multiple sources

208   "He called on . . . " *New York Times*, November 16, 1993

208   ". . . he suggested that . . . " *New York Times*, January 6, 1993

208   "While introducing a . . ." Ibid.

208   "'There is a . . . " *New York Times*, April 15, 1993

209   "'Seemed like every . . ." Robert Parry to JM, interview on February 28, 2000

209   "This was the . . . " *The New Yorker*, February 19, 1996

209   "More recently, Blinder . . ." Bob Woodward, *The Agenda*, p.15

209   "He had also . . . " *New York Times*, September 26, 1994

209   "During 1994's Jackson . . ." Mickey Levy to JM, interview on February 25, 2000

209   "At one point . . . " *The New Yorker*, February 19, 1996

210   "And at the . . ." Steven Beckner, *Back from the Brink*, p.188

210   "So it was . . . " *New York Times*, July 14, 1995

210   "In his own . . ." L. William Seidman to JM, interview on January 20, 2000

210   "He even jumped . . . " *New York Times*, September 26, 1994

211   "His office was . . . " *The New Yorker*, February 19, 1996

211   "'Blinder came in . . ." Mickey Levy to JM, interview on February 25, 2000

211   "'I can see . . ." Paul Samuelson to JM, interview on August 17, 1999

211   "'If they send . . . " *Business Week*, September 25, 1995

211   "Clinton's response was . . . " *New York Times*, February 13, 1996

211   "Within the Administration . . ." Ibid.

212   "Alice Rivlin, director . . . " *New York Times*, June 21, 1996

212   "Now it was . . ." Ibid.

212   "The Fed today . . . " *New York Times*, June 7, 1996

212   "On June 20, 1996 . . . " *New York Times*, June 22, 1996

213   "My own feeling . . ." J. Alfred Broaddus to JM, interview on February 25, 2000

213   "In 1993, Greenspan . . . " *National Journal*, July 24, 1999

213   "Between 1993 and . . . " *Business Week*, June 17, 1996

213   "His mother, Rose . . ." Steven Beckner, *Back from the Brink*, p.10

213   "She played tennis . . ." Carolyn Halpert to JM, interview on February 25, 2000

213   "But in 1987 . . ." Wesley Halpert to JM, interview on May 10, 2000

213   "'He loved her . . ." Joan Mitchell Blumenthal to JM, interview on November 8, 1999

214   "A small graveside . . ." Carolyn Halpert to JM, interview on February 25, 2000

214   "'Alan's dad was . . ." Wesley Halpert to JM, interview on December 14, 1999

214   "'I am guardedly . . . " *Manchester Guardian*, December 7, 1996

215   "He was on hand . . ." Courtesy of the American Enterprise Institute

215   "Greenspan's speech, entitled . . ." David Sicilia and Jeffrey Cruikshank, *The Greenspan Effect*, p. 55

215   "His audience was . . ." James Glassman to JM, interview on February 15, 2000

215   "He discussed Japan's . . . " *Business Week*, December 23, 1996

215   "Directly addressing the . . . " *New York Times*, December 7, 1996

215   "In March of . . ." Courtesy of Federal Reserve

215   "On June 1, 1965 . . . " *New York Times*, December 7, 1996

216   "Glassman snapped to . . ." James Glassman to JM, interview on February 15, 2000

216   "Herb Stein also . . ." David Sicilia and Jeffrey Cruikshank, *The Greenspan Effect*, p. 55

216   "The impact was . . . " *New York Times*, December 7, 1996

216   "The Nikkei 225 . . . " *Newsweek*, December 16, 1996

217   "Greenspan used remarkably . . ." James Glassman & Kevin Hasset, *Dow 36,000*, p. 22

217   "On April 6, 1997 . . . " *New York Times*, April 7, 1997

217   "Greenspan proposed on . . ." Andrea Mitchell to JM, interview on March 9, 2000

218   "It was a garden . . . " *People*, April 21, 1997

218   "The guest list . . . " *New York Times*, April 7, 1997

218   "'It was very . . ." Andrea Mitchell to JM, interview on March 9, 2000

218   "Mitchell wore a . . . " *People*, April 21, 1997

218   "The couple's honeymoon . . ." Andrea Mitchell to JM, interview on March 9, 2000

CHAPTER 15

221   "Question: How many . . . " *Time*, March 13, 2000

222   "Perceived positive comments . . . " *USA Today*, February 12, 1999

222   "Two weeks later . . ." *Wired News*, February 24, 1999

222   "His Congressional testimony . . ." Reuters, July 28, 1999

222   "On at least . . . " *Time* November 10, 1997

222   "... says Milton Friedman ..." Milton Friedman to JM, interview on October 11, 1999

222   "'I spend a ... " *Wall Street Journal*, June 23, 1995

222   "'I'm trying to ..." Ibid.

223   "The idea behind ..." Matt Quayle to JM, interview on February 15, 2000

223   "Web sites started ..." GetExuberant.com

223   "During 1999, a ..." David Gaffen, creator of the Greenspan Game to JM, email exchange on April 7, 2000

224   "Meanwhile, an artist ..." Phillip A. Boyd II to JM, interview on April 7, 2000

224   "Here's a message ..." Bulletin board message posted August 25, 1999

224   "Here's a message ..." Bulletin board message posted August 10, 1999

225   "... Lenny Gilleo had ..." Lenny Gilleo to JM, interview on February 3, 2000

225   "Then there's the ... " *Wall Street Journal*, November 5, 1998

226   "'I am his ... " *Kansas City Star*, December 22, 1999

226   "'He has done ..." Ibid.

226   "'And by the way ... " *New York Times*, December 3, 1999

226   "'If you were forced ... " *New York Times*, January 27, 2000

226   "One was Steve ... " *New York Times*, December 3, 1999

227   "Leonard Peikoff took ..." R.W. Bradford, editor of *Liberty* magazine, to JM, interview on October 20, 1999

227   "'Ayn Rand must ..." Bert Ely to JM, interview on January 19, 2000

227   "'The story of Greenspan ..." Richard Salsman to JM, interview on October 18, 1999

228   "'Greenspan is at ..." Lloyd Grove to JM, interview on January 31, 2000

228   "'He's definitely A-list ..." Kevin Chaffee to JM, interview on February 16, 2000

228   "Over the years ..." Andrea Mitchell to JM, interview on March 9, 2000

228   "... and Katherine Graham ... " *Washingtonian*, April 1995

228   "Greenspan made an ..." Andrea Mitchell to JM, interview on March 9, 2000

228   "Another annual tradition ..." Lloyd Grove to JM, interview on January 31, 2000

229   "The Fed also ..." Kevin Chaffee to JM, interview on February 16, 2000

229   "The U.S. economy ..." Courtesy of the Conference Board

229   "Real GDP had ..." Courtesy of the Council of Economic Advisers

229   "The old record ..." Courtesy of the Conference Board

229   "The Nasdaq climbed ... " *Business Week*, February 14, 2000

229   "During those 107 ..." Ibid.

229   "In January 2000 ..." Courtesy of the Conference Board

229   "In perhaps the ... " *Business Week*, February 14, 2000

230   "Greenspan addressed this . . ." Alan Greenspan speech on September 8, 1999, in Grand Rapids, Michigan, at function co-sponsored by the Gerald Ford Museum

230   "'I don't think . . ." Andrea Mitchell to JM, interview on March 9, 2000

230   "By the year 2000 . . . " *Business Week*, February 14, 2000

231   "According to one. . . " *Business Week*, March 17, 1997

232   "During the credit . . ." Steven Beckner to JM, interview on January 27, 2000

232   "It used to be . . . "*Newsweek*, November 21, 1994

232   "'The laws of . . . " *New York Times*, Oct 9, 1997

233   "'When we look . . ." Alan Greenspan in speech to Economic Club of New York on January 13, 2000

Index